*Sunset*

# LANDSCAPING
## for
## Western Living

### by the editors
### of Sunset Magazine

UNDER THE DIRECTION OF

Walter L. Doty
*Director Editorial Research*
*Sunset Magazine*

Paul C. Johnson
*Editor*
*Sunset Books*

**LANE BOOKS • MENLO PARK, CALIFORNIA**

# Acknowledgments

There is no place in this book for the kind of acknowledgment that says "Thank you for your help." There is no ordinary author-helper relationship here. This book is the record of a search for a special, better way of living.

This record began years ago when *Sunset* joined with a number of architects, landscape architects, nurserymen, and home owners who had in common one obsession—an idea that was, and continues to be, greater than any individual involved.

The idea is this: Landscaping offers a way to take house and garden, building materials and plant materials, the open sky and the stars at night, and blend them all to create a deeply satisfying space for everyday living.

Through landscaping we are finding a way to make the most of our common environment—the West.

A big part of the Western environment is climate; another part is our romantic history; a part is mountains, seashore, rivers, lakes, green hills and brown hills, deserts and rain forests. And the part each individual experiences most personally is, of course, his own garden, his own private out-of-doors. Here he finds relaxation, seclusion, outdoor living, intimacy with nature—sun, plants, wind, and rain.

It is our hope that this book will advance the full and complete purpose of landscaping and that the men and women whose work in landscaping is represented in the pages of the book will feel that it is their book.

For many years of guidance and encouragement we are indebted to Leland Vaughan, University of California; Donald T. Martel, Oregon State College; George Jette, University of Oregon. For collaboration in visual presentation of plans and ideas, we thank Robert Danielson of the University of California.

**Twelfth Printing January 1967**

# Contents

# How to use this book:

This book is planned to help you help yourself to the kind of Western environment you want. You should be able to find yourself in these pages whether you dream of a thousand flowers or a plan of no-work and complete relaxation; whether you see your garden as a background for entertaining with a flair or as a secluded, quiet corner to hide in.

It's our hope that you will leaf through the book slowly and understand its logical sequence.

Regardless of how you read, realize this: Chapter groupings must be in a sense misleading. "Hillsides" can be grouped as such, but in the examples you'll find children's gardens, low maintenance gardens, and other special interests.

No problem stands alone. Every photograph and diagram illustrates a number of ideas. This relationship of many ideas is the reason for planning.

So don't overlook the value of reading a photograph or diagram in several ways. Look at their obvious message, and look again.

In doing so, you'll find that you have some definite opinions about a garden and what it should be.

You may find yourself in the following headings:

**You are afraid that wood and masonry will give your garden a harsh, mechanical look**

While man-made structures may dominate a garden for a short time, if plant material has half a chance it will put any structure in its proper place.

For example, there's an entrance garden on page 77 that started out as a brick garden. Looking at it now you see that the brick is subservient and functions mostly as a display panel for pots.

In the chapter on hobby gardens, pages 62-63, there's a garden designed on a very rigid modular pattern. About 3500 bricks are in view of the camera, yet you feel no harshness.

Sometimes a garden is like an empty pot—sitting there in good design, but dead until planted. Look at these gardens with that in mind: the two-room patio on page 12, the hillside garden on page 13. Judge these paved areas with your fear in mind.

Look at the all-paved garden on page 64 and see what container plantings can do for you.

**Your hobby is growing things, and you don't want a plan that denies that hobby**

There are a number of plans, starting on page 59, worked out for the flower growing specialist. But the hobbyist is not overlooked elsewhere. If yours is a hillside garden, there are suggestions for vegetable and fruit growing on pages 42 and 68. More ideas for vegetable growers on page 164.

For ways to get a lot of growing activity in small space, see pages 38 and 40-41.

For display of choice miniatures, see page 13.

If you are willing to look at any plan with the idea that you can introduce your favorite plants in places where their absence would not be noticeable in winter, you will find many possibilities in this book for including specialty plantings.

**You want quick results—right now**

If by "quick results" you mean shade where you need it or a place to entertain, you can get them with overheads and paving. Good examples of immediate results are these gardens: pages 40-41, 54. Photographs were taken 60 days after the houses were completed.

The means by which you can quickly control sun on a patio are shown on pages 18, 19, 55, 56, 58.

Quick results with plant material is a relative thing. Photographs on pages 52, 53 chart the rapid growth of a garden.

Other ways to get quick results: plant fast growing vines, page 78; use pots and tubs, pages 13, 64, 129, 130, 164.

**You are going to remodel an old garden**

On pages 85 to 100 you'll find a number of "before" and "after" photographs. There should be an idea or two there that will spark your own ideas.

If part of your problem is the front garden, you may find help in the chapter on *Streetsides,* pages 75-84.

How about making an area free of insects? See pages 125-128.

Don't forget the low maintenance ideas, pages 161 to 164.

**You hate angles, like curves**

You will have no trouble finding curved lines in this book. If curved lines mean a quiet, hidden place that is always ready to relax nerves made taut by offices and pavements, you can find such gardens. See pages 50, 52, 88, 132, 164.

Note how often the lines, straight or curved, have nothing to do with the total feeling of the garden. There's concrete and an angular seat wall in the garden on page 97, but in its way the garden is as comfortable as a sofa.

The paving in the garden on page 104 is as rigid as a ruler, but the protected areas—the garden as a whole—are warm and casual.

Bricks are angular until plant material starts to spread over them. See page 107.

**You are a perfectionist and appreciate the results of good workmanship**

The clean finished look of good workmanship is as important to the beauty of a garden as the flowers that grow there. At least, that is how some persons feel.

You may appreciate that feeling when you inspect the details in the garden on page 39. All work was done by the home owner. Note the precisely cut bricks along the edge of the concrete.

See page 100. The painted cap on the raised bed is an important finishing touch here.

For an interesting seat-retaining wall, see page 123. Also see the seat wall on page 134, and the brick seat against the retaining wall on page 13.

Structures in photographs on pages 40 and 41 have the perfectionist's touch.

**Your garden must be a place for children to grow up in**

On pages 49 through 54 there's a collection of children's gardens—plans in which small children get first consideration.

Don't overlook pages 46, 47. Note especially the sandbox-raised bed combination.

When checking plans, remember that devoting a small corner to children's play equipment doesn't make a children's garden. They appreciate space they can call their own, but there must be room to spread out. See pages 88, 89, 91, 163.

**You live in a fog belt**

Do not overlook the ideas that are buried in the shelters to block the sun. For example, if you study the following photographs, you'll see that you can substitute glass or plastic for the solid material in the roof. See photographs on pages 141, 143, 144. Note especially the covered deck on pages 56-57. If this were roofed in part by glass or plastic, you would have an area that would serve as a greenhouse.

See windbreak and shelter on page 64.

Remember that shrubs grow rapidly in the mild coastal climates. Better start with a bold design so that plant growth won't erase it.

### You live where summers are hot

In the interior valleys of the West where it is not uncommon for the temperatures to soar past 100° for 20 days straight, the garden must be planned accordingly.

Although there are gardens in these climates wherein large areas of concrete are exposed to the sun, they are not used until after sundown. Wise planners will provide shade wherever heat-absorbing paving is used.

Good examples of hot summer gardens with paving: pages 13, 15, 144, 159.

Many gardeners make use of the cooling benefits of water—mist sprays, pools, water-cooled fences. For examples, see pages 158-160.

### You live where summers are cool

Probably the best pre-planning exercise you can take is a study of the shade and sun pattern around the house. See pages 11, 18.

Take the many overheads (pages 135 to 144) in stride, and substitute a transparent roof in the structures you like.

There are "cool summer" photographs on pages 16, 43, 44, 45, 82, 83, 87.

### You want a garden that takes care of itself

Gardens don't take care of themselves, but you can make a big difference in the amount of care required for any garden by the way you plan it. There's a chapter on maintenance starting on page 161.

Check the children's gardens, pages 49 to 54, for ideas in minimum upkeep.

Look to these photographs for more ideas: streetsides chapter, pages 77 through 84; raised beds chapter, page 129; decks, pages 54, 56, 57; modular gardens, pages 40, 41, 43.

### How to make use of a $1000 idea when your budget is $200

Don't turn your eyes away from the obviously expensive garden just because you can't afford everything you see there. Many a good plan in brick and stone can be done in wood and gravel.

Many solutions are shown to the problem of getting a smooth relationship between house and garden when the indoor floor level is two feet or more above ground level. Several decks show one way. If the big deck is too expensive, make your own adaptation of ideas on pages 90-91 in the chapter on remodeling.

### Your best exposure is on the street side

If the weather you want to live in is on the street side of your house, why not build your patio there? See examples in chapters on streetsides and remodeling.

### You want to simplify your garden

When you have a suspicion that your garden is growing away from you, it probably has. It's hard to believe that the plants you put in the ground could ever outgrow the place.

Some of the best examples of simplified planting are in the chapter on streetsides.

### You would rather plan on the ground than on paper

The procedure outlined for putting your plan on paper (pages 23 to 34) can be duplicated on the ground by means of a few stakes and some string. By outlining patio, lawn, and planting areas with string, you can check your plan by walking through it. The one trouble is that it's harder to move string than to erase lines on paper.

### You are afraid to "design"

If you feel you "can't get started" because you've heard of so many traps to be avoided, see on page 24 how simple it is to start your plan with doodles, and from there build the final design according to your needs.

# Landscaping for Western living

Along in the 1930's, the outdoor barbecue captured the fancy of the Westerner. In doing so, it changed the course of landscaping.

Suburban home owners went out-of-doors to cook and entertain, and, in most cases, they found the garden or back yard was not designed for that use. There was no privacy, and sometimes the next-door neighbors were embarrassed; tables and chairs poked holes in the lawn; often the sun was too hot, the wind too strong, the evenings too chilly.

Obviously, before outdoor space could be used, it had to be made more habitable. If much the same kind of living was to take place outdoors as indoors, the same problems had to be solved—garden furniture arrangement, hallways (pathways) for circulation, a floor (paving) for tables and chairs, walls (fences, hedges) for privacy, even heating and cooling for personal comfort.

Suddenly, a set of factors seldom dealt with in conventional landscaping became important. Sun and wind control, and areas for dining, entertaining, playing, and working became first considerations in the Western landscape approach. And the Western home owner built "barbecue shelters," "wind controls," "garden rooms," "overheads."

These experiment-minded Westerners presented a fertile field to the landscape architect who understood them. What they were willing to take, the architects were more than willing to give, and a new type of landscape architecture began to flourish in the West.

It was a new type, at least, to the home owner who felt no immediate need to decorate his grounds with plants but was excited about "fixing up the place" to get more living out of it.

He could understand the very practical purpose of landscaping for use. He happily applied the word *landscaping* to paving a patio, planting a wind or sun screen, building a deck, or roofing over a garden corner to create an "outdoor room." Landscaping, in short, summed up all the things he did to make hours in the garden more livable.

The important change was that thousands of families accepted *landscaping* in this new sense as a natural and normal development in modern living.

This new kind of landscaping has not evolved as a style. It has grown out of the belief that landscaping is for people in search of new experiences in living. Call it site planning, or land use, or landscaping; it is planning the garden for use by people.

Because people are its reference points, this new Western landscaping is quite universal in its application. Wherever it occurs—in Seattle or Los Angeles, in Phoenix or Boise—it involves the same guiding principles of weather control and adaptability to people's needs and desires: to accept or reject gardening; to be absorbed in the arrangement of flowers, shrubs, and trees, or to just sit in the shade; to enjoy close communion with plants, or people; to create a garden picture from a kitchen window or to borrow space from a garden by extending the living room into it.

In this book we have brought together the work of more than 50 Western landscape architects. Practically every attitude toward landscaping is in evidence. Every major Western climate is represented—from the frost-free winters of the coastal strip to the zero winters east of the Cascades and in the intermountain area; from the mild and moist springtimes of the Northwest coast to the dry, sun-blasted summers of the interior deserts.

It is not surprising to find great differences in attitudes and techniques in a collection of many gardens in many climates. But it is both surprising and significant to find that underneath the apparent differences there is a basic approach, common to all. The same set of fundamentals underlies the entire collection.

The landscaping we call Western landscaping is based on these fundamentals:

*Western landscaping's first concern is people—their activities and their comfort in the garden.*

*Western landscaping is concerned with beauty—giving people pleasant sensory and emotional experiences.*

The measuring stick of Western landscape design is people—men, women, and children in pursuit of ways to satisfy their widely varying interests out of doors.

- People: Their height measures fences, shrubs, trees, and all vertical and overhead elements.

- People: Their line of vision determines whether a fence will provide privacy or merely separation.

- People: Their relationship to a tree determines the kind of tree to be planted. . . . Shade trees to walk under. . . . Trees to look upon. . . . Trees for privacy.

- People: Their relationship to shrubs determines the best height for a particular planting. Ankle-high to cover the ground; knee-high for direction;

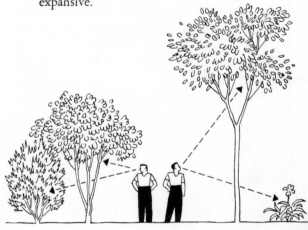

waist-high for traffic control, partial enclosure; chest-high for division of space; above eye level for protective enclosure.

- People: Their height and line of vision measure garden space as small and cramped or large and expansive.

People in motion outdoors require more space than they do when moving through the house. Two people

can walk side by side on a 4-foot garden path, but a 5-foot width gives them freedom to stroll and raise their eyes from the path.

ALLOW SPACE FOR MOTION

The width of a wheelbarrow measured from knuckle to knuckle, the width of a clothes basket from elbow to

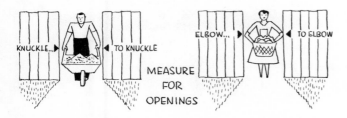

KNUCKLE... ←→ TO KNUCKLE     ELBOW... ←→ TO ELBOW

MEASURE FOR OPENINGS

elbow—these measurements determine the width of gates, passageways, and other openings.

A child on wheels establishes the dimensions of paved play areas. A tricycle *can* stay on a 24-inch walk, turn in a 4-foot circle.

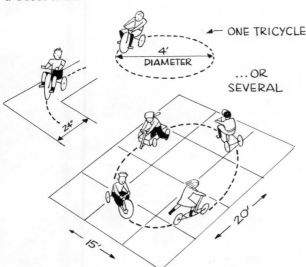

ONE TRICYCLE

4' DIAMETER

...OR SEVERAL

24"

20'

15'

But three or four children on wheels need space for action, high speed turns and races.

The easiest flower bed to weed is a raised bed, with a cap to sit on and a width no greater than a comfortable reach.

Patios without furniture and without people may look like bare, cold spaces in need of planting. But people, more colorful than shrubs, are dominant elements in the picture when the garden is in use.

Outdoors as well as indoors, people need room for their clutter, leftovers, accumulations, whimsy. And when it's time to tidy up, they need outdoor storage places.

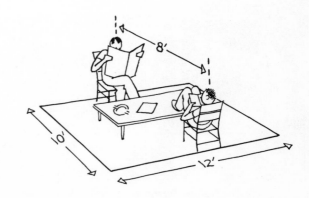

Their sitting position determines the height of a seat wall, benches, and other structures.

The space people need for loafing, conversing, eating, should determine the size of the terrace or patio. Two people sitting on either side of a coffee table take up space like this:

8'

10'

12'

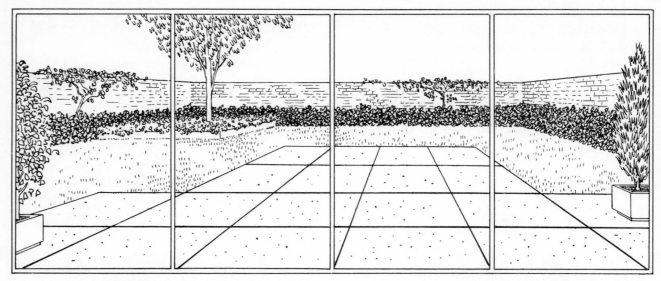

*Some think of the floor of a large patio as being by necessity a cold expanse of masonry*

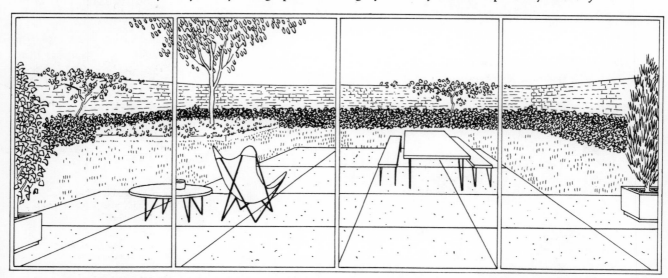

*But, partly furnished, it loses its austerity, becomes a part of the indoors, invites you out*

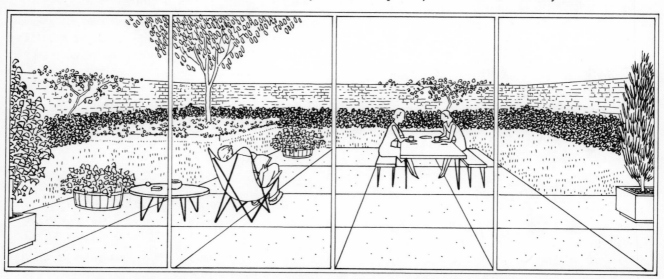

*People are furnishings, too. They complete the picture—as important to design as plants*

• People: Their desire to be comfortable out of doors sets up numerous problems:

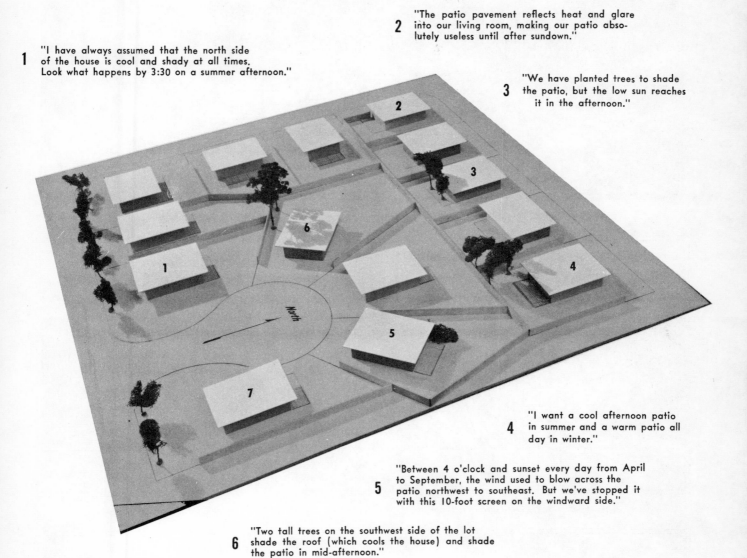

2 "The patio pavement reflects heat and glare into our living room, making our patio absolutely useless until after sundown."

1 "I have always assumed that the north side of the house is cool and shady at all times. Look what happens by 3:30 on a summer afternoon."

3 "We have planted trees to shade the patio, but the low sun reaches it in the afternoon."

4 "I want a cool afternoon patio in summer and a warm patio all day in winter."

5 "Between 4 o'clock and sunset every day from April to September, the wind used to blow across the patio northwest to southeast. But we've stopped it with this 10-foot screen on the windward side."

6 "Two tall trees on the southwest side of the lot shade the roof (which cools the house) and shade the patio in mid-afternoon."

7 "Everybody told me to get a south patio, but for this climate I like it on the east side."

But sun and wind controls, play space, and work space, do not make a complete garden.

*Landscape design is concerned with beauty—giving people pleasant sensory and emotional experiences.*

Satisfying physical needs is not enough. How a human being reacts to his surroundings is equally important.

Will he be excited by movement in the garden, intrigued by variety, soothed by quiet, stimulated by color, kept interested by change?

A beautiful garden harbors secrets and surprises. It is never completely discovered. It contains sentimental values which change with the growth and age of the garden.

There are more depths and dimensions of beauty in the garden to be lived in than in the garden to be just looked at. All the senses are involved. You react to what you touch, smell, hear, as well as what you see.

We are talking about gardens like those shown on the following five pages.

*The philosophy of the oriental garden lightly touches this Southern California terrace. In foreground is the* "active" area. Hidden by planting, shaded by house, furnished with pool and fountain spray, is "quiet" area

*Shallow pool dominates "quiet" area of same garden, carries out oriental feeling with plants, natural rock* forms. Water lilies are planted in pool well. Plants around pool are bamboo, tamarix juniper, and abelia

WALTER AND FLORENCE GERKE

Northwest hillside hangs tapestry of choicest plants around this living room terrace—lovely miniatures for close-up view. Sun filter is matchstick bamboo on wires from house to reinforcing rods in concrete on bank

DOUGLAS BAYLIS

Cool terrace in California's San Joaquin Valley. Brick in sand under wide spreading oak. Insets in terrace get seasonal color—violas, geraniums. Other container-grown plants held in reserve for use in season of bloom

Landscaping for living  13

These tropical plants—anthurium, philodendron, monstera, coral tree—correctly place this garden in Hawaii.

However, by substituting plant materials, this patio could be adapted to almost any area in the West

THOMAS CHURCH

Tree ferns say tropics, but pines, oaks place this garden in Pebble Beach, California. Tree ferns limited

to warm coastal areas, but there are many bold-foliaged plants ready to bring tropical lushness to coast gardens

LEON FREHNER

*Gardens are places to nurture memories. Shrine of stone and water borrowed from Utah's high country.*

*Dainty star flower, Mahonia repens, fringes rocks over pool. Water birch and smooth sumac cast reflections*

**Landscaping for living    15**

ECKBO, ROYSTON, AND WILLIAMS

*There are more depths and dimensions of beauty in the garden to be lived in than in the garden to be just looked at. All the senses are involved. You react to what you touch, smell, hear, as well as to what you see*

ECKBO, ROYSTON, AND WILLIAMS

*This Pacific Northwest garden answers some of the questions about fences. More than walls for privacy, fences can be delicate screens of various designs that complement foliage and glorify colors of the garden*

# Take inventory of your site

"Take Inventory" may be too strong a title—too serious sounding—for this process of getting ready to landscape. To put it another way, look at what you have before you plan what you'd like.

Since this kind of landscaping began because people wanted to do more everyday living out of doors, let's start with the most important factor that will hinder or help you—your climate. How do the sun and the wind affect your property?

## The sun

The path of the sun, the amount of sun, and the intensity of the sun, through the seasons of the year and the hours of the day, affect the location, kind, and amount of your outdoor living areas, and determine the kind of plants you can grow.

If the number of warm sunny days is limited, you naturally seek to develop areas where the sun can be trapped. You appreciate paved areas of concrete, brick, and asphalt that absorb the heat of the sun and re-radiate it to increase temperatures near their surfaces.

Paving that is shaded in summer but exposed to the sun in the winter (as it is under a deciduous tree) is ideal. Where sun and rain alternate many days in the year, glass or plastic overheads multiply your outdoor hours.

Where the amount of sun is limited, look to south walls to reflect extra heat for those plants that need it; avoid plantings that will shut off the sun in the fall, winter, and spring months.

If summer temperatures are high, you not only attempt to avoid the sun by creating overhead screens of foliage or structure, but you also put in a minimum of paving that cannot be shaded.

Of course, the time of day you plan to use the garden will also influence what you do about the sun. Pavements too hot for afternoon use may be just the thing to take the chill out of the after-sundown air.

In western North America, the sun is never directly overhead, although we may mistakenly think of it that way. This means that a tree or overhead structure will never cast all of its shade directly beneath it.

At midday, the sun is always somewhere to the south of a point directly overhead; at sunrise it's always somewhere between the northeast and southeast points on your horizon; and at sunset it's between the northwest and southwest points on the other horizon.

How high the sun may be within this area at any particular time of day depends on the time of the year. As you see in the photographs on the following page, the sun's arc is low in winter, high in summer (but never high enough to be overhead at noon).

To a small degree the sun's angle on any day also depends on how far north of the equator you live. But this, the effect of latitude, makes only a comparatively minor change in sun angles between the Mexican and Canadian borders. Our illustrations were set up for the West Coast's mid-latitude, 40° N, or the line that runs through Red Bluff, California, and Provo, Utah. Shave off a little shadow in the illustrations to get the shadow at Tucson's latitude; add a sliver to get Bellingham's.

In the following diagrams we trace the shadow pattern of two houses through the year. In one case, the patio side of the house faces south; in the other, it faces west. The pattern on the east and north side is also evident.

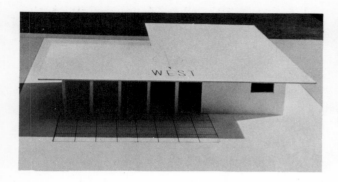

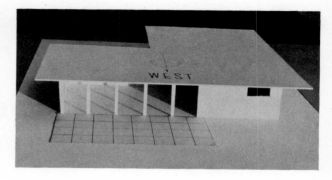

DECEMBER 21, 11 A.M. One pleasure of a mild winter climate is to spend an hour or two of a sunny weekend morning on the patio. Unfortunately, you don't get that sunshine on a west-side patio; you generally get shade when it is neither needed nor wanted. The usual solution is to continue patio around corner on south side.

DECEMBER 21, 4 P.M. The late and low western sun sweeps across the patio into the living room. To many people this angle of sun is uncomfortable; a screen planting of tall shrubs or small trees will block it out. Where a view is at stake, the screen should be designed selectively to obscure and reveal it.

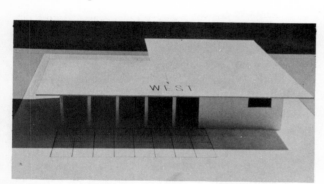

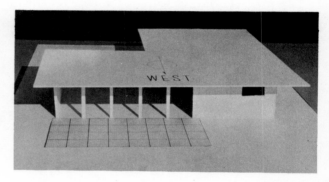

MARCH 21-SEPTEMBER 21, 11 A.M. Throughout spring and summer the west-side patio offers no sun problem in morning hours. And no warmth on cool March mornings. A roof would increase the amount of shade in early afternoon hours, but no overhead can extend far enough from the house to block out late afternoon sun.

MARCH 21-SEPTEMBER 21, 4 P.M. In September when the naturally warm areas receive some of their hottest days, the western sun is at its most punishing angle. To make this exposure livable requires both overhead and vertical baffles of some kind. A line of trees, tall shrubs, vertical screens, or louvers are usual answers.

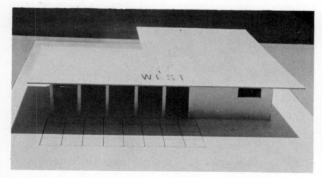

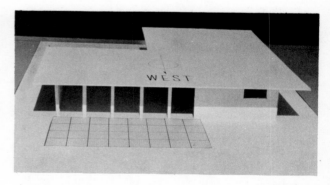

JUNE 21, 11 A.M. Throughout the year the west side of the house is in morning shade, but it's the last place you would use shade loving plants. Conversely, many shade plants take morning sun if they are given afternoon shade. The west-facing plants in warm summer areas should be those that are not disturbed by heat extremes.

JUNE 21, 4 P.M. In all warm summer areas, regardless of where the patio is located, the west side of the house should be shaded. The interception of the sun's rays by vines, trees, or structures will avoid the west wall's input of heat that reradiates into the rooms of the house long after sundown.

**Sun and shade on SOUTH patio through the day and year:**

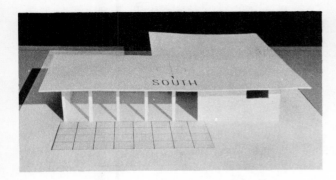

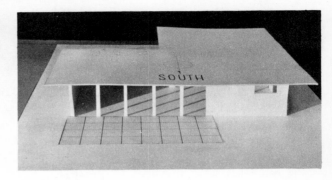

DECEMBER 21, 11 A.M. When sun's arc is at its lowest point on December 21, the sun's rays flood across south patio from midmorning to sundown. If patio is protected from wind, December sun will make temperatures of 50° feel like 70°. December photos show why time-honored advice to plant tender plants on south wall makes sense.

DECEMBER 21, 4 P.M. In cold winter areas there's much to be said for allowing low winter sun unimpeded entrance to patio and rooms facing south. In mild winter areas this pattern can't be had without getting into trouble with too much heat in October and November. Screens of deciduous trees partially overcome problem.

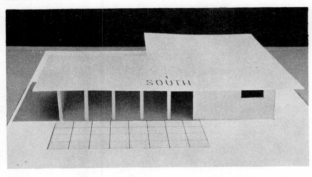

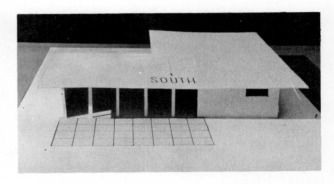

MARCH 21-SEPTEMBER 21, 11 A.M. After December 21, sun's arc is increasingly higher. By March 21, 8-foot wide overhang blocks sun from living room while patio is in full sun. Sun returns to this position September 21, after which sun's arc is increasingly lower. Here patio roof would give shade except at right side of patio.

MARCH 21-SEPTEMBER 21, 4 P.M. Difficulty of getting shade where and when you want it is indicated here. If patio area roofed, most of it would get sun's heat and glare while shadow pattern would be to east as in shadow pattern of house. To get shade in patio, vertical screen must be built or grown on west side of lot.

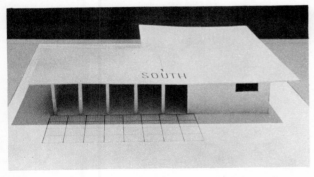

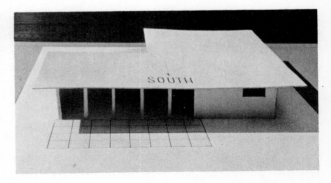

JUNE 21, 11 A.M. South patio is at its best when sun is high over head in June, July. A roof overhead gives adequate protection at this time. Where summers are short and extra warmth is needed in spring and fall, south patio orientation is favored by most authorities. In our experience south-east orientation is preferable.

JUNE 21, 4 P.M. Late afternoon shade pattern leaves much of patio area in the sun. There will be less shade from this day on. Correction can be made by plantings at west side of patio. Visualize angling house slightly to east to see why southeast exposure would be a distinct improvement in shadow pattern during summer.

## The wind

Whether it's cool, dry, hot, or moist, a wind or breeze can change outdoor comfort for better or worse as drastically as changes in temperature.

How can you take inventory of the wind before you have lived in a place for a year? One source of information is your neighbors; you can share their experience. The "lean" of trees in the neighborhood will tell the story of prevailing winds. But the direction of the prevailing wind around your house may not be the same as it is around the house next door. Wind flows like water —spilling over obstacles, breaking into several currents, eddying and twisting.

No one experiences exactly the same temperature as the thermometer at the weather bureau. When the weather bureau says that the temperature is 68°, it means to say that a thermometer *in the shade, protected from the wind, reads 68°.*

If there is a 10 to 15-mile-an-hour breeze, a person in the shade in the breeze may feel that the temperature is about 62°. If the breeze is stopped and the patio is in sunlight, the person will feel a comfortable 75-78°.

Of course, the cooling effect of a breeze becomes an advantage when summer temperatures are above 90°. In

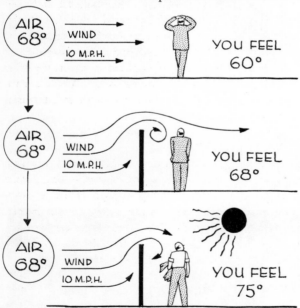

such cases, the path of the prevailing summer wind is an important design factor. You won't want to block the wind with obstacles like shrub plantings and solid fences. You may prefer vertical louvers to literally "catch a breeze."

In checking the wind problem around your house, remember that the house itself is your biggest windbreak but may need additions to be effective. In some cases, the wind spills over the house and drops on the patio.

Remember, too, that a solid barrier is not always the most efficient. Following are the results of a *Sunset* study in wind control. (Lower line of figures shows number of feet from fence; upper line notes sensible temperature differences between these points and the windward side of the fence.)

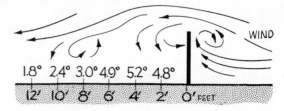

Wind washes over solid fence as a stream of water would wash over a solid barrier. At about the distance equal to fence height, protection drops rapidly. You feel 1.8° warmer 12 feet away than in the unprotected area.

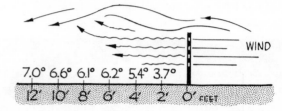

For the fence with vertical laths spaced about ½ inch apart, the lowest reading is close to the fence, the highest, 12 feet away. At 12 feet you would feel 7° warmer than when standing on windward side of the fence.

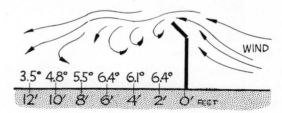

A 45° baffle at top of fence eliminates downward crash of wind. In this pocket, and 6 feet away from fence, you feel 6.4° warmer than without a barrier. Beyond this point, the temperature difference declines gradually.

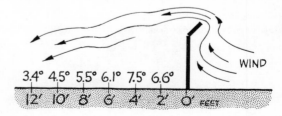

Angling the baffle into wind gives greater protection close to the fence than any control tested. Beyond the maximum 7.5° increase, comfort drop is gradual, extending effective protection to distance equal to over twice fence height.

## The seasons

The opportunities for outdoor living are, of course, fewer in severe climates than in mild climates. But there are two ways to count your opportunities. You can estimate how few days there are, or how many. To the pessimist, 60 days or 120 half days of outdoor living weather is a fraction of 365; to the optimist, those 60 days add up to a total that is four times as long as his vacation.

If you base your decision for landscaping for garden use on the proportion of completely comfortable rainless days to the total of wet or chilly days, you wouldn't do much in any short summer season climate—or anywhere.

Completely comfortable outdoor living, hour after hour and day after day, is very rare. But each step you take to modify the climate increases the use of the outdoors.

If you pave an area immediately adjacent to the house, that area can be used between showers when the lawn would be too wet.

Stop the breeze that sweeps across the terrace, and you can enjoy it in sunlight when air temperatures are much lower than the accepted 78° comfort temperature.

Put glass or plastic over head, and many rainy days become pleasant. (The Northwest, with its days of warm rain, might find an adaptation of Hawaii's lanai a good idea. The lanai takes care of many tropical showers.)

When you take inventory of your climate, note the number of days that might be pleasant in the garden if you did something about them.

## Your piece of land

What is the shape of your lot? How will its form affect your landscaping? Each lot shape has its advantages and disadvantages.

*The inside rectangular* lot sets up a rigid rectangle of clearly defined space. The view of neighboring roofs and windows must come into your planning.

Your back garden may be influenced by as many as five neighboring families. If, by some miracle, all five could get together on a program of tall shrub and tree planting, the problems of getting privacy and of sun and wind protection could be worked out more efficiently and at less expense than if each home owner goes his own way.

*The long narrow lot* has many advantages. You can easily zone it into areas by use—outdoor room, children's play area, work center, etc. The difficulty of getting these various areas to flow together as one garden is the design trick you'll have to solve. There are several examples throughout the book.

*The pie-shaped lot,* with the narrow end toward the street, is probably the most desirable of all. It gives least space on the street and most space behind the house.

*The corner lot* presents a difficult problem when you are trying for maximum private space. Compared to an interior lot where you give up the setback space on the front only, the corner lot makes you give up both side and front to the public. In the corner lot you lose private space, but you get a feeling of openness that you can't have in the more boxed-in interior lot.

(See chapter on *Problem Sites.*)

## Soil, drainage

In a small garden, you needn't worry about a lack of plant food, or whether the soil is sand or clay. You can improve poor soils with chemical soil conditioners and quantities of vegetable matter.

But if your soil is shallow and underlaid with a compacted layer that is impervious to water and roots, or if water does not drain from your lot, you must either correct the situation or plant as if you had no soil. For example, plant above the ground in raised beds.

## Indoor-outdoor relationship

The development of outdoor space for living can give the interior rooms an entirely new dimension. Check to see possible garden views from the windows of the house. Can the patio be built so that it is visually an extension of the living room? Would a kitchen patio be more usable? If indoor floor level is above ground level, are the steps from house to garden easy to negotiate? Would a deck at floor level make the living room larger and entrance into the garden easier?

## Utility connections

Will sewer pipes and septic tank drain field interfere with tree plantings? Are water outlets placed so that future use is possible without cutting through lawns or pavement? Should there be a water faucet in the garden work center? A drain? What connections are there for sprinkler systems? If you plan to light the garden at night, do you have outdoor electric outlets?

## You and your family

It's much safer to plan a garden to fit the natural habits of your family than to aim at changing those habits after your garden is built. If you are careless housekeepers, the garden shouldn't require you to be neat. If the children are rough-housers and are allowed free run indoors, don't plan a garden that can't take punishment.

A good garden is like a good house—it should accommodate the people who live in it and adapt to their changing interests and changing needs. How distant in the future are teen-age parties? Grandchildren?

*What kind of a gardener are you?* Do you garden because you must, or is gardening still a new experience for you?

If you are an experienced gardener and love it, can you expect to be with the garden every week that it needs you, or will you be called away on long trips? Will a sprinkler system, installed the first thing, make routine maintenance easier?

*What kind of workmen in your family?* Can you put together simple structures with hammer and saw? Does the prospect of mixing concrete intimidate you?

How much work do you get from your teen-agers? Is the hard work of building, digging, paving, and planting your family's idea of fun?

*Can you go fast or must you go slow?* Two things are involved here: one is your budget, the other is the leisure time you can devote to installing your garden.

For many home owners working on their own, a reasonable garden-installation timetable is two to four years. Do you tend to over-estimate your ability to carry through a project?

## Space requirements

*Patio area.* If this book does nothing else for you except to increase the size of your garden living room, it will pay its way. Whether the patio will be used for entertaining, or play, or just sitting, it is always more satisfying when over-sized.

*Play areas.* Are your children pre-school age? They will want sand and water and tricycle runs now, but you will probably want to convert this area to another purpose within a few years.

*Game areas.* Garden games are fun; they also swallow up space. Will you want a basketball hoop now or later? Can you use the front driveway for this and other games? Will you want space for badminton, croquet, tetherball, shuffleboard?

*Outdoor work area.* In many parts of the West, the weather is pleasant enough for you to do woodworking, painting, cabinet making, and many other craft and hobby projects outdoors. Teen-agers like to tinker with an old car. Small boys need to build things. You may want to plan space for these outdoor activities.

*Outdoor storage area.* A minimum amount of outdoor storage is essential for garden tools, lawn mower, garden cart or wheelbarrow, paints, garden chemicals, peat moss, fertilizers, ladder, lawn furniture. And where will you store firewood and lumber? If you have no basement or attic, you may want a garden storage structure.

*Trash area.* Most families tend to accumulate bulky trash. It's a good idea to have a place out of sight where you can hide this accumulation between burnings or trips to the city dump.

*Plant shelters.* If you're a serious gardener, or if you become one in time, you may want a garden work center, a lathhouse, a greenhouse. How big should it be? Where will it go?

*Food garden.* You may want to grow some of your own vegetables. You may want a small family orchard. Very often a garden can provide both vegetables and fruit without sacrificing beauty or play space, but you must allow for them in your plan.

*Water.* The sound and sight of water are always pleasant in a garden. You may want a small fountain, a small pool, or a swimming pool. The fountain or small pool are easy, but a 16 by 28-foot swimming pool and the paving around it require a minimum of about 850 square feet.

# How to get your plan on paper

Your first practical step in getting your design on paper is to make a "scale" drawing of your lot—draw a plot plan.

## Draw a plot plan of your lot

The purpose of your plot plan is to show in measured relationship the limiting factors discussed in the previous chapter. You'll save yourself many hours of measuring if you can locate any of the following:

1. *Deed map.* Shows actual dimensions and orientation of your property. If you do not have this, you might get information at the city hall, county courthouse, title company, bank, or mortgage company.

2. *Contour map.* For hill sites this is very important, and it is now sometimes required by law prior to issuing a building permit. Made by an engineer, it shows 1-foot, 2-foot, 5-foot, or 10-foot contours—in other words, it shows the exact *shape* of your site. It sometimes also

indicates property dimensions, streets, sidewalks, utilities, large trees, rocks, etc.

3. *Architect's drawings or house plans.* Should show site plan, floor plan, elevations, how related to site, windows, doors, roof, utilities, hose bib connections, downspouts, footing details. NOTE: Check with builder or architect, or check personally, to see whether any later changes have been made. Often homes are shifted on the lot several feet one way or another to utilize the site better.

Make a large map on graph paper (24 by 36 inches) that will show in clear detail just exactly what you have to work with. Draw to the largest scale the paper will allow—generally, $1/4$-inch equaling 1 foot. This will be your base map. Slipping this base map under the top sheet on a pad of tracing paper, you can later sketch out designs to your heart's content. (You can buy graph paper and a pad of large-sized tracing paper at a stationery store.)

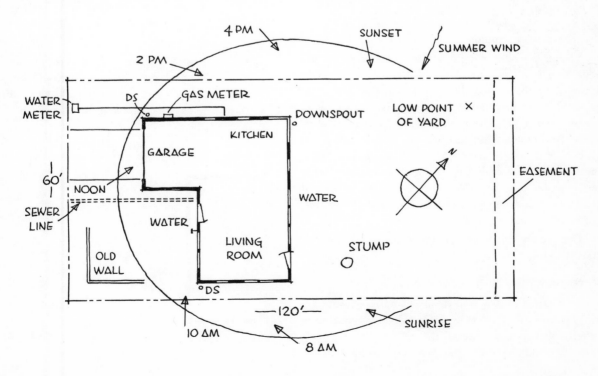

On your base map, show the following:

1. *Orientation to the compass—then indicate hot spots, shade areas.*

2. *Direction of prevailing wind, winter and summer.*

3. *Boundaries and dimensions of the lot.*

4. *Location of easements that may affect your planning—underground telephone lines, trunk sewers. (See deed map.)*

5. *Location of setback boundaries that may limit outdoor building.*

6. *Location of utilities—water, gas, and sewer connections—and depth of each; underground electric or telephone wires; outlets on outside of house for water and electricity; location of sewer cleanouts; septic tank drain field; meter boxes.*

7. *Location of your house. Show all doors and windows and indicate whether they open to or from dining room, kitchen, living room, bedrooms, entrance hall, playroom.*

8. *Soil conditions. Show location of fills, cuts. If you want, make test borings to determine character of soil; show results on map. (Generally not necessary when remodeling an old garden.)*

9. *Gradient. Show contour lines; locate high and low points; indicate contours on neighboring property that will affect your planning by draining water or cold air into your garden; mark downspouts and indicate whether underground drains or sewer connections are included.*

10. *Map existing planting, particularly large, established trees; indicate names of plants if known.*

11. *Alongside plot plan, note the problems beyond the lot line, good or bad views of neighbors' property, hills, trees, telephone poles.*

---

Bring out the check list you have made up from your inventory and place it alongside this basic plot plan. You now have in front of you all of the physical restrictions and requirements imposed by your lot, and a list of all your needs. You are ready to go ahead with your planning.

Lay a sheet of tracing paper over the base map on which you have outlined house and lot. All the work of getting the house and lot on the graph paper is safe from being messed up. If you make a false move, nothing is lost except one piece of tracing paper. You can swing that pencil with abandon.

So now you sit looking down at a piece of paper, and your head is filled with 15 or 20 items which must be arranged on that paper. Don't feel that this design-on-paper idea is a silly crutch for beginners. As you work out any garden, you are forced to make dozens of decisions. And unless those decisions are recorded, they will be lost. A plan is a record of decisions and a constant check on the accuracy of the decisions. No expert planner relies on his memory. Nor does he make off-the-cuff decisions. It costs money to change a line fixed in cement, but it costs nothing to erase it on paper.

But you are still looking at that piece of tissue paper. Afraid to begin?

### Start your plan with "doodles"

If you're afraid to start your design plan, try "doodling." Many landscape architects work from doodles—miniature patterns that set the theme of the design. "If it doesn't look interesting in a doodle, it won't look good when

it's built." Doodles are helpful to many amateurs because by over-simplification they rule out minor details that get in the way of the basic plan. Most important, they do not have the serious aspect of a full-sized landscape plan. They are experiments in approach. They allow comparisons.

Doodles come quickly. You can doodle a dozen plans in miniature while you are getting ready to put one final plan on paper. Just remember that the shape of your doodle plan should be in proportion to your lot.

But how to start the doodle?

We've been collecting doodles of garden plans for some time now. We feel we can establish some principles from them. Out of our collection, we have selected a few that various landscape architects made when they were working on the same problem.

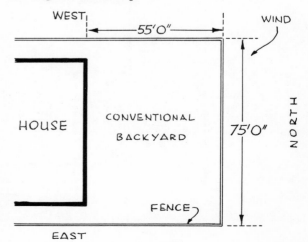

All of these doodles came out of a conversation about how to landscape a conventional back yard—a rectangle 70 feet wide and 55 feet deep.

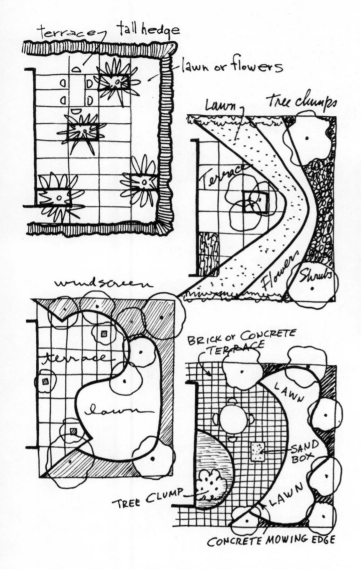

The problem was identical, the features added were about the same, but the designs were as characteristic of each landscape architect as his handwriting.

When we asked each designer how he reached a satisfactory design, he answered in effect, "I can't tell you."

Us: "What kind of guidance do you call that?"

DESIGNER: "Draw some shapes. Look at them. Do they please you? Try again. You'll know when you hit it."

Us: "What about those of us who are design-blind? Surely you have a rule or two to follow?"

DESIGNER: "Rules are for dopes. Rules limit imagination. Every situation is different."

But landscaping is taught. And teachers must guide. They must talk of rules or principles. Perhaps at a school we might collect some doodles that would show why lines are drawn here rather than there.

So we attended a class conducted by Robert Danielson for beginners in landscape design at the University of California.

The following quotes are from our notes. The doodles are from instructor Danielson's illustrations.

Danielson is at the blackboard before an outline of the back yard space of a 70-foot lot. He says:

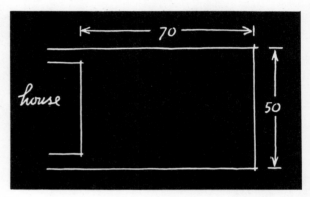

Here in a limited amount of space, we must provide for the occupancy of a family. Let's assume that there is no wind or sun problem, and that the house is properly oriented. In actual practice, the control of the sun and wind is the point of reference that would keep the designer constantly in touch with reality.

In this space, we must measure off room for eating, walking, and conversation; room for hiding, for expanding, for shade, for work, and so on.

We can measure off these volumes in many ways. The activities of the family will dictate the size of the volumes. But the pleasure the family finds there will depend upon how well you fulfill their sensory requirements.

These people must find a sense of shelter, but not the feeling of being cooped up.

Generally, their eyes seek a basic unity and orderliness in what they see. But unity and orderliness are not virtues if they result in monotony.

Variety, variations in visual experience, delight, amuse, interest them.

In a more or less predictable way, they respond to pattern, texture, color, sound.

Most people recognize what they call pleasant proportions on one hand and awkward proportions on the other. If the relation between things is too equal or extremely unequal, the sight of them is disturbing.

If you accept that principle and apply it to a section of the garden, the following would be true.

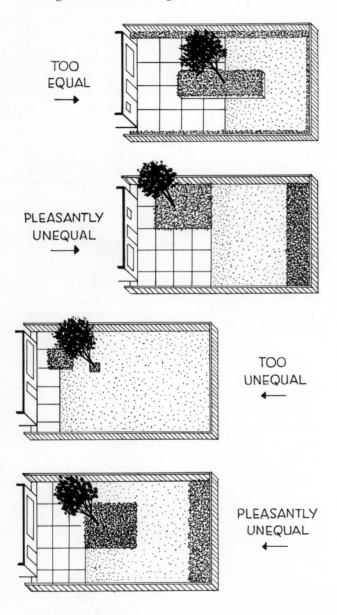

TOO EQUAL →

PLEASANTLY UNEQUAL →

TOO UNEQUAL ←

PLEASANTLY UNEQUAL ←

The sense of proportion cannot be plotted on a chart. One man may feel as tall as the sky and as wide as an acre. He feels comfortably in scale with the tallest trees, the highest mountains. Inside the house, anything less than a 9-foot ceiling is crowding down on him. Another person is happiest when his back is against a solid wall under a ceiling he can reach up and touch.

But even the cave dweller seeks free and easy space outdoors. His eyes measure the sky, the distant trees, as well as the fence.

Space that is completely limited and defined is relatively small; space that is partly limitless and partly closed is big, yet comfortable.

When organizing space, you can lean on the knowledge that most people see orderliness in well known shapes. The simplest shapes the designer can work with are the square, the rectangle, the triangle, the hexagon, and the circle. He has great latitude in variations as long as the basic shape is recognizable.

Let's see if we can demonstrate this:

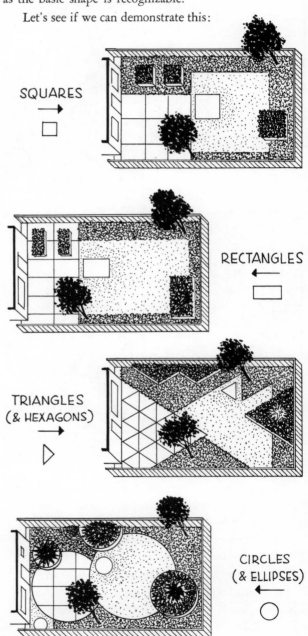

SQUARES →
□

RECTANGLES ←
▭

TRIANGLES (& HEXAGONS) →
▷

CIRCLES (& ELLIPSES)
○

The eye is not disturbed by a change if an easily recognizable shape carries through the central theme. A theme with variations creates a unified garden with variety and interest, without monotony. Here are two examples in which the basic theme is heavily strained by many variations in paving, overhead, fence, lawn, and raised bed:

The safe way to impress the eye with a unified design is to create a rhythmic arrangement of units as a pattern. For example, here are the same units arranged with and without thought of pattern.

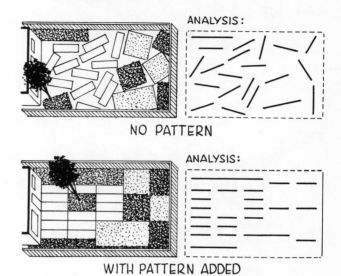

NO PATTERN

WITH PATTERN ADDED

In grouping shape or mass, it is much easier to make them seem unified if you join or interlock the units rather than if you separate them and put them in tension with one another. Here we take the same units and arrange them in three different ways:

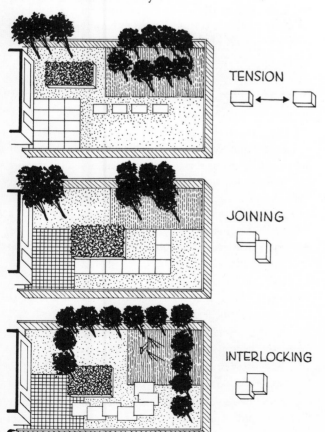

TENSION

JOINING

INTERLOCKING

Plantings and structure should be arranged to satisfy man's need for the feeling of shelter. However, to carry it to the point where it prevents him from walking and playing in the garden may give him a cooped-up feeling— the very feeling the small-house dweller comes into the garden to escape.

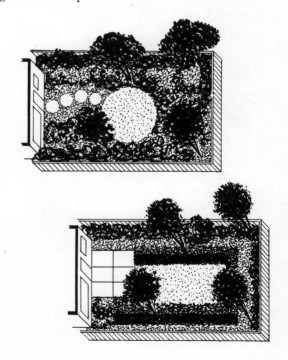

Here, on page following, are examples of cooped-up space compared to open space.

GREATER APPARENT SPACE

You will find that many people will agree with this statement: Curved lines are restful, natural; angular lines, zig-zags, suggest speed, force, thrust.

Here are two schemes composed of the same units. Supposedly the upper plan is calm, the other, exciting.

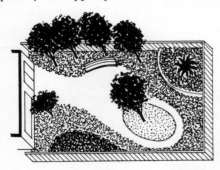

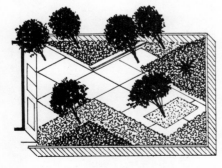

Fortunately, the lines on the ground are not as dominant when you see them from eye level as they are when you look at a plan. Movement in the vertical elements can contradict the surface lines. By planting the so-called "exciting" plan, you can make its angularity disappear at eye level.

Use the curiosity of man to sustain his interest. Create an invitation to explore what he cannot clearly see—around a corner, behind a tree—by restraining parts of the picture from his view. In first sketch below, everything is seen at a glance from terrace; in second, part is hidden, part open.

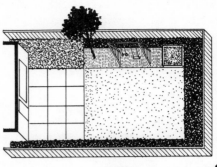

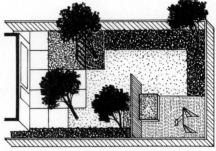

If the size of the lot or any area within it is too long or too narrow or too rigidly fixed to be interesting, create new boundaries or shapes that destroy the original fixed shape and give an illusion of greater space.

— — — — — — — — — — — — — — —

From the foregoing lecture, it seems to us that the so-called principles of landscape design have value only when you question them. They can help you by making you look for the reasons why you like what you like. The principles are not design guides to be followed blindly, but are guides that enable you to look at a garden, or a garden photograph, or a landscape plan, and see the essentials that make it a success or failure as far as you are concerned.

The trap to avoid in looking for guidance in design is the belief that "design" as such exists free and separate from your specific problem.

Of the principles that have been advanced in the previous chapters, this is the most important:

*Design is for people—for their activities and comfort in the garden.*

You'll be on your way to a usable garden if you follow this principle by providing adequate patio and play space;

by blocking the hot summer sun (but inviting the warming winter sun); by deflecting the disagreeable wind (or sometimes catching a refreshing or cooling breeze).

Since the sun and wind will, in general, control the placement of the major elements in your garden, you may find yourself placing these elements in such a pleasant relationship that no thought of design as such is necessary.

If they do not arrange themselves so easily, consider these main points in Danielson's lecture:

1. *To avoid confusion, to get simplicity and order in your design, plan with the recognizable shapes of the square, the rectangle, and the circle.*

2. *In the small garden with fixed limits, create the illusion of greater space by not allowing the eye to measure the complete space at a glance.*

In working out your own design, you should be aware of the special devices used by the leading landscape architects. The photographs of their work say over and over again:

1. *Design generously, then count costs.*

To get a feeling of luxury in the garden (and where else can it be bought so cheaply?) you need only take a step here and there beyond necessity.

A 2-foot wide brick walk, laid in sand, can be changed to a luxurious 5-foot walk for 90c a lineal foot.

A 10 by 16-foot patio seems more than adequate to most builders; but a 12 by 30-foot patio, part concrete, part ground cover, part gravel, is a luxurious thing.

In most builders' houses, the usual step between the house and the patio is only as wide as the door. Lengthen it and widen it and you not only go in and out of the house with ease, but you have a garden seat as well.

2. *Design boldly so that later plant growth will not completely erase your design.*

Design should make a strong and definite statement. Unless you lead from strength, growing plants will erase the design almost as soon as it is executed. What may appear too strong the first year is gentled and quieted by plant growth in the third year. The low wall, the wide mowing strip, the raised bed, are strong, built-in, permanent lines used boldly by the designer.

3. *Design can direct the steps of people, spread them out through the garden, bring them together, draw them to an entrance or an exit.*

For example, if the patio floor appears to be a part of the house, the edge of the patio will set the limit for movement of most people. However, if a wide path flows from the patio to another paved area in the garden—under a tree, perhaps—people will spread out through the garden. A second sitting area at a distance from the house gives everyone visual permission to move into the garden.

---

Now, let's get started on the plan.

On the sheet of tracing paper you have laid over the basic map, indicate the general areas you will need and their approximate location; show where sun protection and wind protection will be needed. When you remove the tissue, it may look something like this:

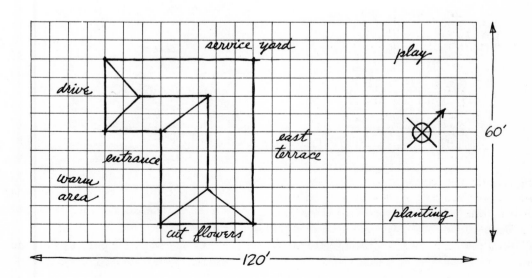

With this start, based upon the use of the space and on sun and wind control, we might continue to play with the relationships of space and plane, of form and line, until the design suits us.

But since the circle is already suggested, let's take it as our basic theme. So draw the biggest circle you can, leaving room on the north side for trees. Draw another circle in front of the house to define the streetside patio.

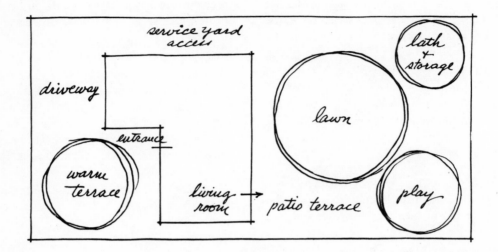

Next, let's take care of the entrance areas, the patio, and the paved surfaces.

Since the patio should be an extension of the living room, its location is fixed. Since we expect to roof the patio, it should be rectangular in shape. So we put it down on paper.

The partial circle of windbreak trees might be continued around the circle for partial enclosure of spaces indicated for play and lathhouse on the first rough plan.

Next, let's get traffic under control, from driveway, entrance, to paths around the house and in the garden. The plan now looks like this:

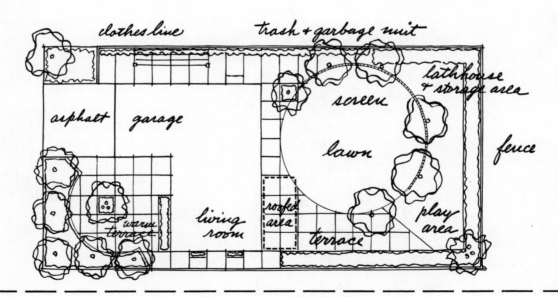

With the exception of the trees, all planting up to this point has been on the ground. The trick now is to think in the vertical plane with plants and structures.

At this point, don't think of specific plants or specific structures. Think of both in general terms of height and width.

As we develop the plan, we will indicate each step by a letter on the plan opposite.

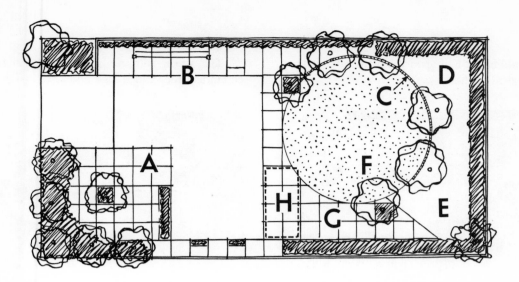

A. Entrance court (south side of house) is partially screened from street by shrub and tree planting. Will be used as outdoor sitting room when sun is wanted.

B. Clotheslines are screened from view from street by front fence panel.

C. Since the circle of trees planted to slow down the wind from the northwest won't amount to much the first two years, a circular 6-foot-high screen fence is built.

D. Area back of fence will be used for cutting garden or garden work center or both.

E. For children's play yard equipment. Actually, children have choice of lawn for games or paved area completely around the house for wheeled toys.

F. Lawn panel.

G. Paved terrace in 5 by 5-foot squares with 2 by 4-inch headers between the squares.

H. Lath overhead takes care of hot late afternoon midsummer sun on north side of house.

Making plan views—looking straight down at your lot, seeing it in two dimensions—is the easiest way to make preliminary arrangements of space and volume. Plan views show at a glance the relationships between all the items on the lot at one time. However, you should also try to think in perspective—in three dimensions—as you plan on paper.

If we visualized the garden as it would appear from a nearby hill, we would see it in perspective. It would look something like this:

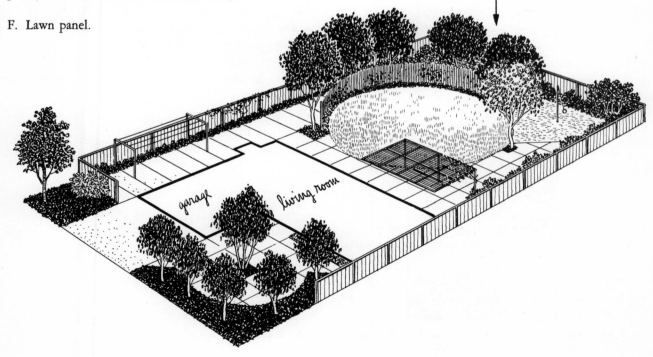

This would be the back garden looking from the seat wall back toward the house.

The screen and tree planting indicated along the entrance garden might look like this:

## How to plan with rectangular shapes

Now, let's take an entirely different approach; and instead of using the circle as a guide, let's take the square and rectangle. Many an amateur has found it helpful to work with a uniform "module" (e.g., a unit of space, repeated again and again, like squares on a checkerboard or bricks in a wall).

Your module might be 3 by 4, or 4 by 4, or 4 by 5 feet, or almost any larger rectangle that suits your needs.

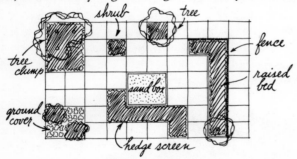

Using the rectangular module, we can make everything fall neatly into place. There's no question about what spacings to use or what sizes to establish.

Let's say you decide to use a 4 by 5-foot module. All of your walks would be 4 feet or a generous 5 feet in width. Your patio would divide up into 4 by 5 rectangles. One or more of these might be an open 4 by 5-foot planting island within your patio areas. Plant beds would be 4 feet across. A sandbox might be 8 by 10 feet, a raised bed 4 by 5 or 4 by 10 feet, a tree well 4 by 5 or 8 by 10 feet. Every design line in your garden, and every structural dimension, would be in relation to every other. You would benefit from a general sense of order and tidiness in your garden scheme.

The module system offers other advantages. With the dimensions suggested above, you have only 15, 16, or 20 square feet of paving to worry about at any one time. You can mix and pour concrete for just one rectangle at a time. You lay one rectangle of bricks before you start another. If you're a little bit off with your brick courses, you get a fresh start with the next rectangle.

Here are some of the ways you can go about selecting a module.

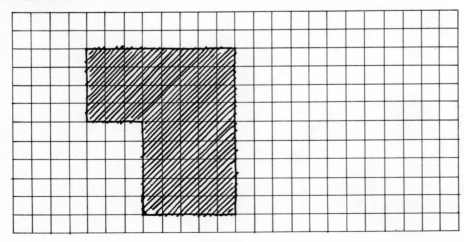

*Entire lot ruled off in 5-foot modules is start of plan on following page*

A path or walk that is about 4 feet wide will offer easy passage for a wheelbarrow, a wagon, or a bike. A narrower path seems restricted; a wider path may eat up too much space.

The patio wall of your house may be 24 feet wide. A 4-foot division in your patio paving would make 6 modules exactly fit your wall dimension.

If you work with bricks, you will avoid brick cutting if your module is an exact multiple of brick dimensions.

Most professionals urge a module no less than 3 by 3 feet; amateur landscapers say a generous module saves work.

Now let's take the same problem, the same base map, and work out a design using the module system.

On our first try, we'll use a 5-foot square as our unit. The length of the house divides by 5 and the walks at the side of the house will be 5 feet wide.

So we rule off the entire lot in 5-foot squares.

This grid pattern is our guide from now on. With it under a fresh piece of tissue, we start to register our decisions. Whatever we do anywhere will have some relationship to the rest of the garden.

First, let's get a paved area out from the living room. Marking out 3 squares gives a generous width of 15 feet. We try for a length of 8 panels—40 feet—with the mental reservation that we may end up planting a portion of it.

Next, we decide to protect the terrace from sun and wind with an overhead of lath. To get protection from the north wind, we'll wall in the north end with lath.

Now imagine that we are sitting on this terrace looking out at the empty back yard. We have a play area and a utility area to take care of. And we haven't forgotten the north wind.

The raised bed becomes a part of the terrace and lath cover. The seat-wall of the raised bed invites full use of the lawn and terrace. It indicates that the entire area is to be used.

Looking at the outline of screen fence and the terrace, it is obvious that without planting we'll have a rather harsh, structural garden. Since we need trees for shade and wind protection, let's get away from the rectangular feel by swinging the tree planting in a circle.

What would happen if we partially enclosed a portion of this total space, and blocked the rest from view? Couldn't we get a feeling of more privacy and protection?

So we follow the module lines to build a screen fence that will make a garden room out of the terrace. The screen fence will be the room's far wall. Like this:

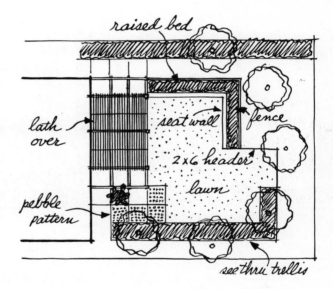

The design so far is reasonably satisfying. We've taken care of all the space requirements. Can we check it? How does it rate on these points:

- Could anything be done more simply and work even better?
- Did we make our design strong enough—bold enough—to hold its effect as plants grow?
- Can we get through the garden and around the house with a wheelbarrow?
- Have we provided adequate sun and wind control?

If it passes these tests, you are ready to give it the further refinements that you will pick up by studying (we hope) this book.

The sketches on the following page show other ways this problem might be worked out.

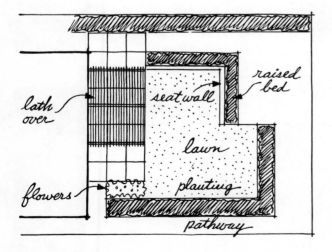

Here are four plans for a 60 by 120-foot lot. Consider that in no example has space been set aside for storage and service. However, according to your habits, interests, and needs, you can locate storage and service alongside house or take it away from planted area. Modular squares are 5 by 5 feet.

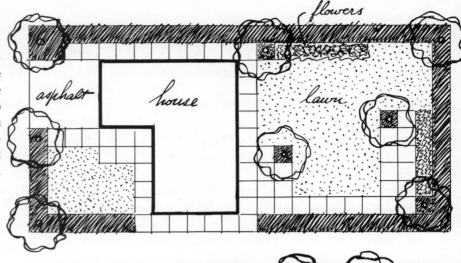

Entrance court and circular lawn are featured here as in all plans. The pattern of squares that are planted or paved is almost entirely as you like it. In the courtyard planting, clumps of trees are suggested in plant squares.

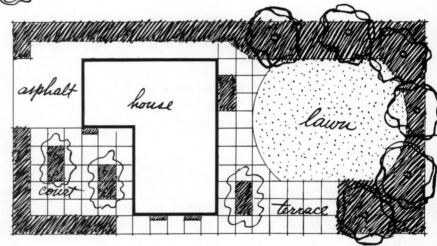

Planning takes into consideration the amount of work necessary to maintain the garden. Border planting may be as simple as a ground cover plus trees or a mixed border that is changed with the seasons. Paved squares could be concrete, brick, gravel, or combinations of all three.

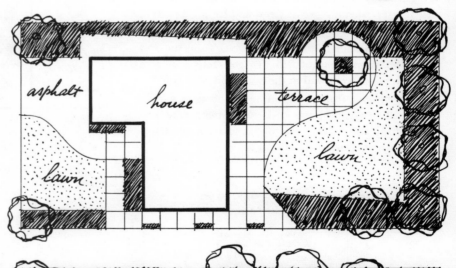

Concrete or brick squares cross the driveway and circle the house. Taking a contrasting type of pavement across the driveway does a lot to take away the idea that the driveway is for the exclusive use of the automobile. Angled borders give plant material better display.

# Planning for problem sites

There are no stock plans in landscaping. No two situations are exactly alike. No one plan could be made to exactly fit several situations.

But there are great similarities as well as differences. In the preceding chapter we accepted the very common rectangular interior lot for our problem. The solutions shown are usable in similar lots. The plans can be successfully copied if the necessary adjustments are made for differences in sun and wind problems.

We now explore the possibilities of adaptable solutions to such sites as the corner lot, the pie-shaped lot, the sloping lot, and so on.

First, let's take a look at a typical subdivision lot plan and see how landscape problems differ by types of site. A glance at the map shows that due to the uniform setback from the street, there's a great difference between the amount of streetside or "public" area and private area. In the map below, a 25-foot setback is required.

It's obvious that if you want the largest private garden you'll try for the pie-shaped lots.

On the other hand, it's hard to believe that a 10,000-square-foot corner lot will give no more private garden space than a 6,000-square-foot interior lot.

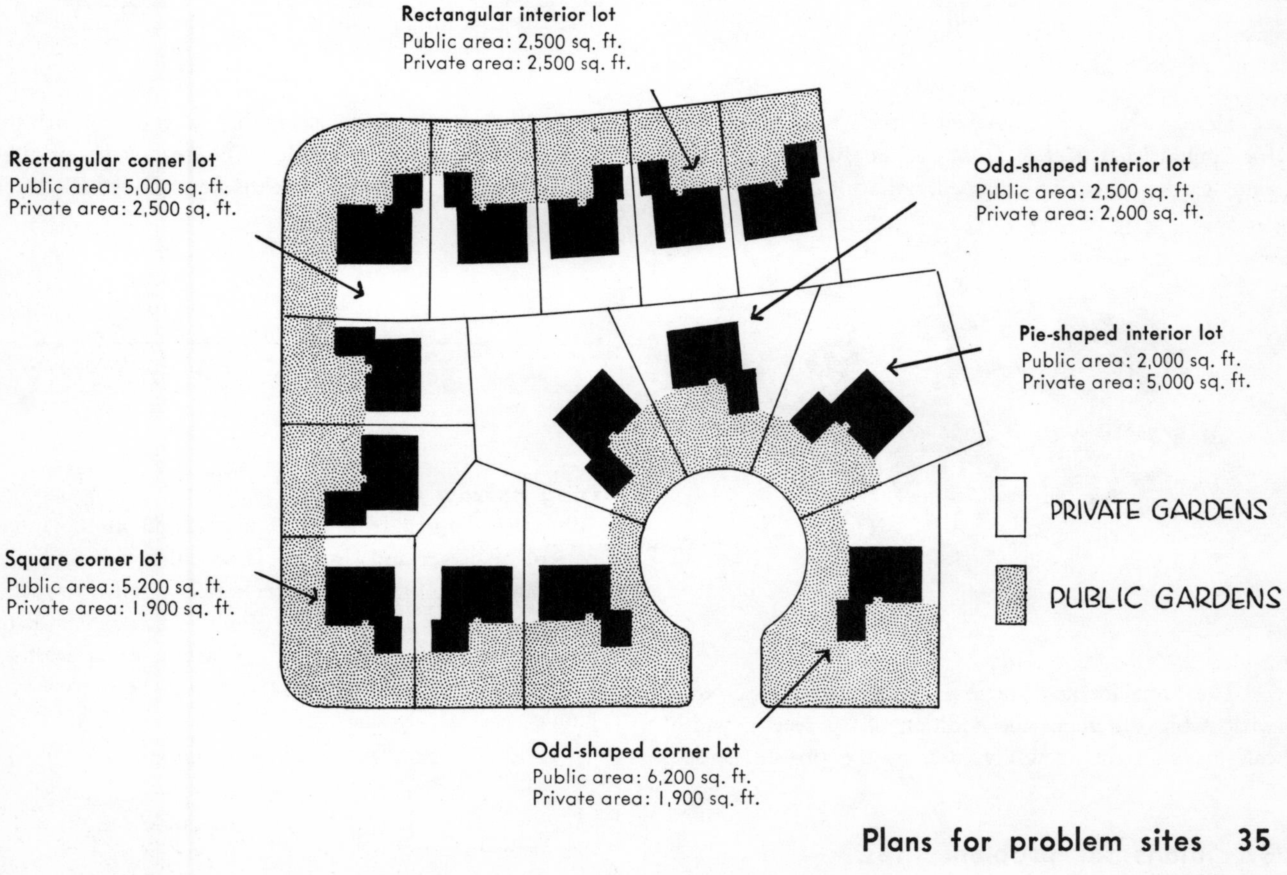

**Rectangular interior lot**
Public area: 2,500 sq. ft.
Private area: 2,500 sq. ft.

**Rectangular corner lot**
Public area: 5,000 sq. ft.
Private area: 2,500 sq. ft.

**Odd-shaped interior lot**
Public area: 2,500 sq. ft.
Private area: 2,600 sq. ft.

**Pie-shaped interior lot**
Public area: 2,000 sq. ft.
Private area: 5,000 sq. ft.

**Square corner lot**
Public area: 5,200 sq. ft.
Private area: 1,900 sq. ft.

**Odd-shaped corner lot**
Public area: 6,200 sq. ft.
Private area: 1,900 sq. ft.

☐ PRIVATE GARDENS

▨ PUBLIC GARDENS

## Corner lots

Several ways have been used to overcome the unequal proportion in space for the public's eyes and space for private use. If you drive around looking for suggestions on how to handle the corner lot, you'll see many solutions that might be denied you. The newer subdivisions are generally more strict in enforcing setbacks. In older residential sections, the problem of privacy was often solved by planting a hedge on the property line next to the sidewalk and letting it grow to 8 feet or more. Some of the later subdivisions allowed a property line fence, 6 feet high, 5 feet from the sidewalk, along one side only. The general rule seems to be that 6-foot fences are allowed only on the secondary street side. A low fence or wall is permitted nearly everywhere, but check local ordinances.

Illustrated below are various ways in which more private space can be obtained.

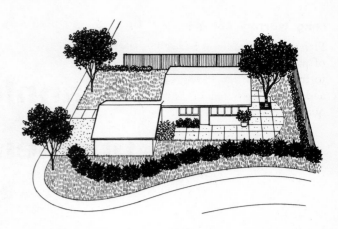

Here, where garage determines the setback, private space is gained through establishment of informal hedge. When making such plans, avoid creating a blind corner.

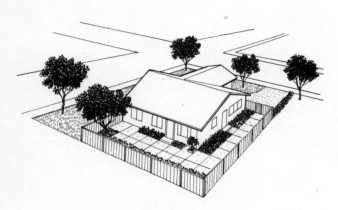

Here's what happens when setback restrictions take for "public" use 25 feet from two sides of the lot. Private garden area is cramped, difficult to landscape.

In the sketch above is another way to get private living space on the streetside. The entrance court becomes a patio. Screening fence is kept on setback lines.

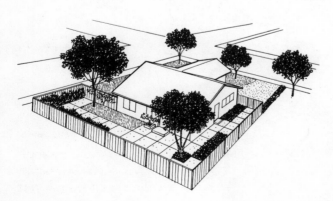

The same lot and house as in sketch above. Note what a big difference the addition of 20 feet in width can make in the livability, use, of the private garden.

## Long narrow lots

When the long narrow lot is landscaped in the usual pattern of flower and shrub beds on either side and end of a lawn panel, the garden feels like a hallway with a narrow green carpet down the center. The problem is to find ways to give the illusion of width, or at least to prevent the eye from quickly measuring the narrow rectangle.

Here are examples of narrow lot solutions:

## Long Narrow Lot No. 1

Plan features a series of hedge panels set at angles. Series of paved terraces, partially hidden from the terrace next to the house, invite the viewer to explore. Paved areas and curving lawn panel make it impossible for the eye to quickly measure the dimensions of the lot.

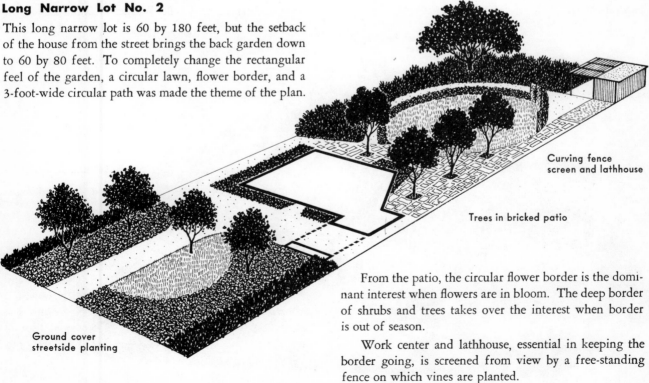

Compost pile
behind hedge

Drying yard

Older home
with detached
garage

Might have
panel fences with
vines instead of hedges

Screen hedge planting such as illustrated here will do a good job of wind control when needed. Terrace behind middle hedge would be a good place to build a work center if you wanted it out of sight.

## Long Narrow Lot No. 2

This long narrow lot is 60 by 180 feet, but the setback of the house from the street brings the back garden down to 60 by 80 feet. To completely change the rectangular feel of the garden, a circular lawn, flower border, and a 3-foot-wide circular path was made the theme of the plan.

Curving fence
screen and lathhouse

Trees in bricked patio

Ground cover
streetside planting

From the patio, the circular flower border is the dominant interest when flowers are in bloom. The deep border of shrubs and trees takes over the interest when border is out of season.

Work center and lathhouse, essential in keeping the border going, is screened from view by a free-standing fence on which vines are planted.

## Long Narrow Lot No. 3

By opening and partially closing space, all sense of a long, narrow garden is lost.

Owners are enthusiastic gardeners specializing in camellias, rhododendrons, azaleas, and hydrangeas.

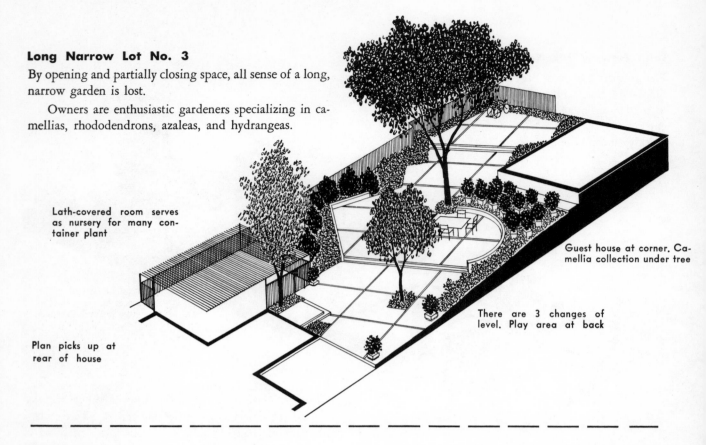

Lath-covered room serves as nursery for many container plant

Plan picks up at rear of house

Guest house at corner. Camellia collection under tree

There are 3 changes of level. Play area at back

## Pie-shaped lot

The pie-shaped cul-de-sac lot can give you the greatest proportion of private space to public space of all the lot shapes in a subdivision. The streetside is narrow; the backside, deep.

Here, the large lot is divided into several departments: entry garden, children's play area, living room patio, barbecue patio, lawn area for games, utility area, food garden, dog run. In spite of the variety in uses and departments, the garden holds together as one unit.

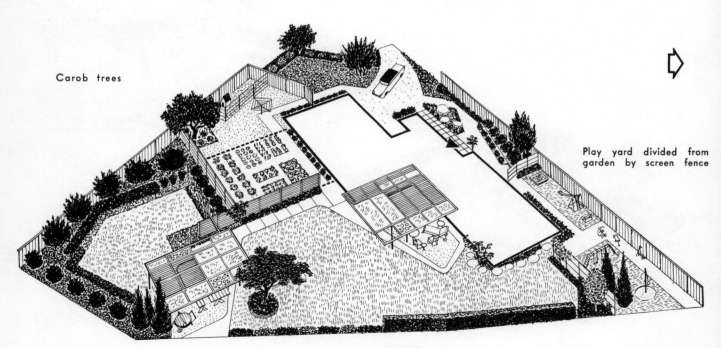

Carob trees

Play yard divided from garden by screen fence

Lawn area behind garden gives chance to roam around

MARY GORDON

*Overhead uses combination of materials—solid, open, plastic. Brick was laid in sand on a crushed rock base. Blue-gray concrete edge strip provides color contrast to brick, defines edge of patio, extends as path to the barbecue patio beyond. Placing a second patio away from house invites exploration, spreads out use of the garden*

*Front entry garden uses gravel as ground cover, with evergreen plants and concrete circles as design elements. Entry porch on right. Fence screens play area*

*From barbecue patio, looking back to the house. Overhead repeats patterns and materials of living room patio roof. Fence screens vegetable garden, service yard*

**Plans for problem sites 39**

DOUGLAS BAYLIS

*The free-standing section of the arbor is given extra wind and sun protection by the reed screens at the back and vertical lattice at both ends. The raised beds are used for vegetables, berries, seasonal color*

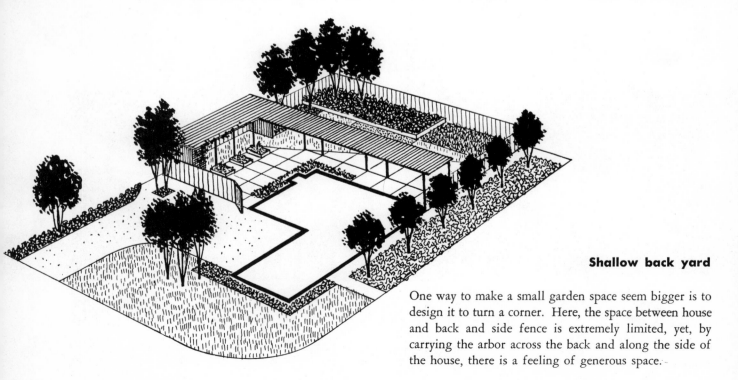

### Shallow back yard

One way to make a small garden space seem bigger is to design it to turn a corner. Here, the space between house and back and side fence is extremely limited, yet, by carrying the arbor across the back and along the side of the house, there is a feeling of generous space.

At end of arbor is small garden work center. Hanging fuchsias. Plant bed in foreground contains 3 tomatoes on stakes. Outdoor dining area adjacent to kitchen

Overhead along back of house is roof eave height. Constructed of 4 by 4 posts, 2 by 8 cross pieces, 2 by 6 rafters, lath cover. The lath should be 1 inch thick

Designed for a hot summer climate, this lofty lath-covered arbor put the sun under control immediately.

It's attached to eaves along back of house (north), and set out 10 feet from the house on the west side

## Deep setback of house

In this house, streetside area has been remodeled to provide off-street guest parking and to give all the space possible to children's play. Back garden is divided into

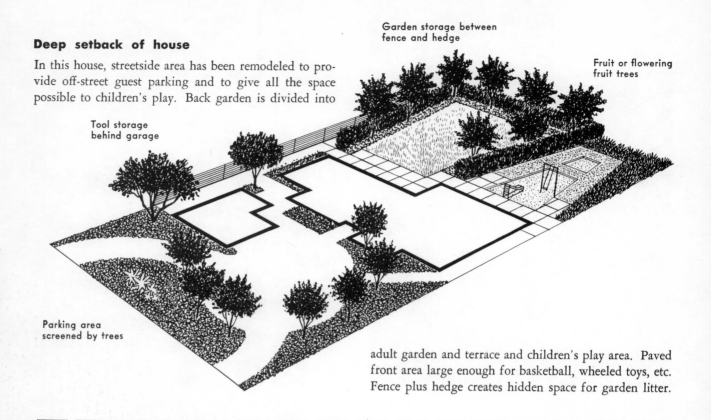

Tool storage behind garage

Parking area screened by trees

Garden storage between fence and hedge

Fruit or flowering fruit trees

adult garden and terrace and children's play area. Paved front area large enough for basketball, wheeled toys, etc. Fence plus hedge creates hidden space for garden litter.

## Garden to look down upon

Owners, enthusiastic gardeners with time on their hands, wanted a garden to work in and to look down upon from the bedroom-sitting room windows in the second story. Old-fashioned formal garden feel is maintained in design and by mixed planting of flowers and vegetables.

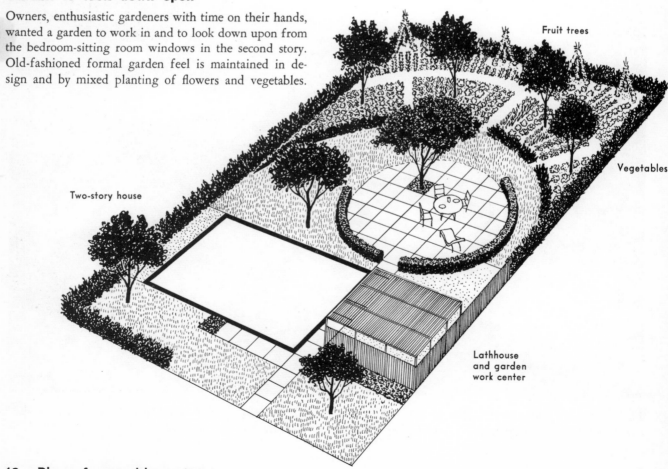

Fruit trees

Vegetables

Two-story house

Lathhouse and garden work center

# Planning for comfort . . . ease

"Give me a beautiful garden that will take care of itself"
—that seems to be the fervent wish of most homeowners
when they start to landscape their places.

If you don't take "take care of itself" too literally,
you'll find many pointers in this chapter on how to plan
for beauty and easy maintenance too.

*Modular panels of dichondra in variation with grid
pattern act as green transitions between unified sections of gravel and concrete, softening lines with color*

SCHUYLER REED HAFELY

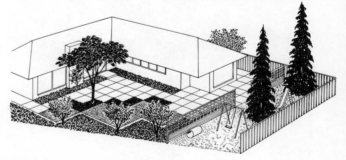

## Planned to sit in, not work in

Here is a case in point—a garden that is livable and easy
to take care of. The great variety in flooring materials
is kept in order by modular panels.

Raised beds add to the sense of order.

Maintenance confined to whatever is done to the
raised beds.

Trees will furnish effective shade in two to three years.
Meanwhile, patio not used until in shade in afternoon.

Owners hoped to sit and enjoy the garden, rather than
work in it. Wanted place for grandchildren to play.

*Living room wall of vertical bleached cedar continues into garden as patio wall. Teal blue cap on garden wall extends into living room. Rhododendron A.T. de la Mare carries trusses of white, pink-flushed flowers opening from deep pink buds. Rhododendron foliage is crisp dark green, stands sun*

*Border has Snow azaleas, red Vulcan rhododendrons, dwarf juniper. Clematis armandii on fence opposite*

## Planned for comfort and beauty too

When living room and garden room are separated by a glass wall, there is no visual division between them.

Here, the garden is as much a part of the living room as its furniture. By extending wood wall of the living room as a fence, at wall height, the close relation between indoors and outdoors is made undeniable.

The glass wall on the garden side makes the fence and forest of trees above it the visual "wall" of the living room.

The garden is planned with the same careful attention to color, form, and line as the indoor areas. It is seasonally "out of bloom" but never out of design.

Because of the paving and excellent wind protection, it is comfortably usable whenever weather permits, even when the permission is but for an hour between showers.

*View from living room. Paving is gray Mt. Adams stone. Dwarf Sargeant flowering crabapple in bloom; shore pine, left; Sargeant flowering cherry, right, with Gumpo and Hexe azaleas. Flowering cherry offers spring bounty in large dusty pink single flowers in spring, bronzy orange foliage in fall*

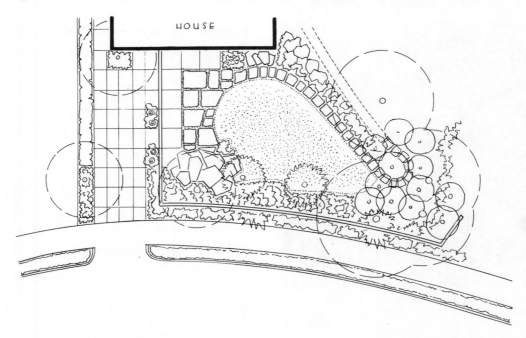

HOUSE

*Four different paving textures: brick in garden patio, lawn at right, concrete under house patio roof, and red rock in the children's play area seen in the background*

*Sand box is made as part of the seat wall that borders the children's play yard. Such low walls are efficient garden protectors where children play, give neat effect*

## Planned for comfort and easy maintenance

The requirements for comfort and low maintenance were met by building the basic form of the garden with fences, raised beds, and trellises, by sun control, and by simple arrangement of large areas for sitting, for entertainment, for play. But the structural background of the garden was designed to enhance and dramatize plant material; designed into the plan were countless ways to give shrubs and vines and flowers more importance than they would have had without the structures.

The result was that as they lived in the garden, the owners found themselves becoming enthusiastic gardeners—as excited by the plants themselves as by the landscape pattern in which they grew.

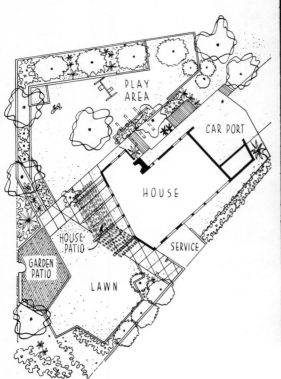

GERALDINE KNIGHT SCOTT

*Spacing between lath gives variation in sun control. The widely spaced laths filter sun on patio; narrowly spaced laths cut down sun shining on glass, into house*

*Narrowly spaced laths extend to block sun in spring and summer (March 21 to September 21), but admit it to warm house during cool fall and winter months*

*Raised bed at the base of the board fence which defines children's play yard. The trellis in left foreground supports clematis, screens play yard from entry garden*

*With the fence defining its limits and acting as outdoor walls, the garden becomes a place for living as well as looking. Besides providing privacy, the fence transforms a yard into a private garden room. Boxwood hedge lines lawn*

## Garden to live in, work in, look at

Here's a garden that shows recognition of the fact that interests are often mixed.

Built where rains are expected even in early summer, the major outdoor living area is arranged for moving portable table and chairs at a moment's notice.

The garden is always a pleasing view from the living room. It recognizes that plant material and building material complement one another.

The garden can be handled with very little attention, or speeded up to absorb the most intense of gardening interests. Whether the greenhouse, vegetable garden, and planting squares are in full operation or closed down is not important to the appearance of the garden.

*From living room, the French doors open into garden. Low stone steps at rear lift view, give a sense of depth*

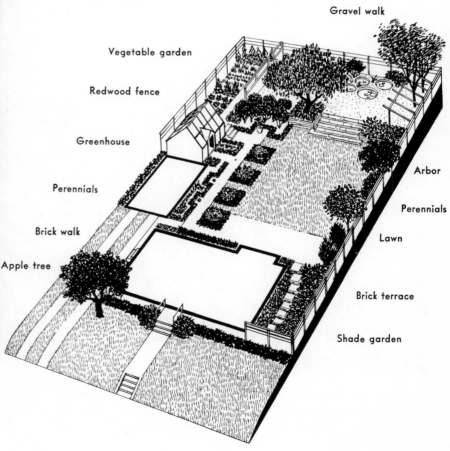

Gravel walk

Vegetable garden

Redwood fence

Greenhouse

Perennials

Brick walk

Apple tree

Arbor

Perennials

Lawn

Brick terrace

Shade garden

# Plans for children's gardens

If you turn loose a couple of 5-year-olds—boys or girls—on an acre of land where play places are a beautiful lawn, a cattle-loading chute, a full stand of tall grass and weeds, an old tree, a broken down truck, a pile of scrap lumber, a regulation jungle gym, where would you find them most of the time? Not in the places you prepared for them.

When you set aside a corner of a 60-foot lot and label it for "child play," the very best you can say for it is that it acknowledges that the children have rights to a place strictly their own. But if you're wise, you'll allow for

garden use beyond the sandbox, swings, and basketball hoop.

Garden use by children will mean a different thing in each family. In some families, gardening and growing children are not incompatible. In other cases, the garden must be all play space.

In the next few pages and scattered throughout the book, you'll find plans that have been developed with children in mind. Look at them with an eye to the complete space for play and the provision for change with changing interests.

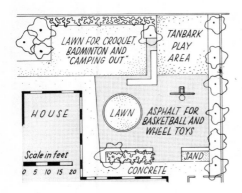

*Asphalt paving for wheels and basketball. Plants are protected in raised bed which can also serve as a seat wall*

THOMAS CHURCH

*Since children like to climb and fly through the air, here are bars for climbing and swings combined on one circular pipe frame, set over tanbark. Includes climbing rope, rings, trapeze, ladder*

THOMAS CHURCH

*In this remodeled garden, the old garage was converted into a roofed shelter by removing one wall and by carrying the fence line under the roof. In the shel-* *ter, behind the fence, is a potting bench, work center, and generous garden supply storage space. The garden is noteworthy for its simplicity, its easy maintenance*

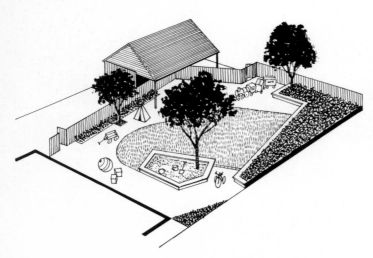

## Planned for hard use

Simple design avoids confusion and minimizes maintenance.

Asphalt paving, carried to the fence, gives a large and interesting space for wheel toys. Lawn panel serves same purpose as a soft rug in a playroom.

Raised bed protects flower border from scooters and tricycles.

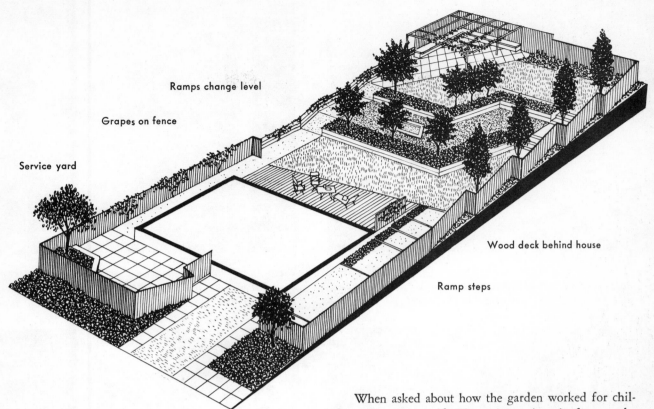

Ramps change level

Grapes on fence

Service yard

Wood deck behind house

Ramp steps

## Planned for variety in interests and play

Great variety in planes and plants is held together by strong lines of retaining walls.

Interesting and efficient circulation through use of ramps, ramped steps, and steps.

When asked about how the garden worked for children, the owner said, "Steps, trees, jogs in fence make wonderful forts . . . 'Dead' warriors who have staggered down steps ambushed from behind a tree too numerous to mention. . . . Fourth of July spectacle of ours and 13 neighbor kids making circuit tour up steps, around, down ramps, waving sparklers, like something from Disney—and proves the circulation is good."

DOUGLAS BAYLIS

*Looking up terraced hill from house. Tanbark is spread on the level where children are playing. Vegetables, fruit at left; grape arbor shelter in background*

*Wood deck is bridge between house and garden. Natural grade drops to about four feet below the house floor line. Screen on left is for privacy from neighbors*

Children's gardens 51

LAWRENCE HALPRIN

*Here, in 1950, all the bare bones of the design dominate picture. The garden looks too fenced-in, and you can't see much reason for the overhead structure*

*Two years later, the overhead trellis is a green roof of wisteria; its shadow pattern changes the surface design. Fence begins to lose its harsh stockade look*

*By 1955, flowering purple-leafed plums cut down the glare, screen the kitchen and bedroom windows, cool*

*the house, contrast leaf color against its gray painted exterior. The elms block the view of neighbor's roof*

*In 1950, view from house shows the screen built to hide service area dominating picture. Arbor has no apparent purpose. There's very little garden feel here*

## Planned for children's changing interests

Gardens and children grow up before you know it. Here, in the brief time it takes a child to grow out of tricycles into bicycles, a garden becomes mature.

LAWRENCE HALPRIN

*In two years, purpleleaf plum arches directly overhead. Ash tree rises above trellis. Ivy covers grapestake fence. "Structure" becomes arbor as wisteria takes over*

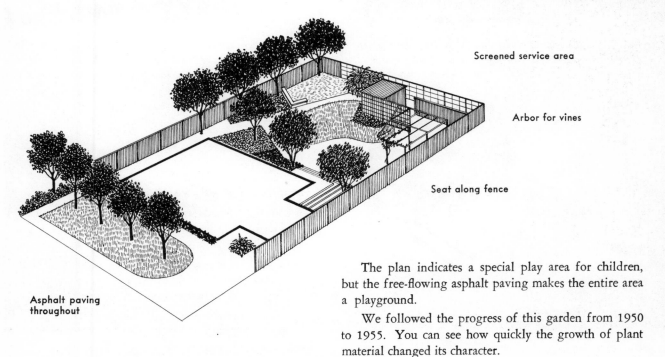

Screened service area

Arbor for vines

Seat along fence

Asphalt paving throughout

The plan indicates a special play area for children, but the free-flowing asphalt paving makes the entire area a playground.

We followed the progress of this garden from 1950 to 1955. You can see how quickly the growth of plant material changed its character.

DOUGLAS BAYLIS

*Another example of what can be done when house is above ground level. Simple deck at living room level is more serviceable than usual paved terrace reached* *by steps from house. Decking is 2 by 3-inch fir. Seat fixed to posts makes full width of deck usable. Canvas at corners rolls down for protection on rainy days*

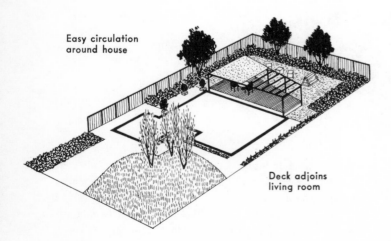

Easy circulation around house

Deck adjoins living room

## Planned for all weather use

Wood deck extends indoor room, creates a rain-and-sun-protected playroom.

In this 36 by 60-foot back garden, a deck is built at the floor level of the living room and connected with it by sliding glass doors. Half the deck is roofed solid, half open to the sky, sheltered only by a vine trellis.

By making the deck 12 feet wide at one end, 8 feet at the other, more space is available for tanbark play area, without losing the generous feeling that the 12-foot width creates.

# Plans for climate control

Here is an example of the kind of problem that prompted a new kind of landscaping. With this house to start with, here's how to create a livable, pleasant environment both indoors and out . . .

Western sun hits glass—heats the room

Two-foot change of level from living room to ground—awkward and restricting

West wind sweeps across patio area

Outdoor area in full view of neighbors

This solution—at first glance unorthodox and costly—illustrates by exaggeration the change in the approach of landscaping.

The garden changes size and climate of living room

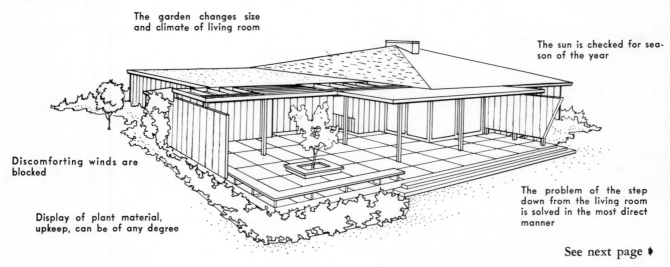

The sun is checked for season of the year

Discomforting winds are blocked

Display of plant material, upkeep, can be of any degree

The problem of the step down from the living room is solved in the most direct manner

See next page ▶

## Planned to extend indoor living

Pictured on these pages is the solution to the problem in climate control outlined on the previous page.

It's a solution that deserves careful study, as it can be adapted in many ways.

LAWRENCE HALPRIN

*Looking from garden to house. Baffle at right stops wind, screens view of neighbor's house. Wide, strong-lined steps change level easily between new deck, lawn*

*Fence and house wall provide wind screen, form sun pocket. Overhead structure is a combination of lath and open space here, but is solid around living room*

*To some people, a deck offers more comfortable out-door living than a brick or concrete terrace, and lumber cost can be held to less than $1.00 per square foot*

LAWRENCE HALPRIN

*Deck creates an almost unbelievable sense of spaciousness inside the living room since both of the floor levels are even and the roof overhang repeats the line of the ceiling*

There is good evidence here that decks are not just for hillsides. They can correct that very common fault of changing level from the indoors to the garden. Previously, when house and garden were only remotely related, this step down was of little consequence; but with the use of large openings of glass and sliding glass doors, the need for one continuous level becomes most important.

The increased use of glass also makes sun control a necessity.

*The addition of a few shrubs or trees quickly brings garden feeling to a deck or a terrace*

**Patio turns the corner . . .**

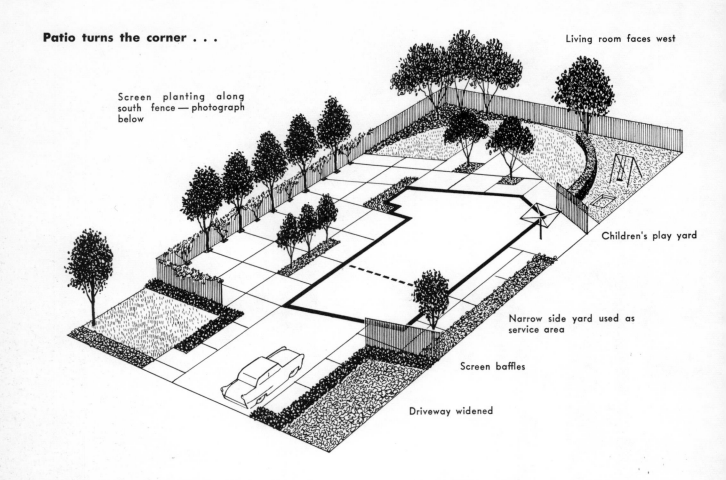

Screen planting along south fence — photograph below

Living room faces west

Children's play yard

Narrow side yard used as service area

Screen baffles

Driveway widened

DOUGLAS BAYLIS

*Side yard patio in this garden is screened from neighbors after only three years' growth of* Eucalyptus polyanthemos *trees along fence. Opening off protected lanai, paved area is tricycle race track and winter playground*

Continuing the patio around the corner of the house gives the rear patio a sense of much greater space and also provides a warm winter southern patio.

The glass wall of the living room, facing west, received sun from 2 o'clock to sundown during the hottest months of the year.

Two quick-growing trees were planted close to the glass of the living room to create a vertical screen to block the sun's rays and give a leafy umbrella when sun is overhead.

# Plans for hobby interests, favorite plants

*A hobby garden can be of any size or disposition. Here's protection and display for the great group of shade-loving plants. But sun-loving container plants can be added to give color to garden*

Plant enthusiasts and specialists generally look with suspicion at the work of the landscape architect. To them, the apparent denial of the existence of so many of the best-loved plants in the world doesn't make sense.

Of course, the only reason more landscape plans do not show roses, iris, gladiolus, chrysanthemums, and the like is that most gardeners specializing in one plant aren't interested in design. They are interested in more planting space. And we have no quarrel with them.

The ideas presented here are for the specialists who happen to want both a complete garden and a show place for their favorites.

It's strange but true that the most effective way to handle most of the favorites is to design a garden that looks good without them. By designing the basic framework so that it is attractive throughout the year, you almost automatically provide more attractive backgrounds for your favorites than if you planned directly for them.

To illustrate the many ways that a garden can be designed for both the owner's horticultural hobby and his family, we have taken the same background and followed four different design themes.

Note these points:

- Garden beds are arranged to give access to hobby plants from both sides to make it easy to give constant care.

- Beds are placed to give maximum display to blooms and plants.

- Hobby plants are separated from lesser breeds because of peculiar cultural requirements.

- Plans provide room for eventual expansion. No hobby gardener has the strength of will to stop buying plants.

- Since most specialties look their worst in winter, plants or structures should be placed to soothe the eye during the bleak months.

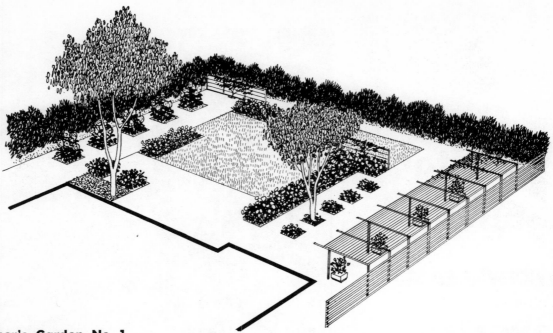

### Gardener's Garden No. 1

Designed for a family with chrysanthemum project. The planting squares to the left of the terrace take care of the chrysanthemums that need staking. Since that area is graveled, there will be no difficulty in adding more planting squares as the collection increases. A portion of the lath shelter at right will be covered with plastic to take care of chrysanthemums in containers after the fall rains start. The possibility of later converting a portion of the lathhouse to an all-weather garden workshop with potting bench, propagation frames, was considered.

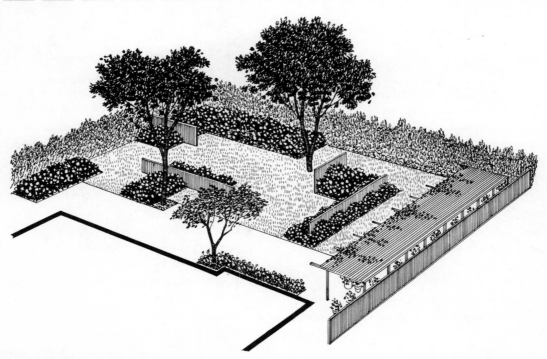

### Gardener's Garden No. 2

Another suggestion for the same size lot illustrates the use of baffles or screens to hide portions of the garden so that experimental plant material will not conflict with the garden picture. The gardener who is collecting and developing fuchsias and day lilies would find this garden to his liking. The lath shelter and the trees give sufficient shade area for the specialist's use. Note that although the projects are a part of the garden design, they do not take full command, nor are they slighted.

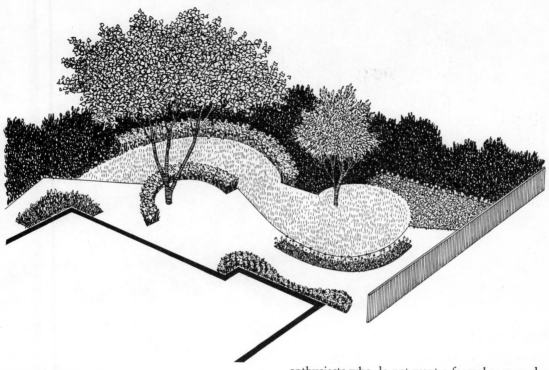

## Gardener's Garden No. 3

In this case, the flower display cases take a more prominent place in the garden. The plan might appeal to rose enthusiasts who do not want a formal rose garden. There are six good-sized planting beds. The evergreen background is strong enough to hold the interest when roses are out of leaf.

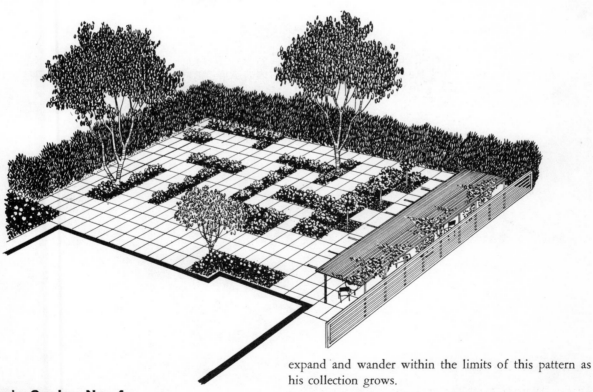

## Gardener's Garden No. 4

Here the rigid grid pattern is compromised and dominated by plant material. The enthusiastic gardener can expand and wander within the limits of this pattern as his collection grows.

The iris specialist would enjoy this garden. He could work with color, new introductions, expanding supplies, with the greatest of ease.

DOUGLAS BAYLIS

*Here, in 1950, the bricks are in place to fix the alternating 6 by 6-foot panels of brick and planting space. The canvas overhead is laced to a pipe frame*

## Garden reflects changing interests

As gardening ideas and interests change, the garden plan should be flexible enough to take care of them. The plan here has that quality. It came into being for a family that wanted to be free to experiment. In its first stages, 1950, the garden took care of a great miscellany of flowers and vegetables. In 1952, the garden acquired new owners. They saw the garden as an æsthetic experience rather than as an horticultural experience.

*In 1952, permanent plant materials replace seasonal plantings. Without changing floor plan, it becomes an entirely different, better disciplined type of garden*

*Three years later than photograph at bottom of page 62, Canary Island pines have developed characteristic form. The gray pittosporum has changed fence to a*

*gray-green, textured wall. Moss-covered rocks, miniature cotoneaster, and juniper provide close-up interest. Dwarf pine in tub. Ship's table benches at left*

*Bricks in sand in 6 by 6-foot squares or multiples thereof—some 3 by 3, 3 by 6*

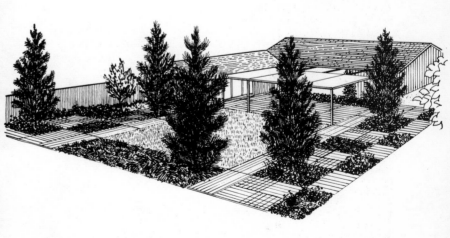

STRUCTURE BY STUART ROSE

*Container gardens offer plant collectors opportunities to pursue their hobbies regardless of size of garden, or type of soil, or climate. Here, a glass shelter between house and garage stops prevailing wind, protects pot rack, and provides a garden work bench and sink. Banked tiers display pot collection*

C. JACQUES HAHN

*Pool is surrounded by 18 by 18-inch terra cotta containers planted with echeveria, sempervivum, crassula, sedum. Pots flanking gate contain myrtifolia oranges with white petunias at base. Cissus hypoglauca on fence. Seasonal color from pots of bleeding heart, marguerite, cyclamen, lily-of-the-valley, and camellia*

**64  Hobby gardens**

# Plans for hillsides
# and the sloping lot

In this discussion of ways to landscape a hillside, we accept all sloping sites as hillsides. The site may be anything from a natural slope with a fall of only 4 feet in 100, to a carved out "bench" with a sudden sheer drop in front and a high cut bank in back.

Every slope is a different landscaping problem, but all slopes have features in common.

When the bulldozer made it possible to grade out a level lot almost anywhere, most hillside home sites changed from slopes to a series of benches. The bulldozer created a flat pad for a level foundation, and leveled some additional space beyond the foundation.

The bulldozer did much the same kind of a job on the hillside sites for individually built homes as it did in the subdivision, except that in the subdivision it carved the bench pads in a series.

The result: a great variety of hillside situations. Some have a short level lot with a bank sloping down in front and up in back or vice versa; some have a narrow level space with an up-bank on one side and a down-bank on the other; some have variations in two-way slopes; some have natural slopes.

To get at solutions which would apply to each group, we have gathered together in the following pages examples of several types of hillside landscaping. If you study these plans, you'll see that the sloping site offers many advantages in outdoor living and gardening and many opportunities for imaginative planning.

A well planted steep bank can become the backdrop of your own private garden amphitheater. A hillside with a 12-foot rise, planted with shrubs and ground cover, gives a house as much privacy and wind protection as does a line of 5-year-old trees.

A two-level garden offers mystery and surprise as you move up or down.

A planting of trees on a hillside below you can blot out the view of roof tops and often convert a commonplace view into a spectacular panorama.

If your slope faces south, you can enjoy growing many more tender or heat-loving plants than the gardener down on the flat. South slopes warm up earlier in the year and receive more total sunshine. Cold air flows downhill, leaving you from 5 to 10° warmer than the cold pockets below you.

Hillside topsoils are usually thinner than the soils of valleys, but you can concentrate your good soil in the terraces needed in most hillside gardens.

On a slope, even your next-door neighbors are often out of your line of sight.

But there's a price. Hillside gardening means drainage and grading problems—water flows down hill and water erodes. It means digging out or building up for a level patio. It means putting in steps or ramps from one level to another. In short, the sloping site demands more thought, more work, and sometimes more expense.

## Shallow natural slope

Can be converted into a series of level areas. Minimum of grading. Steps and raised bed serve as low retaining walls. Here, the owner created a level lawn area in front by raising grade at the street and lowering it in front of the house. Two terraces, with both steps and ramp between, take care of the back grade. Taller screen of trees around rear terrace is needed for privacy and wind protection.

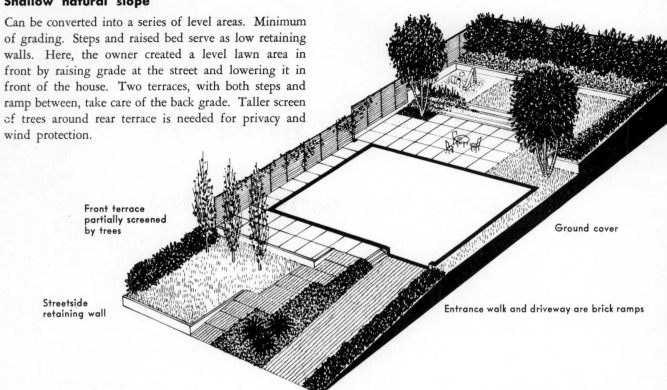

Front terrace partially screened by trees

Streetside retaining wall

Ground cover

Entrance walk and driveway are brick ramps

## Shallow graded slope

As usually handled in a subdivision. The only difference between this and the level lot are the two short banks front and back. Bank at rear serves the same purpose as a hedge or fence as far as privacy is concerned. Landscape problem is the same as for the level lot, except for taking advantage of the two short banks. Here, owner planted a row of fruit trees to serve as a summer screen from neighbor to the rear of the lot.

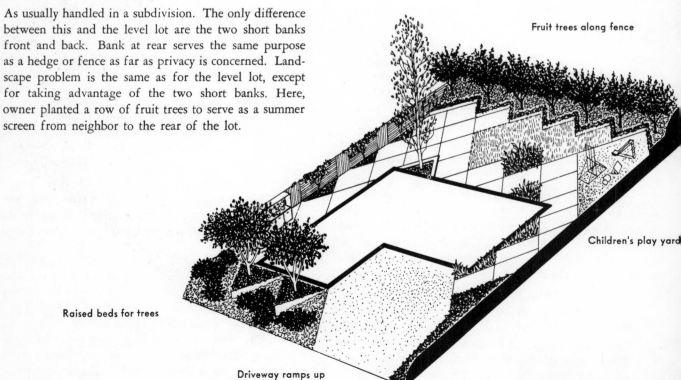

Fruit trees along fence

Children's play yard

Raised beds for trees

Driveway ramps up

## Medium natural slope

A series of low retaining walls creates a series of different levels on this medium sloping site, so there are no radical cuts and steep banks. Seemed better to change levels than to cut back deeply for one large floor level. Front garden is terraced into five levels, the back garden into four. The back lawn ramps down so the mower doesn't have to be lifted or pulled up and down stairs.

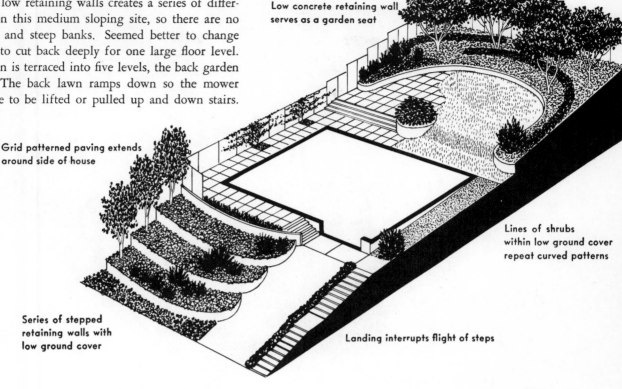

Low concrete retaining wall serves as a garden seat

Grid patterned paving extends around side of house

Lines of shrubs within low ground cover repeat curved patterns

Series of stepped retaining walls with low ground cover

Landing interrupts flight of steps

## Medium graded slope

Steep banks fore and aft on a lot may seem like a problem when you first move onto a side that has been deeply cut by the bulldozer. Actually, however, you can turn these banks to your advantage. With an evergreen cover, they can be made into attractive wind screens. With spreading shrubs, rear bank may do in two years what trees do in five years or more.

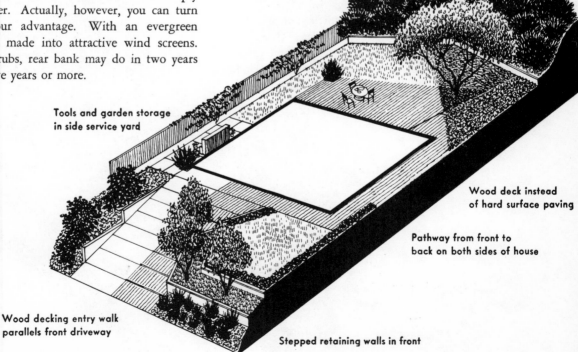

Shrub ground cover on back slope

Tools and garden storage in side service yard

Wood deck instead of hard surface paving

Pathway from front to back on both sides of house

Wood decking entry walk parallels front driveway

Stepped retaining walls in front

## Steep natural slope

In many cases, the simplest and least expensive way to get level space at floor level is to build a deck. If a tree planting is made that brings foliage to deck height, the high-perch feeling disappears, and a sense of protection takes over. Gardening, of course, can be carried on most satisfyingly in containers.

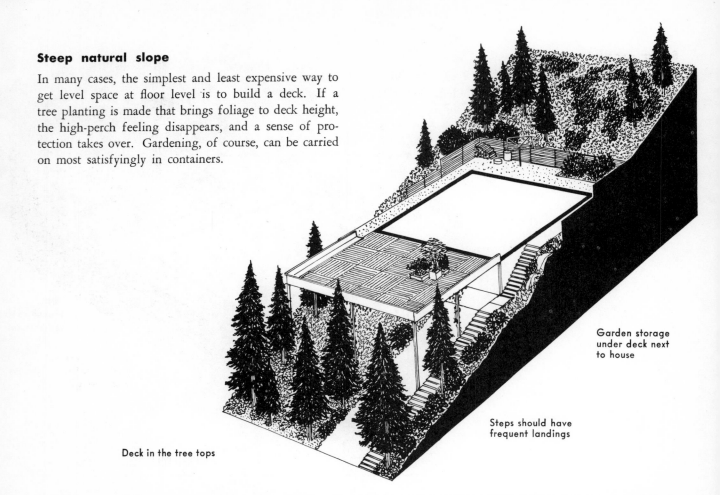

Garden storage
under deck next
to house

Steps should have
frequent landings

Deck in the tree tops

## Steep natural slope

One of the oldest ways to conquer the steep hillside. Terraces provide great variety in gardening and use. Here, in 4 levels, is space for outdoor living, vegetables, cut flowers, fruit trees, and children's play. This hillside receives strong afternoon winds from below. A row of small trees at each level successively bounces the wind upward, leaving each terrace quiet and comfortable.

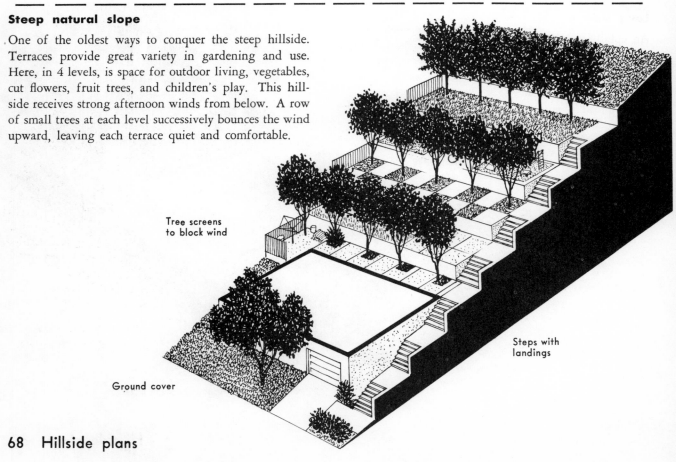

Tree screens
to block wind

Ground cover

Steps with
landings

## Steep graded slope

When banks are steep enough to create a possible erosion problem, they must be completely controlled. The front and back banks here are solid with shrubs and ground cover. The drop-off at the front of the house has been minimized by extending a deck from the patio over the steep bank.

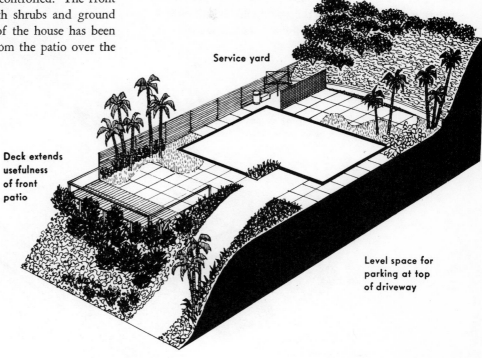

Service yard

Deck extends
usefulness
of front
patio

Level space for
parking at top
of driveway

## Long side to the street

An uphill lot, with long axis to the street, needs seclusion and feeling of width. Vine trellis, which is built out over slope, makes a kind of horizontal fence, and carries a carpet of vines at the patio floor level. Good evergreen vines for this situation: ivy, honeysuckle, or star jasmine (slow to get established).

Children's play area
screened from terrace

Shrubs set against
property line wall

Vine trellis gives visual
extension of paved terrace

## Back garden slope with bank in view

With a steep bank to the rear, you can landscape the lot much the same as a level site—if you can find a good solution for the bank. Left half of this bank has been made into a play area for children, hidden by tall trees; right half has a curving path.

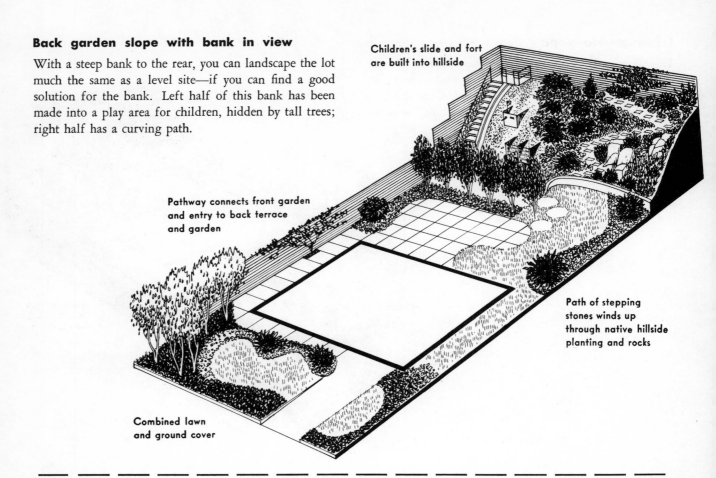

Children's slide and fort are built into hillside

Pathway connects front garden and entry to back terrace and garden

Path of stepping stones winds up through native hillside planting and rocks

Combined lawn and ground cover

## Back garden slope with bank out of view

A back slope that is completely out of view is no great problem where there is no adjoining lot. But when your bank adjoins a neighbor's site, both drainage and erosion become important to him. Also, your bank may be the most dominant feature in his view. It's a good idea to work the planting out together.

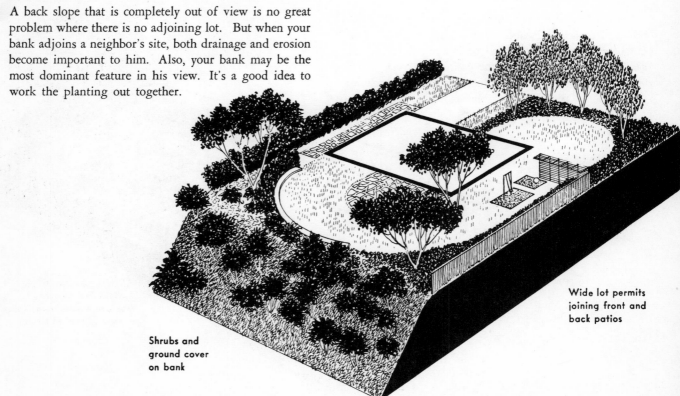

Wide lot permits joining front and back patios

Shrubs and ground cover on bank

## Streetside slope with street above

This situation is handled in several ways. For example, rather than having a driveway down to the house level, as illustrated, a garage is built at street level. In any case, this type of site provides private space both in front and back of the house. Here, the owner took advantage of the privacy provided by the bank and built an entrance courtyard.

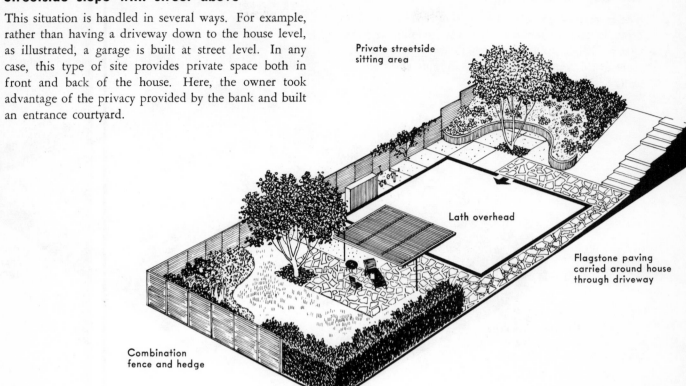

Private streetside sitting area

Lath overhead

Flagstone paving carried around house through driveway

Combination fence and hedge

## Streetside slope with street below

Where slope is gentle, rising from the street, you can design the entire street garden as a large entrance court. Here the angle of the raised beds (right of the driveway) gives direction to front door, offers a more interesting approach than a head-on walk from the curb. Back garden has sitting area, space for plants.

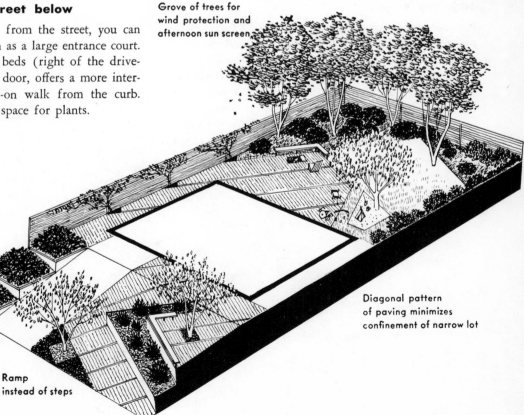

Grove of trees for wind protection and afternoon sun screen

Diagonal pattern of paving minimizes confinement of narrow lot

Ramp instead of steps

## Two-way slope

The two-way slope here takes curving retaining walls to create a series of terraces. Makes a retaining wall that changes height to follow a contour, as shown in the front of this garden. May be too difficult a task for the skills of an amateur mason.

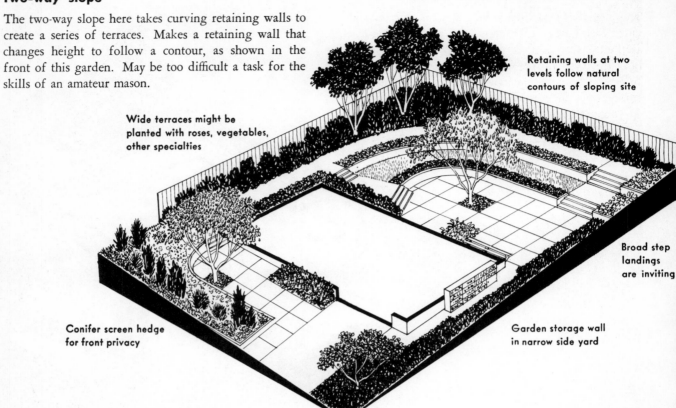

**Retaining walls at two levels follow natural contours of sloping site**

**Wide terraces might be planted with roses, vegetables, other specialties**

**Broad step landings are inviting**

**Conifer screen hedge for front privacy**

**Garden storage wall in narrow side yard**

## Two-way slope

Another way to handle the two-way slope: Cut and fill to create large level areas, but allow natural slope to prevail around those areas. Here, soil from excavation to form small dunking pool was used to level out the lower terrace. Here, again, the one difficult job is the construction of retaining walls. In this case, since there are no curves, the wall could be made of wood. The front garden could be simplified by omitting the level area for lawn or ground cover and substituting a planting of low shrubs on the natural slope.

**Lath shelter**

**Level area with ground cover will be protected by conifers**

**Entrance court**

PEGGY SULLIVAN

*Flight of steps leading up to lathhouse in background is strong feature here. Blue slate combines well with interplanting of ajuga, blends with the redwood risers*

GERALDINE KNIGHT SCOTT

*Steps of massive, split redwood timbers are matched in weight, contrast in color, with light-colored granite boulders. Landings are redrock with gravel topping*

ECKBO, ROYSTON, AND WILLIAMS

*Steps with frequent landings, red clay tile treads, redwood risers, drop from carport, upper left, to house level. Bridge leads to second story of house*

DOUGLAS BAYLIS

*Change of level from street made by ramp, right foreground, and flight of steps, cutting through terraces that are solidly planted with juniper and cotoneaster*

ECKBO, ROYSTON, AND WILLIAMS

*Here designer creates second change of level for no purpose other than making garden more interesting. As plants grow, they will cover rawness of construction*

*Steep slope of decomposed granite soil planted to create backdrop of variegated ivy ground cover, drought resistant shrubs—elaeagnus, ceanothus, and genista*

*Zig-zag retaining wall, with cap for seat, allows for topsoil-filled planting bed for Algerian ivy trained to climb steep cut. Native plants above are not disturbed*

*A good example of the rewards of planning boldly. By carrying risers the full length of the slope, but filling in only a portion, a feeling of luxury is obtained* *that is not possible with the ordinary steps in a planted bank. Large boulder is surrounded with low juniper, lambs ears, and Convolvulus mauritanicus*

# What to do about the streetside garden

Planning or remodeling the front "public" garden generally calls for a different set of considerations from landscaping the private back yard.

You don't want to let the neighborhood down. The people who drive by must be considered. But you don't want to get trapped into spending all your garden time

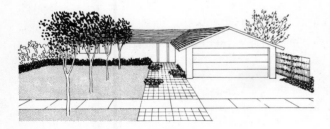

and money in an area you can't use. Low maintenance is an important streetside planting consideration.

Possibly you would like to set your house apart from all others in the block. In a new subdivision where houses are all the same age and much alike in appearance, the desire for individuality is a natural one.

If the public area is extensive because of an unusually deep setback, as in many older neighborhoods, you may want to take back some of the public space and work out a front patio.

First, let's look at the problem in a subdivision where houses have identical setbacks and a series of driveways at exact right angles to the street.

In such a situation, if you wish to set yourself apart from the neighbors, you must think out two problems simultaneously. Your plan must work as a unit with the house and at the same time break up the uniform pattern of the street.

Let's consider both angles.

The quickest way to break the uniformity of a subdivision street is to work with strong vertical elements such as hedges or rows of trees. Fences, high for privacy or low for the division of space, raised plant beds, will quickly vary the over-all appearance of the street.

The change from lawn to ground cover breaks the uniform pattern, especially if the ground covers are selected to create a pattern by contrasting textures and colors. Pattern planting with ground covers, confining the plants with header boards to prevent intermingling, offers the bold gardener many opportunities for individual expression. Couple pattern planting with wide paths and generous paving, and the departure from other homes on the street is even more pronounced.

The parking strip takes well to imaginative ground cover treatment. This area offers visitors a preliminary welcome. Make some provision for foot traffic—welcome your guests with a dry, paved, landing area. Here are some suggestions for paving-plus-planting.

*Alternating two kinds of ground cover*

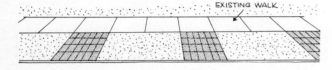

*Brick landing strips in grass parking strip*

*Ground cover, header boards, and gravel*

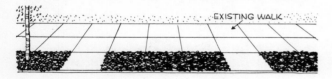

*Concrete to curb with ground cover panel*

You may want to change the stiff line established by your driveway. You can do this in many ways. You might put in a raised bed on one side of your driveway, with a low planting on the other side. Or you may pave a step-out strip along your driveway and then join this strip to your entry walk with a generous area of connecting paving.

If you have both a straight path to the street and a straight driveway, you may want to consider a more drastic solution. In this illustration the original walk was broken up (the pieces were saved for later use in raised planter beds), and a front entry garden with planting beds and paving was developed.

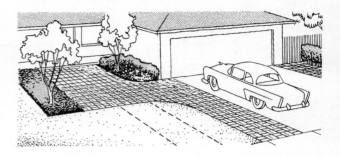

*Caution:* Use low, clear-vision plantings along a driveway. Screen planting along a drive can be dangerous where small children are likely to run out or be playing on the drive when driver backs out.

You have much to gain by carrying out your streetside planting plans in cooperation with your neighbors. Such cooperation is not always easy to enlist, but in a new subdivision where everyone is interested in the appearance of the neighborhood as well as that of his own house, you have a decided advantage.

Here is an example of the special effects to be achieved through cooperative planting. In the sketch below, you and your neighbor on your left (A) jointly plant a ground cover that runs from your driveway to his driveway right across your property line. With the neighbor on your right (B) you plant lawn, again right across your property line. To define your properties, you and neighbor A plant the same trees on either side of your property line. You and neighbor B do the same thing, using different trees.

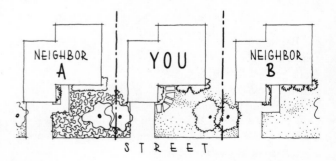

This results in a pleasant harmony between your own garden and the gardens on either side. It also achieves a very generous feeling, instead of a tight, cramped feeling, in your entry garden.

*Parking strip is part of front yard design. Both areas planted with Hahn's ivy. Liquidambar offers seasonal change. Olive good contrast against brick wall*

*Interesting interplay of informal planting with formal structure. Low perennials break definite lines of paving. Added color from pots of geraniums and petunias*

In many recently built subdivisions in California, front fencing goes from house to house, frequently repeating the structure and line and color of the house itself. Some home owners like the simplicity of this approach; others would prefer not to be so directly linked to their neighbors.

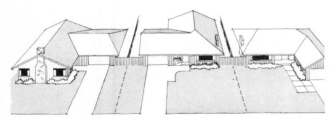

Below are two ways to terminate the property line fences between your house and your neighbors' in the front garden. Notice how both the T solution at the left and the L solution at the right create pleasant planting situations for trees and shrubs.

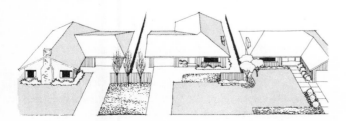

## Make the entire front yard an entrance court

Whether you want to set your house apart from the neighbors' or to cut down on public garden maintenance, one of the best approaches is to consider the entire front yard as a grand entrance court.

The conventional landscaping approach that concentrates on the front of the house as an architectural unit to be enhanced by shrub and tree planting fails to work when houses are so closely joined that it is impossible to look at them as individual units.

By concentrating on an entrance court and forgetting the face of the house for the moment, you are likely to end up with an attractive entry garden that takes care of all the "foundation" planting generally associated with landscaping the front of the house. Your planning should start with the correction of any awkward situation caused by the house itself. These are the kinds of problems you may face:

How to get out of a car without stepping on grass or planting?

What to do when a front picture window or a wall of glass looks out on your entry garden?

What to do with the narrow walk from sidewalk to front door?

How to help guests reach the entrance easily from both the street and driveway?

**Streetside plans   77**

*Entry along garage wall is set apart from other entries by violet trumpet vine with branches spaced for pattern. As vine grows, it will eventually cover overhang*

*Walk to front door features posts, overhang supporting Burmese honeysuckle vines. Fence provides privacy from street. Pyracantha trained against garage*

**Here are possibilities to consider in planning**

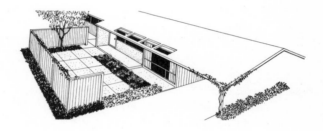

By adding a deck to this split-level house on a hillside lot, you gain an inviting entry and an outdoor room, and reduce its apparent height. Paving along drive against house clearly identifies approach. Espalier breaks large wall expanse. Rock garden minimizes steepness of steps.

Courtyard is screened from street but open on drive side, offering approaching guests an opportunity to enjoy the garden as they approach the entry. Planting bed in the front of window is conversation piece, and reduces glare inside. Vines, low planting soften fence, house roof.

This enclosed entry garden has enough privacy to serve as an outdoor living area, yet the light, partially open fence does not appear as an unfriendly barrier. Carpet of evergreen ground cover in front of window absorbs the glare of afternoon sun, is a soft contrast to paving.

Trees and well balanced space divisions transform the front of this tract house into a distinctive courtyard. Trees on right provide leafy canopy; slender upright trees, left, separate drive from entry, relieve streetside monotony. Planting pockets break up largest paved area.

*Let the visitor find his way to your door along these large concrete pads, cast in the ground, set in dichondra and sedum ground cover. A live oak shades entry*

*Here parking area, driveway, walks are continuous. Podocarpus trees frame entry. Light textures of ferns in pots, tree fern, papyrus, good against dark house*

## entire streetside garden as an entrance court . . .

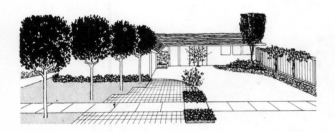

Entire front of the house, including the parking strip, is included in this entry garden. Line of trees creates illusion of depth, leads you to door. Low planting makes green panel between asphalt, brick paving. The fence and house walls offer opportunities for good use of plants.

Simply planned entry with minimum paving, emphasis on plant material. The simple curved path is pleasing foil to the straight lines and angles in rest of the area. Six-foot evergreen hedge next to the garage screens the front door, and emphasizes horizontal lines of the house.

Small trees irregularly spaced across the front of the property, interlocking ground covers of different foliage texture and color, and nicely handled division of space distinguish this inviting entry. The trees are pruned high and kept open to maintain a look-through quality.

An existing tree and a special need for low maintenance influenced the planning and planting of this streetside garden. The area outlined by the perimeter of the tree is paved to avoid the necessity for watering. Ground cover plants have been chosen for low moisture needs.

*Pleasant entry garden, sheltered terrace, in space formerly occupied by garage, driveway. Ceanothus is planted on slope to screen the entry garden from street*

*Informal and welcoming is this natural planting combined with a generously paved area of quarry stone. Plants are mainly rhododendrons, petunias, violets*

*Sometimes front terrace is logical choice—when living room faces street, or where streetside exposure offers more comfortable outdoor living. This terrace is completely fenced for privacy. Pool is design feature*

*A fenced streetside area need not be unattractive. This orderly planting arrangement of olive trees and ivy is as handsome and as interesting as an open yard.*

*Clipped teucrium hedge continues feeling of trimness, its gray foliage gives contrast against weathered fence. Parking strip paved with tamped and rolled red rock*

*Slatted fence, with sweet alyssum at base, makes friendly barrier between garden, parking strip. Young live oaks and Pfitzer junipers screen house from the road*

*Purpleleaf plum, red winter berries of cotoneaster, yellow flowers of sedum offer year-round color in front of plastic screen. Lawn strip lends unity to the street*

GEORGE JETTE

*In Eugene, Oregon, this small front entry terrace offers perfect sun control. Dense shade of native bigleaf* *maples keeps area cool even on hottest days. Paving is exposed aggregate. Planting under trees is ajuga*

## Streetsides when setbacks are deep

The older house with the generous setback from the street presents a different problem—and different rewards—from the new subdivision home with a shallow setback.

As costs of garden upkeep mount, and as home owners increasingly look to their private back yards as extensions of living space, the devotion of large, well mannered front areas to the public seems out of line for the little pleasure and usefulness that it contributes to the family.

More and more, home owners are thinking about streetside gardens less as generous display pictures and more in terms of full-time usefulness—or at least good looks with minimum care. With fences and hedges, some of the public area is reclaimed and made private. In many neighborhoods and in many parts of the country, a high fence or hedge is regarded with suspicion; however, a small area, well planted, in front of a fence or hedge can give just as much delight to the passerby and just as much pride to the owner as a more elaborate setback.

You can obscure or partially obscure the board structure itself. The boards in your fence, in time, will weather and warp. Yet, if your fence is planted, the deterioration of the fence itself is not really serious. The eye goes to the plant material, not to the structure. Against the fence you can train vines or espaliers.

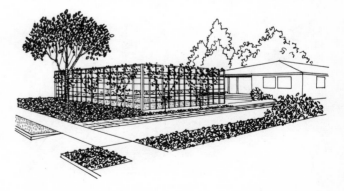

The area between the fence and sidewalk, like the parking strip, should be handled as a part of the over-all landscape plan. Remember that such strip areas, where

*Same entry garden shows streetside privacy fence. Its placement on setback line, as seen here, still gives a* *wide open appearance to the street. Shade of trees invites planting of azaleas, vine maple, and sword ferns*

your garden meets the street, often will be outside the regular garden area. Plant it with low-maintenance, undemanding, year-round material.

You can take back for private use a part of an overly generous streetside area by construction of light baffles. By training vines on them they soon lose all the look of

get more sun. Note examples in chapter on remodeling. Such deep setbacks also offer opportunities for large entrance courts which can be used as garden rooms.

A simple screen planting or a hedge will also give you the desired privacy.

a fence. On sites in cool summer climates where the house faces south or southeast, the recapture of enough space for an outdoor patio garden gives you chance to

When setbacks are deep, you have the opportunity for providing off-street parking. See chapter on *Remodeling* for plans and details.

Streetside plans 83

THOMAS CHURCH

*Trim, uncomplicated offstreet parking area—interrupted only by elm trees. Fancy leaf geraniums offer color at base of tree, against house with pyracanthas*

*Here, entry walk and driveway are one. Step-up separates parking area from entry. Tobira on left of entry, geraniums on right. Ivy ground cover, teucrium hedge*

THOMAS CHURCH

*Entry from driveway leads forward to front door, right to kitchen. Redwood board-and-batten fence gives privacy, provides background for golden bamboo*

*This low maintenance streetside and entry garden uses three main plants: Teucrium fruticans, clipped to a neat hedge, variegated ivy ground cover, silver maple*

# How to remodel

# the established garden

———  ———  ———  ———  ———  ———  ———  ———  ———  ———  ———  ———  ———  ———  ———  ———

The urge to remodel an older garden strikes in various ways and for many reasons.

You buy a home that has been landscaped by a person who loved the very plants that you can very well get along without.

Or after a three-year try, you look at your own handiwork and are sick of it. The shrub you thought would be gray-green is as lively as green grass. The shrubs that were supposed to remain low are covering the windows. The patio is too small and too hot.

Or you find yourself with an overgrown, 30-year-old garden, rich and lush in plant material but poor and cramped in living space.

Or the family is growing up. Tricycles have changed to bicycles; you need a basketball court instead of a sandbox.

Don't resist such reasonable urges to change.

Even changing just for the sake of change has its rewards. It is one of the ways you can enjoy the satisfactions that come with being a designer—the refreshment to the eye, the sense of creating something beautiful, the new ability to see the form and texture of plants.

To exercise your designing eye, drive through a street of pleasant homes and look at the streetside planting of each with the question, "Would I choose this as an example of a good planting arrangement?"

Most plantings would be too spotty, too jumpy. Some would be too sparse; many would be overgrown.

After looking at a hundred gardens, you might be ready to re-examine your own with fresh eyes. Often as not, *then* will come the urge to remodel.

## Doing over the mature garden

If you are living with a garden someone else planted 15 or 30 years ago and it does not satisfy you, you very likely face a drastic job of garden remodeling.

Is this older garden your master or your servant?

Does it tax your time and budget to keep it up?

Does it give you the space you want for outdoor entertaining, for sun-bathing, for growing the plants you want to grow?

The charm of many an old garden is in its overgrown foliage, its sheltered pools of deep shade. Little by little over the years, the domestic jungle closes in, and without anyone's quite knowing when it happens, the garden no longer has a place for sun-bathing, for growing dahlias, roses, or other sun-loving flowers, and the service yard has no place for drying clothes. Even indoor living suffers; foundation planting has overgrown the windows, blotting out the sun.

When you study the planting in such a garden, you often find in the mixture of shrubs and trees many that were originally planted for quick effects or were selected without thought of eventual size.

Woody plants grow higher when treated as trees than when allowed to grow as shrubs. With energies diverted into a single upward channel, a plant that has remained 12 feet high as a mature shrub may reach 20 feet as a tree. By training old shrubs as trees, you not only relieve congestion and gain new planting space around the base, but you also improve them in health and appearance.

OSMUNDSON-STALEY

**After:** *Lath overhead cuts off view from neighbor, makes room out of open space. Glass screen deflects wind from room. Exposed aggregate paving reduces glare. Raised bed simplifies area*

PROBLEM: To bring livability to a wind-swept open-to-the-world patio.

SOLUTION: Open patio becomes a comfortable room. Winds are blocked by glass panel, in foreground, and plastic screen, seen beyond lath shelter in background. Lath overhead, built for afternoon shade and privacy, is stopped short of reaching the eaves of the house so that indoor rooms would not be darkened.

**Before:** *There was no protection from the wind, no screening from the glare of afternoon sun, and no privacy from neighbors*

---

Plants in any older garden may gradually shade the windows of a house until finally most of the sun is cut off. Pruning, rearranging, adding plants will get pleasant results.

penetrate will give the undergrowth a chance to develop.

These thinning and clearing operations should allow you to see and appraise the basic frame of your garden.

BEFORE PRUNING

So the first step in remodeling an overgrown garden is to move in with saw and pruning shears. Clear away enough of the excess growth to see what you have.

Next, thin out the overhead canopy. Most old trees will benefit from thinning; the shafts of sunlight that

AFTER PRUNING

If you are remodeling an old garden to get play space for children, don't overlook its special opportunities for tree house, "camp" sites, hide-outs. A private, overgrown path leading nowhere can give as many hours of pleasure to children as a jungle gym. For other ideas, see section on play space for children in another chapter.

PROBLEM: To create a floor level protected patio on two-level lot.

SOLUTION: Grade was cut back at house floor level at varying distances from the house. Stone retaining walls define reclaimed areas. Garage roof is extended into the garden. Partially enclosed extension gives rain protection to outdoor living-dining room.

WALTER AND FLORENCE GERKE

Before: *Change of level of hillside made too close to house creating an unusable moat only a few feet wide*

After: *In creating usable area at house floor level, grade was changed in two jumps as in foreground, creating wide raised bed, and maintained at full width for outdoor living area and overhead extension*

## Remodeling for easier maintenance

Many older gardens were designed for regular maintenance by a hired gardener. Today, with garden help both scarce and expensive, these gardens present a formidable maintenance problem. Even with the help of power mowers, electric hedge clippers, and wheeled fertilizer spreaders, the garden simply takes up too much of the owner's time.

The first step in remodeling your garden for easier maintenance is to take a close look at your over-all plan. In many older gardens, the plan is a formal one such as this:

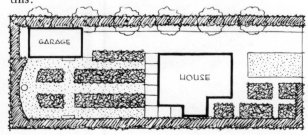

Highly symmetrical plans usually call for meticulous edging. The great variety in plant material makes maintenance difficult. There may be edges to trim, lawn borders to clip, annual beds to cultivate and change, and individual specimens to shape and care for.

Simplifying, arranging mass groupings of plant material, confining lawn and plant beds with header boards, using ground covers and pavings, and building raised beds will all result in lower maintenance. For details, see chapter on *Low Maintenance*.

## Remodeling for outdoor living

If you want a protected terrace closely related to the house, the first point of attack in an older garden often is the long driveway to the garage at the rear. By building a carport toward the front of your property, the old garage can become a garden shelter, a garden work center, or a hobby shop. Part of the long driveway you can convert into a patio area. Note the possibilities for outdoor living in the remodel on the following page.

ECKBO, ROYSTON, AND WILLIAMS

*Deck is all important. Its bold size and shape is appropriate to the large house and tall redwood tree.*

*From the living room (center) the deck angles out around garage to the barbecue area. See photo below*

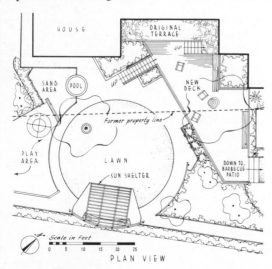

PLAN VIEW

HOUSE · ORIGINAL TERRACE · SAND AREA · POOL · UP · UP · NEW DECK · Former property line · PLAY AREA · LAWN · SUN SHELTER · DOWN TO BARBECUE PATIO · Scale in Feet 0 5 10 15 20 25

PROBLEM: To bring greater all around livability to an old house on a hillside.

SOLUTION: Deck extends indoor space. Unused front lawn and driveway converted into play area.

*View of length of deck from steps to play area, as it surrounds trunk of old redwood and bridges to barbecue area in background*

**88   Garden remodeling**

ECKBO, ROYSTON, AND WILLIAMS

*Lawn play area on lower level is contained by curved see-through fence made from horizontally spaced 1 by*

*1-inch lumber. Overhead repeats airy fence design, and is supported by the fence and steel pipe columns*

*Children's play yard consists of tanbark area with jungle gym and swing set, large sand area, and con-*

*crete wading pool. Asphalt path circles around the lawn, a high speed freeway for the tricycle crowd*

Garden remodeling    89

*Note excellent handling of changes in level: combination steps and low retaining wall in foreground; change of heights in retaining plant beds; use of light* *screens throughout the garden; the gently curving lath screen at left, fence of horizontally spaced 1 by 1-inch redwood at right; screen and fence in photo at right*

---

### Remodeling with decks and terraces

The foundation of most old houses is above ground level. A deck provides an easy, attractive way to move between the house and garden. Here are two examples:

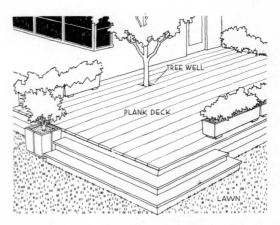

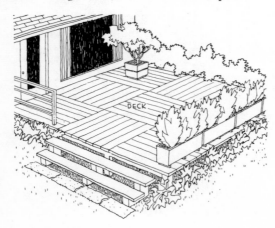

Another way to get level garden space next to a high foundation house is to build up with soil, as illustrated below. This method is most sensible where change of level is not too great. Watch this construction point: Soil should not be added higher than the concrete of the foundation unless a new protective wall is built to give the wood complete protection against the moisture.

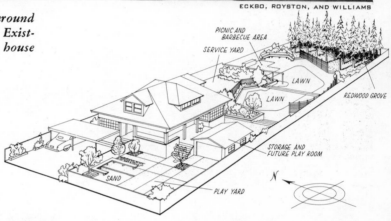

*Picnic area. Water-bound macadam paving around lawn serves as garden path and mowing strip. Existing lilacs saved to screen area from drying yard, house*

ECKBO, ROYSTON, AND WILLIAMS

PROBLEM: Old garden; sloping lot; too much front yard; too much maintenance.

SOLUTION: Unused front lawn and driveway gave way to paved play yard for children. Garden and picnic area make the garden live big. Lawn areas are small and level.

If the area between the indoor and outdoor levels is not to be used for outdoor living, a series of terraces, part planting and part steps, is attractive and easy to negotiate. Here, the grass treads bring the lawn right up to the door. At left, tile or other masonry steps serve for wet weather use. The lawn steps should be at least mower width. If 4 by 6-inch lumber were used as edging—instead of 2 by 6 as shown here—it would also serve as the mowing strip.

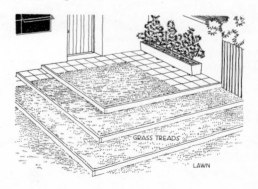

Garden remodeling 91

THOMAS D. WILLIAMS AND RICHARD MEYERS

**Before (top):** *A much loved 50-year-old house but small windows made rooms too dark. Foundation height prevented relationship between house, garden*

**After:** *Lines of old house are cleaned up. Larger windows installed. Addition of weather-protected terrace brings new use and spaciousness to indoor living area*

PROBLEM: To extend the living of a small-windowed, high-foundationed old house and bring more light to living-dining area.

SOLUTION: Enclosed and roofed patio was built at house floor level on fill contained by concrete wall and made a part of living-dining area by replacing house wall with glass and sliding glass doors.

THOMAS O. WILLIAMS AND RICHARD MEYERS

*No shut-in feeling in patio garden. Fence and louvered baffle give privacy and protection from summer winds but allow participation with activity of street. Egg-* *crate roof, supported by steel pipe, made rainproof by partial covering of corrugated plastic, does not rob the area of light. Moon vine and clematis on fence*

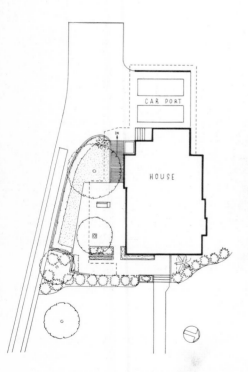

*Sliding doors open to patio from dining-living room. Night lighting not only adds to use of outdoor area but creates dramatic outlook from inside. Covered walk at left ramps to garage*

KATHRYN IMLAY STEDMAN

*Streetside outdoor living room is actually an entry garden that is built as a part of the old front porch. View from entrance is masked by the panel fence at right. Quick color brought in by marguerites and ivy geraniums in containers. New carport is under oak and partially screened by large shrubs against house*

---

Each of the low retaining walls below matches the height of one garden step. The area behind each is back-filled; the outer edge is planted. Steps are long and leisurely. If you need more terrace area, enlarge on the plan.

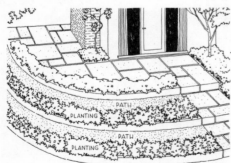

### Remodeling to get more private space

Many old garden layouts gave generously to the public. The more exclusive the neighborhood, the greater the setback. With garden labor and water prices what they are, keeping up a front area that you can't use in any way becomes a burden.

The simplest way to get privacy is to build a 6-foot fence at the setback line. If this type of fencing is incompatible with your garden, or your neighborhood, or your city ordinances, you can grow a dense screen with plant material. Vines on a trellis or on a wire-filled frame will also give you privacy. (See the chapter on *Streetsides* for entry garden ideas in gardens with deep setbacks.)

You may want to remodel your front garden for off-street parking. Chances are that many more cars park on your street today than parked there when your garden was planned; seldom, if ever, do you or your guests arrive on foot.

First, you want a convenient spot to park your own car, preferably only a short walk from the door. You may also want to provide off-street parking for guests' cars, a second family car, or a teen-ager's "customized" convertible.

PROBLEM: To carve out sunny patios in a large pleasantly overgrown garden.

SOLUTION: Streetside entrance area received good afternoon sun—so front lawn became a brick paved terrace. New carport, close to street, eliminated long driveway and made room for a second terrace that caught the morning sun.

KATHRYN IMLAY STEDMAN

*High view of streetside patio taken from balcony showing tall screen hedge of Prunus ilicifolia. Mid and late afternoon sun warms area. Bricks laid tight-joint on the sand by the owners*

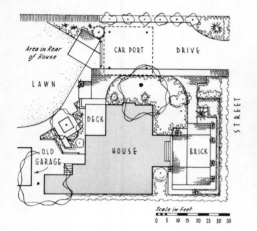

*A new carport was built close to street. By eliminating old driveway, which cut across side and back gardens to garage, space for a second outdoor terrace (good morning sun) created*

A deep setback now devoted to lawn can be reshaped and partially paved. Planting can screen cars from the street and/or from the house. Here are three plans for off-street parking at the front of the lot:

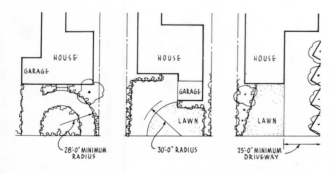

Remember these points when you plan for off-street parking:

• Make it simple for your guests to park. You might indicate car spaces by changes in pavement material, flush header boards, or built-up dividers and bumper strips.

• Make it possible for any guest to leave easily at any time. If the cars have to be packed bumper to bumper, a wholesale car-moving is necessary if one person wants to leave early.

• Don't skimp on the minimum provisions indicated in the sketches below. Try to keep all traffic headed forward—as a rule, no guest likes to back out of an unfamiliar driveway or parking area.

Even though garages or parking lots with attendants may use less space, your plans for parallel, diagonal, and vertical parking should stick to the recommended minimums, as diagrammed on the following page.

Garden remodeling  95

*Streetside garden remodeled to provide guest parking paralleling street. Gravel ties in with rock garden, and can be raked to avoid showing grease stains*

*Where garage is at back of lot, reached by long drive-way, reclaim garden space by converting portion of the streetside garden to an entrance court and carport*

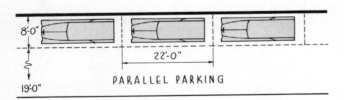

PARALLEL PARKING

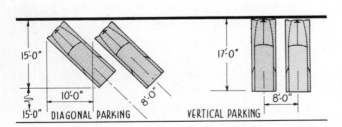

DIAGONAL PARKING  VERTICAL PARKING

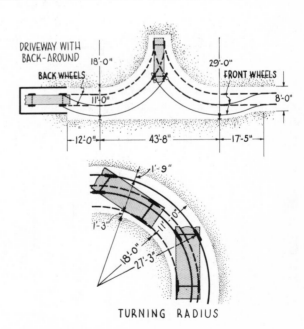

DRIVEWAY WITH BACK-AROUND

BACK WHEELS  FRONT WHEELS

TURNING RADIUS

The illustration at the right indicates the minimum requirements for the turn-around if the car is to be backed out of the garage or carport. (Allow more space if it is to be backed *in*.) The broken lines indicate the back wheel tracks, and the solid lines the front wheel tracks. Note the added 3 feet necessary for turning.

Add 10 feet to the outside of the turning radius if you want to park cars on the turn. Front and back wheels do not follow each other precisely when the car is making a sharp turn.

*In old neighborhoods rich in existing plant material, there are plenty of chances to get garden living by combining the new with the old. Note how easily con-* *verted garage and new outdoor area become a part of this luxuriant old garden. New area makes most of level change with low steps and raised bed-seat wall*

PROBLEM: To effectively use an old garage and driveway, since owners bought adjoining lot for new garage and off-street parking.

SOLUTION: Old garage was converted into an informal garden house. Driveway repaved to give adjoining outdoor living area.

*Gravel and concrete flow through garden, create an inviting terrace that belongs in spirit and function to the new garden room-old garage and the garden itself*

*View from inside garden room shows how you can sit anywhere on the terrace and enjoy the beauty of well established trees and feeling of privacy that they give*

Garden remodeling 97

GERALDINE KNIGHT SCOTT

Before: *Addition of a bathroom to the original box appears to give adequate protection to this small terrace. Actually this corner proved to be quite windy*

PROBLEM: Reaching the age where a large family house is neither needed or efficient, couple decided to buy and remodel this rather awkward little house. After interior remodel, they sensed opportunities to get a combination indoor and outdoor living that would add enjoyment to their everyday living and provide entertainment space as well.

SOLUTION: Generous concrete and brick terrace was built to practically surround the house. Baffles, garden-like in texture, create areas of changing interest and work to quiet the wind in a normally windswept area.

*Looking past the baffle extending out from the bathroom addition (see plan) into rear garden now protected from wind and view of neighbors, panel fence changes pattern throughout the day with movement of shadows highlighting and backlighting the area*

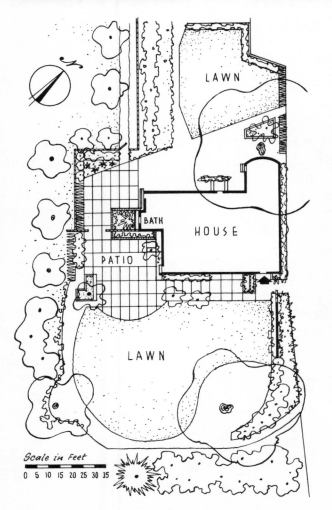

*Shows opposite side of fence panel from photo above. Brick-walled raised bed in foreground has sun rose ground cover. At right of panel is redwood-walled raised bed that appears in foreground in photo at top left. For detail of entry garden see next page*

Scale in Feet
0 5 10 15 20 25 30 35

Garden remodeling 99

GERALDINE KNIGHT SCOTT

*Entry before remodeling was confusing. Visitors would pass by small opening along drive, park car, wander into bedroom-kitchen side of house (see plan). Now guests can't miss seeing inviting screened entry*

### Coordinated remodel—house and garden

Often the best starting point in landscape remodeling is the house itself. The new patio may work a lot better if you step outdoors through a sliding glass door. Removing an old porch and building a generous roofed deck in its place can change the entire character of your garden.

When either modernizing or adding a room to your house, you may want to think of a landscape remodel as a basic part of the total job. By coordinating the two, both house and garden might benefit, as shown in the sketch below. Here, by opening the living room to a deck, the owners not only gain much more living space but greatly improve the appearance of the house.

*Caution:* Before tackling any construction job that is connected in any way with existing buildings—house, garage, lath structure, etc.—have all foundations inspected. If you go ahead without knowing the exact condition of existing structures, you may find yourself in trouble with the new ones.

If you live in an incorporated area, check with the building inspector to learn what can and what can't be built without a permit. In some cities, all structures—carports, lathhouses, fences, overheads, garden houses—must be approved in the plan stage.

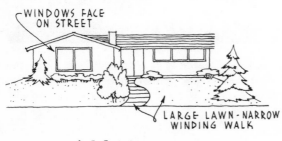

WINDOWS FACE ON STREET

LARGE LAWN—NARROW WINDING WALK

BEFORE

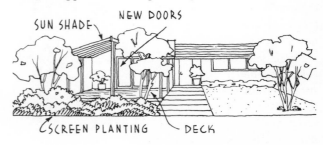

SUN SHADE    NEW DOORS

SCREEN PLANTING    DECK

AFTER

# Ways of flooring the garden

Every outdoor flooring material has its limitations. But each has a place where it serves better in some way than any other material.

You cannot base your selection on one value alone if you intend to satisfy your eyes, your needs, your sense of fitness, and your budget.

Keep in mind the basic idea of your garden plan when you think about garden floor coverings. If you wish to create a mood of a woodsy retreat, slick concrete would be an intrusion. Wood blocks would be more suitable. Or tree rounds. Or stone. If you want the garden to take care of dancing parties and a shuffleboard court, concrete of the slickest finish is in order. If there are children and wheeled toys, the surface can't be too soft and it shouldn't have a knee-scratching roughness nor a skull-splitting hardness. If there are no children and the point of the garden is to quiet and soothe, the click of heels on any hard paving may be irritating. If one of the purposes of the garden is to invite the sun for outdoor living, a pavement of bricks, concrete, or asphalt will husband the warmth of the sun. (If you have too much sun, such pavings might only make your problem worse.)

Whether you do the labor or hire the work done will influence your choice of materials. Many home owners prefer brick to concrete because bricks are easier to handle in a leisurely way.

Your selection need not be one material against the field. Combinations of two materials are often more attractive than one used alone. Amateurs and landscape architects before you have worked out variation upon variation. More than half the photographs in this book show effective combinations.

Let's look at the various paving materials.

## Concrete

Most versatile of all garden paving materials is concrete. The surface can be plain and smooth enough for dancing or roller skating, or it can have a hand-crafted, rough-textured look.

Because concrete is a plastic material, you can blend it with other materials and cast it into an endless number of shapes and forms. Circles, ovals, curves, and flowing lines can be handled more easily with concrete than with pre-formed materials. Where patterns of rectangles and squares are called for in a plan, concrete can be poured in forms to fit specifications.

Concrete gives you more material for your money than any other hard paving surface. For as little as 15 cents per square foot, exclusive of header boards, forms, and special equipment, you can pave your own patio, terrace, walks, and game areas.

The disadvantages of concrete are considerable when it is handled thoughtlessly. A smooth, uncolored and unrelieved slab will reflect heat and light into the house if the terrace adjoins the living room. It's hard to the touch, cold in winter, hot in summer. Because it is porous, concrete shows stains.

It is possible to buy concrete for your own use in any of the three following ways:

1. *Bulk dry materials.* You buy the required amounts of sand, cement, and gravel. Unless you have ample storage space, buy only what you will need for the project at hand. (You can also buy a sand-gravel mix to combine with the cement.)

Advantages: Buying the materials dry and in bulk is the cheapest way you can get them. You can mix any amount that is convenient for you to use.

*Concrete in redwood grids. For rough texture, pebbles pressed into wet concrete, then surface water-washed with hose. Path of random-sized circular con-* *crete stones cast in place. Plant by window is cyperus; tropical* Tetrapanax papyriferum *to right. Fatshedera climbs branch. Strawberry and dichondra along path*

Disadvantages: You must have a place where you can store sand and gravel. The sacks of cement must be kept absolutely dry. This generally means covered storage.

2. *Transit mix.* Concrete in this form is delivered to your door, ready to set in place.

Advantages: No mixing equipment is needed. It can be prepared according to any specifications before delivery. You get consistent, well mixed concrete. Cost for larger quantities is only slightly more than for bulk dry materials.

Disadvantages: An extra charge is made for delivery of any quantity under 2 cubic yards. Some plants will deliver as little as ½ cubic yard under this arrangement, but others will deliver nothing less than 1 yard. There is another extra charge for any time a truck must wait beyond a minimum interval while delivering materials, usually about $7.00 per hour. Delivery to the actual site is often difficult. The trucks are too large for some driveways.

3. *Dry ready-mix.* You can buy sacked dry mixtures containing correct proportions of sand, cement, and gravel for an all-purpose concrete suitable for most home uses. The 100-pound sack contains enough materials to make approximately 4 square feet of 4-inch paving. A 60-pound sack is also available, but is too small for anything except most minor paving.

Advantages: There is no guess work. All you have to do is add water, mix, and pour the concrete. It is ideal for patching old jobs or doing piecemeal work.

Disadvantages: It is quite expensive. The cost is about four times that of materials sold in the other two forms. Although it is a practical way for the home owner to buy concrete for a small job, it is usually not a good choice for large jobs such as paving.

You have an unlimited range of textures when you do your own concrete finishing. Be sure that the finish you choose is the right one for the service it will perform:

1. *Smooth:* For the smoothest surface, use a steel trowel. Add a non-skid texture with a broom. Experiment with different bristled brooms to find out which of the many possible finishes you prefer. For the roughest "smooth" surface, use only the wood float—don't finish off with the steel trowel.

2. *Exposed aggregate:* One of the most popular patio surfaces, and one of the most difficult to handle, is exposed aggregate. (See photograph.) Some contractors

**Scored smooth concrete**

CLARENCE PRENTICE

*Low retaining wall handled as separate unit, makes easy transition from concrete terrace to stone, from house to garden. Heath ground cover. At right, azaleas, rhododendrons*

**Redwood headers in smooth concrete**

HENRY VAN SIEGMAN

*Smooth-troweled concrete loses its hard look in patterned shade of spreading trees. Barbecue designed to repeat shape of terrace. Kitchen entrance at right, behind apricot tree*

**Redwood headers in exposed aggregate**

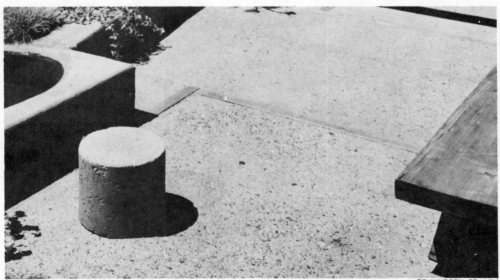

OSMUNDSON-STALEY

*Concrete seems less a material for city streets and more of a garden material when pebbles in the aggregate are exposed by brushing and washing while the mixture is still wet*

ECKBO, ROYSTON, AND WILLIAMS

*Concrete paving squares, separated and rimmed by 2-inch redwood, form geometric pattern. Its precise look depends on regular edging. Acanthus and tetrapanax* *in planting squares in good scale. Outdoor living room protected on three sides by living room, den. Outdoor dining room screened from utility area by plastic panels*

*This concrete paving can be poured in place between removable headers or poured in molds and laid as blocks. In either case, owner has choice of amount of pouring to be done at any one time*

ECKBO, ROYSTON, AND WILLIAMS

*Wild strawberry ground cover matches rough texture of rock, forms interesting contrast with smooth concrete squares*

**1•** Bright colored smooth stones, set in bottom of mold, concrete poured over

**2•** Loose gravel thrown in bottom of mold, concrete poured over

**3•** Creek washed broken glass, hand-set in concrete

**4•** Aluminum triangles, bright smooth stones hand-set in colored concrete

**5•** Tan exploded shale sprinkled into dark brown concrete

**6•** Aluminum strips, dark green, white stones, hand-set in concrete

**7•** Red marble chips sprinkled into white concrete

**8•** Fist-size beach rocks hand-set in concrete

**9•** Steel grate set in bottom of mold, concrete poured on top

and craftsmen do the job with a hose, forcing out the top layer of mortar with the pressure from the spray. Others use a stiff wire brush or broom first, and then clean off excess mortar with the hose.

It is difficult to make two jobs look alike, and many times different panels on a terrace or patio won't be consistently "exposed." However, the natural appearance won't ordinarily be spoiled by slight inconsistencies.

Make sure that your surface is level—a wood float finish is satisfactory. Then let concrete set up only until this top layer of mortar can be removed easily. Knowing when this stage has been reached takes at least a minimum of experience, or some experiment to get the "feel" of the material. If the concrete has set too firmly, it will be too late to remove the mortar. If the concrete is too wet, the exposed pebbles will come loose under the pressure of your hose or brush.

The job must be done in sections that can be worked at exactly the proper time. If you do let the concrete set too firmly, scrub the surface with a solution of muriatic acid and water. This will often remove some of the cement-and-sand mortar.

### Pebble mosaic

Pebbles from the beach or a stream are pressed into a ½ or 1-inch layer of damp mortar laid over a 2 or 3-inch base of concrete. (If cars will drive over it, make the base 5 or 6 inches thick.) The mortar should be about 1 part cement to 2 parts of sand, with enough water for a mix that spreads easily but doesn't run. The mix should be elastic enough so that a little mortar moves up around the side of each pebble.

The pebbles should be wet before being set into place. Check to see that they are keeping a true level surface by occasionally tapping with a long, straight board. You can add color to the mortar to match or complement the pebbles.

It is wise to lay out an approximate pattern on paper beforehand; but since you will have to work fast, some of the design will have to be freehand.

Since you are really working with an art form when you start a pebble mosaic, you can't estimate how much time it will take to do any particular job. It's slow work but can be fun. You won't use more than one shovelful of mortar at any one time.

### Brick

Brick is, in some ways, the easiest of all hard paving materials to install in the garden. It combines well with concrete, asphalt, or any other material. It has been associated with gardens for so many years that it no

*Pebbles seeded into mortar; intricately carved slabs; concrete made to look like stone. Such handcraft requires patience, careful selection of the pebbles*

*Roman brick accented by black-stained headers, some set flat, some on edge, gives an unusual sense of elegance. Bricks are laid in sand. Headers are 2 by 4's*

---

longer seems to intrude. It can be laid in strong or unobtrusive patterns.

Brick introduces a warm color in the garden, and provides a non-glare texture. It is non-slip in dry climates, but sometimes a slippery moss grows on it in moist areas. Well handled, brick can become a dominating part of the garden floor without taking away the garden feeling.

Brick is porous and soaks up water like a sponge. This quality is a real advantage in hot, dry summer climates. Flow water over a brick floor and it becomes a cool surface.

The porous quality is a disadvantage when brick is subjected to food and grease stains. If not properly fired, brick is sometimes damaged by freezing.

Contractor-laid, brick is a costly paving; home owner-installed, it's another story. A home owner doing his own work can get a paved area for less than 30 cents a square foot that costs more than $1.00 a square foot when installed by a contractor.

Brick can be put down in many ways and in many patterns. (See photographs for various patterns and designs.) You can lay bricks on a cushion of sand, on a mortar bed, on sand and cement mixed dry, or on a concrete slab. You can use tight joints, or joints filled with

mortar, sand, or sand-cement dry mix wetted down after you finish the job. For dry setting you need no equipment except a level, but you can use a brick set and/or a mason's hammer. For wet mortar setting, you will also need a trowel and a jointer, or grooving tool.

To get a good looking and permanent job with bricks on sand, these factors must be watched carefully:

1. Confine them rigidly by an outer course of bricks laid with wet mortar, an edging of concrete, or by header boards. The smaller the area between the fixed edgings, the less trouble you will have with buckling.

2. Put the sand cushion, ½ to 1 inch thick, on tamped hard ground that will not crack. If you have adobe soil that cracks when dry, most contractors advise you to put down a 2-inch layer of base rock, wet and roll it, and then the sand pad.

3. Prevent washout of sand—or, at least, keep it to a minimum—by mixing cement (1 part cement to 3 parts sand) with the sand that is swept into the cracks.

Be sure the bricks are bone dry before the sand and cement are thrown on them. Wash off all cement with a fine spray. Apply long enough to wet the cement-sand mixture.

*Bricks in mortar cap walls of pool; bricks in sand surround it. Trim lines of pool, brick repeated in clipped box hedge. Guava above wall breaks definite pattern*

*Casual combinations of plants and brick are always pleasant. Here Vinca major spreads over wire-cut bricks tightly jointed for design pattern, laid in sand*

4. Get bricks flush with the headers by laying them ¼ inch higher than headers and then forcing them level by tamping.

Where temperatures drop below 0° brick on sand is seldom recommended. In these cold areas, the standard practice is to set brick in mortar on a 4-inch concrete slab.

Common brick is adequate for garden use. There are three types:

1. *Wire-cut brick* is square-cut and rough textured. Use it when laying a tight joint pattern.

2. *Sand-mold brick* is smooth and easy to clean. Because it is turned out of a mold, it is slightly larger on one face than on the other.

3. *Clinker brick* has black patches and surface irregularities from over-burning. It cannot be used in tight patterns. Use where a rough, cobblestone effect would cause no trouble.

Supposedly a brick is 4 by 8 by 2½ inches. But there is enough variation within one load of bricks from one kiln to make it worth your while to pick and choose if you are fitting them within a tight pattern. There are variations in color, too.

## Hand-crafted accents

Choices in paving do not have to be as simple as either-or. You can drop a block of pebble mosaic in a brick area, or combine smooth stones with concrete, or play with contrasting colors and shapes, combining colored concrete, colored gravel, or brick.

On these pages there are several photographs of pebble blocks from Western gardens and from experiments conducted at *Sunset*. For complete details on how to make them, see the August 1953 issue.

## Asphalt

Asphalt offers a few unique advantages. It's a resilient material, with no glare. It gives back no heel clicks and absorbs rather than reflects sound. Asphalt is a good selection for paving for children's play areas.

For best appearance, it needs the contrast of plants, brick, concrete, or wood borders.

For texture variation: After surface has been rolled once, scatter sand or pebbles, then roll again. With exposed colored pebbles in the surface, asphalt paving loses some of its parking lot look; with surface texture it seems more suitable in the garden.

OSMUNDSON-STALEY

*Asphalt is inexpensive solution to large paved areas, but needs contrast of plants, brick, or wood border to relieve parking-lot look. Star jasmine in raised bed*

*Handmade ceramic tile in Sunset's reception room, corridors, outdoor covered areas. Tile comes in many sizes and finishes. Wise choice where finished look wanted*

It has these disadvantages: If not given a solid foundation, it will sag and crack. Where summers are hot, it increases already hot temperatures. Its black surface causes it to absorb more heat than any other paving material. Heat softens it. The prints of sharp-toed furniture will show. It does not maintain a uniform color. Weeds and Bermuda grass will penetrate it.

The secret of good asphalt is a solid base of crushed rock, firmly compacted with a heavy roller. The base should be held in place by forms or headers so the edges of the asphalt won't crumble.

The hot-mixed, hot-applied asphaltic concrete is the most durable; it is the best to use if you have it contractor-applied with heavy equipment. One of the cold mixes is the choice for the gardener who is doing his own work. The handyman will need a heavy roller to compact the asphalt properly.

### Tile

Tile is the most finished-looking of all the garden paving materials. It can be waxed for a gleaming, formal finish, good for dancing. This air of formality and the generous discipline of its pattern can overwhelm the small garden if it is not carefully used.

The most pleasing uses are on surfaces that are direct extensions of indoor areas, or under overheads where the house feeling rather than the garden feeling is uppermost.

The principal objection to tile is its high cost. The high quality materials and precision workmanship that go into its manufacture make tile much more costly than common brick.

There are several sizes, colors, and shapes to choose from. Outdoor floor tile is rough-surfaced in contrast to the glazed varieties used in kitchens and bathrooms. Patio tile comes in brick red; quarry tile is obtainable in tones running from gray to brick color.

The large, foot-square tiles are commonly known as patio tile; the others—9 by 9, 6 by 6, 4 by 4, 9 by 6, 8 by 4—are called quarry tile. Patio tile is not made to such close tolerances as quarry tile and consequently is cheaper per square foot.

To save cutting or chipping, plan out surface requirements to stay within the dimensions of the tile you intend to use. Allow $3/4$-inch mortar joints for the large tiles, $1/2$-inch for small sizes.

*Planting beds in flagstone entry court. Cobblestones in cement, foreground right. Plants are Mugho pine, juniper, Viburnum davidii, pine; ajuga in interspaces*

*Stepping stones in carpet of ajuga. For drainage, ground level is ¾ inch below surface of stones. Other plants: strawberry saxifrage, sword fern, hellebore*

---

For a permanent surface, set in a bed of sand mortar (5 parts of clean sand to 1 part cement). Push the mixture between tile; keep the area wet until all the mortar sets up. Tiles should be laid over a bed of concrete, as they are liable to become chipped or broken if put down over soil. They can also be laid on decking.

## Flagstone

Where the spirit of the garden is entirely natural, none of the man-made pavings seems appropriate. In situations such as a terrace on a wooded hillside where the paving is associated with ferns, flagstones come into their own.

Laid by a craftsman with the eye of an artist, flagstone can present the line and pattern and color of an abstract painting. The harder types give a surface as permanent as the house itself, and they will survive in cold where bricks fail. If you live in a severe-winter area, shop carefully, because soft flags are sold in many yards. Units should be scaled to the size of the area; in a heavily wooded area, play up the material's natural elemental qualities by using large scale blocks.

Care must be taken with flagstone to avoid a cold, quarry-like effect. The surface is sometimes rough or slippery.

Slabs can be irregular or roughly rectangular in shape. Thickness most often ranges from ½ to 2 inches, although sometimes you will get stones as thick as 6 inches. For paving over a sand bed, a 2-inch thickness is essential to prevent cracking; thinner stones are set over a concrete slab.

For limited areas such as walks, where soil is stable and well drained, flagstones can be put down directly over the soil. Dig out the soil to a depth slightly less than the thickness of the flags and fit them in place. Fill joints with turf, or pack in some good soil and plant grass seed, or set in clumps of a creeping ground cover.

For a permanent surface, set flagstones on a 2-inch slab of concrete in a mortar bed (1 part cement to 3 parts sand). Work in small areas—set only one or two flags at a time.

Whatever method you use, avoid getting a pattern that is too busy. Begin by laying all the stones loose, shifting them to please your eye.

## Adobe blocks

Adobe is a traditional material in California and Arizona. Informal and an ideal earth color for garden paving, it is an exceptionally flattering background for flower colors. It is soft looking, without glare or reflection.

**Flooring the garden  109**

*Adobe blocks in Sunset's patio are used in combination with hand-finished tile. Blocks set an inch apart on a sand base and interspaces filled with soil for planting of thyme, chamomile, and other herbs that are historically associated with adobe. Adobe blocks give natural look of swept earth, are unusually wear-resistant*

The usual block is 8 inches wide, 16 inches long, and 4 inches thick. Such a unit weighs 30 pounds. Because dimensions vary slightly, adobe blocks are usually difficult to lay in patterns that call for snug fitting. Open joints, 3/4 to 1 inch, compensate for any irregularities. Buy only stabilized adobe blocks.

Like brick, adobe blocks can be laid on a sand bed. Take care that the bed is solid, stable, and quite level—the blocks will not bridge a hollow or straddle a hump without cracking when weight is put upon them. Joints may be filled with dirt, sand, or dry mortar. A dirt filling permits crevice planting.

Buy extra blocks for replacements—a few may develop flaws or disintegrate. It is difficult to match the color and texture later.

Unless there's an adobe maker in your locality, transportation costs will rule out this material.

### Crushed rock

Paths of crushed rock do not call attention to themselves and they feel as natural underfoot as a mountain trail. In service and storage areas, this material is as practical as it is inexpensive.

There are disadvantages. Weed killers must be used to keep the weeds from taking over. The rocks spread into plant beds and lawns, but this problem can be lessened by confining the path or area with header boards.

If crushed rock is too coarse, the surface will be too uneven for high heels; if too fine, the small particles will stick to shoes. To select the right size for his garden, one of our friends took his wife to the gravel pit and asked her to walk on the gravel that had dropped on the ground beneath the bunkers. He found that her heels didn't teeter on the 1/2-inch rock, and the open toes of her shoes didn't pick up the 1/4-inch rock. He bought a mix of the two.

Gravel stands up best when put down over a more permanent bed of base rock or decomposed granite. But it will give several seasons' service when put right on the ground.

The usual method of application is to spread a 2-inch layer, rake, dampen, and roll with a heavy roller or hand tamp. Most contractors recommend 1/2-inch rock; however, some landscape architects say you can use any size you like—as long as you put down a layer only the thickness of one piece of gravel. Roll into soil or any other binding agent; renew, rake, and re-roll as necessary.

*Unlike brick or concrete, gravel never overpowers the garden. It should, of course, be contained by some sort of border. Here the border and steps are railroad ties*

*Crushed rock and gravel offer excellent low-maintenance planting beds and utility surfaces. Here succulents are added as color interest in gray field of gravel*

### Base rock, decomposed granite, sandy gravel, redrock

These and other similar names, differing by localities, designate a general class of fill material—part rock and part dirt—taken from hillsides and often used as a base for asphalt paving. They can also be used to surface garden paths and secondary areas. Ideally, the "fines" and larger aggregate compact to form a water-repellent, non-dusting surface. Too much dirt among the rocks makes the surface impassable when wet. Too much rock in relation to dirt makes it stay loose and crumbly.

A good way to handle these materials is to put them down in three or more 1-inch layers; dampen, and then roll or hand tamp.

Advantages: They are inexpensive and quickly applied, easy to maintain, and can be used as a base for later paving.

Disadvantages: They track into the house. Some kinds get muddy in rainy weather.

### Crushed brick

Crushed brick gives an excellent color contrast to plants; however, it has too intense a color for large areas. It is not especially durable, and may track; it turns to powder under traffic. It is best used as an accent on small areas that receive light traffic.

Crushed brick is not strictly a "budget" paving material. In bulk it costs 10 times as much as base rock, for instance, but if applied lightly over stable soil or a base rock base, it can be put down for a moderate cost.

### Colored roof rock

In areas where paving gets very little traffic and in pattern paving, the green, tan, or white roof rock is useful for color.

### Tanbark

Next to the pine needle floor beneath old forests, tanbark is the most natural surface in color and walking "feel" offered to the gardener. It has a good, reddish color, is soft and springy, and is not harmed by moisture. Since it scatters easily, it is best confined between header boards. Use it on a path, as a generous cushion for a play yard, or in a part of the garden leading out to a natural, woodsy area. It is widely used in municipal and school playgrounds under equipment that is used actively by the children—swings, jungle gyms, slides, rings, etc.

DOUGLAS BAYLIS

*Redwood rounds serve as stepping stones. Here you see them interplanted with ground cover of 3 kinds of thyme—woolly thyme, mother-of-thyme, silver thyme*

*More than play yard material, warm reddish brown tanbark is compatible material for garden where natural feeling of forest floor is wanted. Easy to maintain*

Put right on top of the soil for a path, but over 2 or 3 inches of gravel (for drainage) in a play yard. When tanbark wears out, it still makes excellent compost.

Tanbark is available only within trucking distance of a tannery.

### Sawdust

Sawdust is sometimes used for paths through woods. It is not as serviceable as tanbark in playgrounds as it clings to clothing.

### Wood blocks

Wood blocks contribute warm color and soft texture to the garden.

Wood blocks are best used in shady spots, since they may crack and warp in sunny locations. They freeze and split in heavy frosts.

If you can find rounds of redwood or cedar that have no sapwood, you can count on service from them for several years. Any other blocks should be treated with pentachlorophenol or other wood preservative. Blocks should be 4 to 8 inches thick. Put them on any firm base; fill joints with sand, gravel, or well tamped soil.

### Tricks of the trade

By leaving generous open spaces for planting, you can make any paving material cover a much larger area and achieve the feeling of a bigger patio.

You can use 180 square feet of brick paving in this manner:

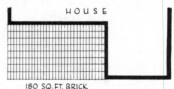

Or, by adding 10 square feet of brick and two areas of planting, you can double the size of your patio:

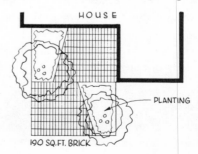

Or, you can make the space apparently larger by freeing it from the house and tying it to a unit of planting:

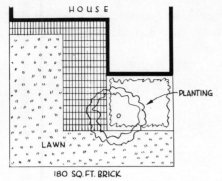

180 SQ. FT. BRICK

Or you can enlarge the patio and still keep the feeling of brick by combining it with a cheaper material such as concrete:

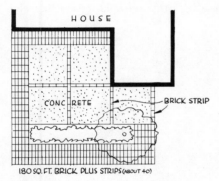

180 SQ. FT. BRICK PLUS STRIPS (ABOUT 40)

## Concrete pointers

Concrete is *heavy*. Make it and mix it close to where you will want to use it. If your yard slopes, remember that it is easier to let a loaded wheelbarrow roll downhill than to push it uphill.

Any foreign matter tends to weaken the concrete. Water should be clean, and, most important of all, sand and gravel should be free of dirt or vegetation.

Concrete will set up more quickly on a hot, dry day than on a cool, damp one. Never mix more than you will be able to use in an hour's time.

Wood eventually will rot in concrete. To retard this action, you can treat header boards with pentachlorophenol or one of the copper sulfate solutions, fence posts with pentachlorophenol or creosote.

Never attempt to re-mix concrete that has begun to set.

Unfortunately, most ready-mix plants don't operate on Saturday or Sunday. Be sure to check with the ones in your area before you make any plans for week-end concrete projects.

*For measuring ingredients.* When you hand-mix concrete on a flat surface, the bottomless box sketched below

is a welcome time-saver for measuring dry materials. The 6-inch boards are your measuring lines. Full, the box holds 2 cubic feet. After measuring, lift the box off and you're ready to start the mixing.

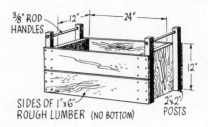

*For cleaning up.* To clean off mortar from brick, use commercial grade muriatic acid. Mix a 32 per cent solution with 2 parts tap water to reduce it to about a 10 per cent solution. One gallon cleans at least 300 square feet. Apply vigorously with a stiff brush; flush surface with a full stream of water from the hose after acid stops bubbling. Keep it off plants and away from surface roots and grass. Caution: Wear rubber gloves and shoes, and protect your eyes with goggles while you mix and apply the muriatic acid solution.

*For checking the slope.* So that it will drain properly, you'll want some slope on any large area of paving. A drop of 1 inch per 6 feet is usually adequate. One good method for establishing and checking this slope is shown below.

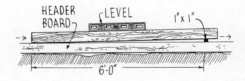

## Header boards

Practically, it's impossible to consider paving—concrete, asphalt, gravel, or brick—without considering header boards.

Header boards have established their place in the Western garden. They make a neat demarcation between lawns and plants, they keep grass and weeds out of plant beds, and they hold water within the root area of shrubs and plants. They also make handsome edging and division strips in brick, concrete. or other garden paving.

Redwood and cedar are the woods most often used, since they contain their own preservative. You can leave them alone, or treat them with any of the commercial preservatives; the difference in longevity won't be considerable.

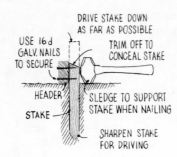

USE 16d GALV. NAILS TO SECURE

DRIVE STAKE DOWN AS FAR AS POSSIBLE

TRIM OFF TO CONCEAL STAKE

HEADER

STAKE

SLEDGE TO SUPPORT STAKE WHEN NAILING

SHARPEN STAKE FOR DRIVING

Illustrated is one standard procedure for driving stakes and attaching the header board in average soft soil. The stake should be driven level with the header board, then beveled off—a keyhole saw will help.

On header boards surrounding any planting area where you might use a power rotary tiller, try to place the stakes on the side of the board where they won't be disturbed by the machine blades.

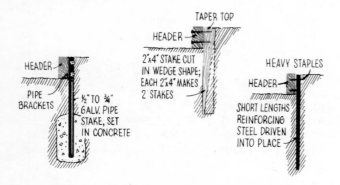

HEADER

PIPE BRACKETS

½" TO ¾" GALV. PIPE STAKE, SET IN CONCRETE

TAPER TOP

HEADER

2"x4" STAKE CUT IN WEDGE SHAPE; EACH 2"x4" MAKES 2' STAKES

HEAVY STAPLES

HEADER

SHORT LENGTHS REINFORCING STEEL DRIVEN INTO PLACE

If you are working in firmly packed soil, you may want to try one of the suggestions above for driving stakes. They will drive into the ground more easily and stay put once they're there.

The galvanized pipe set in concrete is a special solution, applicable only where you want added strength in the stake and permanence in the header board.

Here is a way to use stakes and headers to control and define brick paving laid in sand. For a minimum of brick cutting, try to keep the dimensions between headers equal to any desired number of whole bricks. If the walk is raised off the ground, locate stakes inside headers, low enough not to interfere with the sand bed. The "ears" of the screed rest on the headers as it is pulled along, leveling the sand to a smooth foundation for the bricks.

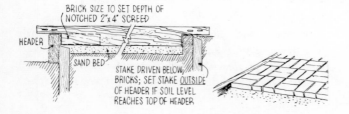

BRICK SIZE TO SET DEPTH OF NOTCHED 2"x4" SCREED

HEADER

SAND BED

STAKE DRIVEN BELOW BRICKS; SET STAKE OUTSIDE OF HEADER IF SOIL LEVEL REACHES TOP OF HEADER

If you have areas of different widths to be screeded, you may want to add these extensions to your screed board. Assemble the board and extensions with wing bolts as shown. As the areas to be screeded vary, loosen the bolts, then slip the extensions out to rest on the headers.

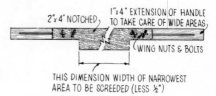

2"x4" NOTCHED

1"x4" EXTENSION OF HANDLE TO TAKE CARE OF WIDE AREAS

WING NUTS & BOLTS

THIS DIMENSION WIDTH OF NARROWEST AREA TO BE SCREEDED (LESS ½")

*For easier stake driving.* One way to make the job of driving stakes easier is to use steel tent stakes (available at most sporting goods stores). These stakes, made of bent sheet steel, have two edges that bite into the side of the header board and hold it very securely.

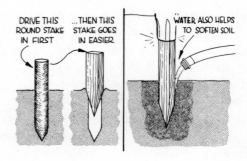

METAL TENT STAKE

STAKE BITES HEADER AND HOLDS

VERY HARD SOIL

These are other ways to make wooden stakes go into the ground more easily:

1. Use a sharply pointed round stake (an old broom handle is long enough for two or three stakes) to make a preliminary hole. This hole will serve as an opening for a larger square stake (about 2 inches thick) as illustrated below.

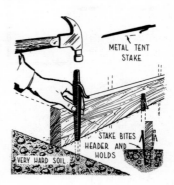

DRIVE THIS ROUND STAKE IN FIRST

...THEN THIS STAKE GOES IN EASIER

WATER ALSO HELPS TO SOFTEN SOIL

2. Let a trickle of water run down into the hole into which you are driving the stake. Water will soften the soil below the point of the stake.

# Ways of enclosing the garden

Once you think of a garden as space to live in, you have a whole new set of requirements for its planning.

You think of it more as a room than as a piece of ground. And you expect and desire much the same visual privacy you would enjoy in an indoor living room.

No matter how friendly you are with your neighbors, you have no right to embarrass them by making them watch your outdoor activities. For outdoor dining, entertaining, sun-bathing, or just sitting and talking with a friend, you need at least a semblance of privacy.

Privacy means walls or screens of some kind. In an outdoor room, the walls may be of trees, shrubs, vines, brick, stone, wood, and many other materials. The walls and screens may or may not be on the perimeter of the lot. You may consider the garden room as a room within the garden.

In several localities, fences along highways, arterials, or railroads must be either chain-link wire or masonry.

The concrete block fence is a basic fence in many Southern California localities. Several subdividers provide a 4-foot concrete block wall with the house.

Since the 4-foot height is not enough for privacy, new home owners face the problem of increasing the height.

One way is to drive pipe or iron into the wall and string wire for vines.

Another way of increasing height of concrete fence to bring necessary privacy is to attach panels of grapestakes, lattice, or other light wood to the face of the wall. Such panels can be made as screens or left open and planted with vines.

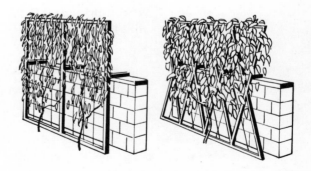

The amateur builder finds concrete blocks easy to handle for low fences and walls. All walls should be built up on a level, continuous foundation of concrete

*In Sunset's garden this fence is both enclosure and background for planting. Heaviness of solid panels of 1 by 12-inch boards lightened by alternate panels of spaced 1 by 4's. Figs espaliered on the fence give lush foliage in summer, reveal branch pattern in winter. Row of purpleleaf flowering plums above fence*

wider than the wall. The concrete block can be set up dry—without mortar. The final step of pouring concrete into the cells of the blocks can be taken when you feel like doing it.

If you object to the machine-made appearance of the concrete, you can lay up the blocks with mortar. If the joints are not raked and the wall is painted, the mechanical look is lost.

In choosing materials for walls, it's well to remember that your selection need not be just the choice between building material or plant material. It can be a pleasant combination of both.

A hedge along property lines seems less offensive than a fence to some people, but a completely surrounding hedge may seem just as confining as a fence.

In the following combination of shrubs, trees, and fence, each element benefits from the presence of the others.

Where space permits, you can enclose with masses of foliage. Like this:

Such enclosures as those illustrated above are not to be had immediately. A home owner on an interior lot in a new subdivision is joined by five neighbors (counting the two at the rear corners). More and more often nowadays, his living room and all the neighbors' living rooms open into the back garden. How can he use his garden?

*This fence of combed cedar stakes, woven with copper wire, is purchased as assembled unit. Advantage of woven fence is the ease of building it in curved lines*

*Board fence of 1 by 8-inch resawn redwood with 2 by 6-inch cap. Flowering quince trained against fence gives interesting pattern both in flower and out of leaf*

He doesn't want to wait three years for shrubs and trees to give him privacy. The obvious answer is a fence.

The need for fences is so universal in such cases that many newly built subdivisions in the West provide the fence with the house. The usual method is to enclose the back garden completely with a 6-foot board fence on the property line.

Left to itself, the 6-foot board fence creates a rigid, confining, boarded-up feeling. It isn't too high for the eye, but it pens you in, and you sense other pens around you. Like this:

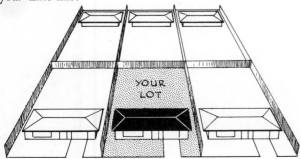

Nothing is gained by lowering the height of the fence. Anything less than 6 feet is useless as a privacy screen. Even a 6-foot fence does not block out the view of the neighbors' heads and shoulders if the houses are even a foot above ground level.

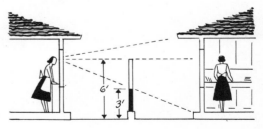

Planning the walls of your garden room calls for an entirely different set of judgments from planning the walls of an indoor room. Six feet indoors is entirely different from 6 feet outdoors.

In an indoor room, the lines of sight are almost constantly below the 6-foot level. Walking through the

*Horizontal strips of 1 by 1-inch redwood make light screen that is in sympathy with the garden. Here the screen, related in design to the raised bed-seat wall,* *sets stage for gray-white* Helichrysum petiolatum *and disappears into large clump of lilac. Mowing strip of gravel at base of raised bed avoids hand clipping*

---

house you watch the floor far more than either ceiling or walls. In conversation, the lines of sight are seldom above 4 feet.

In an outdoor room, the eye is more conscious of the tall trees and sky than of the floor of the garden.

Even a 6-foot fence is just a part of the wall of the garden room.

The house roofs next door, the trees a block away, the hills beyond, the clouds in the sky, all combine to make the wall and ceiling of your garden. Your problem is to work with all of the elements to create a pleasing environment, of which the fence is only one part.

Let's say you find yourself boarded in like this:

The first possibility is to change the nature of the fence by vines.

*Plastic screen on frame. Posts are 4 by 4, spaced 8 feet apart. Interspaces are framed with 2 by 4's that are 2 feet square. Two 1 by 12-inch redwood boards at base*

*Night lighting is built into simple solid board fence by stretching a translucent plastic cloth over 3 by 6-foot panel. Light behind it gives soft glow, silhouettes ivy*

The enclosing walls are really the neighbors' houses. So you use trees:

Note that the trees are not used as a continuous high wall, but are placed to screen out what you don't want to see and to frame the views you find pleasant.

Even though the fence is just a part of the garden enclosure, it is prominent enough to cause those who design suburban gardens to focus a great deal of attention on its design. In the past 20 years, just about every possible variation in design has been tried.

After trying everything, the commercial fence builder has found that the most acceptable fence is a simple one,

built with 4 by 4 posts, 8 feet apart, with 2 by 4 stringers. The popular commercial fences include a basket-weave design using ½-inch boards horizontally, and straight line arrangements using 1-inch boards horizontally or vertically. Of these, the fence with vertical boards is usually the most unobtrusive. In a subdivision, you get either the outside or inside of this fence.

BACK-FRAME EXPOSED

FRONT-BOARD SURFACE

One argument in favor of this fence is that it can be changed without much trouble. By working with your neighbor, you can easily change the fence to alternating panels as shown in the sketch on the next page.

Enclosing the garden 119

*Shadow pattern is part of the design of this translucent plastic wire screen and redwood tongue-and-groove fence. Panels vary in height, create abstract pattern*

*Leaving the mortar joints unraked in masonry walls— either brick or concrete—will avoid a factory-like precision, provide a more natural background for plants*

Again working with the neighbors, you can lessen the confining quality of a perimeter fence by giving it a see-through panel or two. The boundaries of the lot are less distinct. If wire or a plastic-covered wire panel is backed by interesting plant material, the effect of more

space is even more pronounced. In changing from boards to a light material, use an additional stringer and brace.

If you do not wish to knock out boards or alter the existing fence, the addition of light members—such as 1 by 1's and 1 by 2's—will relieve the heaviness of the fence. If the light members are painted a contrasting color, the slender vertical lines will dominate.

This scheme creates a good vine trellis.

If the fence is treated as a series of panels, you'll find yourself working out panel design and using similar panel units in other parts of the garden.

*Gray-stained cedar board fence is designed to create a definite visual separation between paved entry court area that belongs to the house, and hillside of native* *growth of ferns, alders, maples, and conifers. Each area seems to be more interesting because of it. Space behind fence has been left for garden tools, storage*

---

Say that you are content to get along with only the frame to start with . . .

You fill in the portion that will give needed privacy. You set two panels, free-standing, where they add to privacy and give the garden the direction you want it to have.

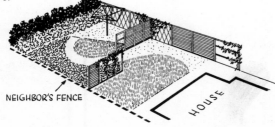

In a deep lot, there is much to be gained by using a screen fence to set aside a section for a cut flower garden, storage, compost, or other garden requirements.

The use of screens within the property line, with or without perimeter fencing, permits many interesting divisions of space—rooms within the garden room. In divid-

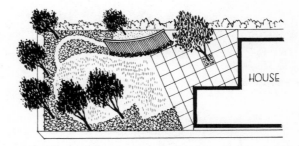

ing the garden into smaller areas, take care that space flows between all areas of the garden. It is possible to make the total appear to be larger by dividing it.

*Here plastic-coated screen panel hides service yard. Framework of 4 by 4-inch posts, 2 by 4-inch stringers, and cap. Fatshedera trained to eventually reach panel*

*Tall privacy screen is a series of panels of 1 by 1-inch redwood, resawn to form triangular strips, applied to frame in alternating vertical and horizontal pattern*

Don't forget as you work with the fence that it can be changed more by planting than by construction. One of the best ways to make the boundaries of your garden less distinct is to plant so that portions of the fence disappear.

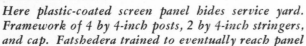

Some of the most important materials used for enclosing a garden room are the tall shrubs that don't take up much space. See *Plant Materials* chapter.

Generally in localities where ordinances limit the perimeter fence to 6 feet in height, the height of struc-tures inside the setback lines is not limited. For example, a wall of the house or garage can be carried out at eave level; a vine trellis can be 8 feet or more when inside the setback lines. Watch for these opportunities when look-ing for ways to screen winds or views that are not con-trollable by the 6-foot fence.

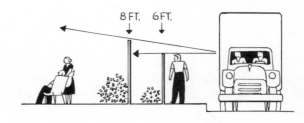

The use of materials other than wood in portions of the fence is most practical when the fence is constructed in a series of panels. This is especially true when you plan with the idea that fence sections can be used as independent panels, screens, or baffles.

ECKBO, ROYSTON, AND WILLIAMS

*Hillsides offer many opportunities for ingenious combinations of enclosing garden room. Here two retaining walls function beautifully as seat wall and display* *case for plants. Cap on walls and interlocking raised bed and wall give a trim finish to the unit. Screen of 1 by 1's adds interest through a change of texture*

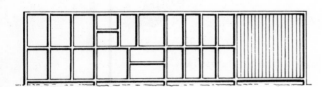

For special panels in the fence, consider any and all building materials that will stand the weather—asbestos, aluminum, plastic, glass, plywood; reed screen, composition board, and wire. See chapter on *Costs,* for complete list.

Generally panel materials are more easily and less wastefully assembled if used in modules equal to the standard size of the material. Plywood, asbestos, and other sheet materials are commonly available in panels 4 by 8 feet. This size sheet works smoothly into an 8-foot section of a 6-foot fence. With one knife or saw cut, the material can be sized to fit. Like this:

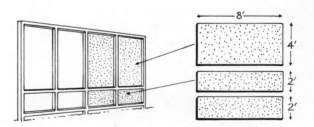

Certain materials have characteristics and qualities that make them more adaptable for certain uses.

1. *Asbestos-cement* panels are a heavy, compact material that stops both vision and motion. They "resist" children—they are almost harmproof. They are indestructible in sun, rain, cold.

These panels are especially suitable for use in children's play yards as a baffle, wind screen, and even as a blackboard. (Chalk writing washes off easily with water.)

2. *Glass fiber-reinforced plastic* is a translucent material that can be obtained in various permanent colors—in flat or corrugated form. When applied to a frame correctly, it will not break or scuff easily. It is especially useful in dark areas where a solid frame would cut off light. (See chapter on *Costs*.)

3. *Glass* can solve the problem when the best view is located in the same direction as hard-blowing, cold, prevailing wind. It is valuable in interior lots where wind protection is necessary within a garden. To avoid breakage, the usual solution is to make the wall part wood and part glass.

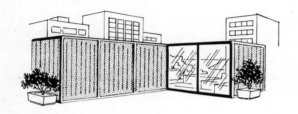

4. *Plywood* can be used in any part of the garden. Its smooth finish is usually stained or painted to withstand the weather. It is frequently used as an element of simplicity to contrast with some more exciting form, color, texture or shadow. If you buy plywood for garden use, remember to specify "exterior grade."

5. *Plastic-coated screen* is translucent and light in feeling, and it blurs out anything located behind it. These qualities make it excellent for use in dark corners where privacy is preferred, and in a small side yard or cramped area. Because you can actually see forms and shadows on the other side of the screen, you get an effect of spaciousness rather than enclosure.

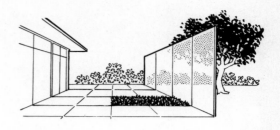

6. *Wire* comes in many mesh sizes and gauges. (See chapter on *Costs*.) It is frequently used in conjunction with a pool area; when the pool is not in use, the wire fence keeps out people but doesn't block the view or breeze. A heavy wire fence solves many play yard problems—parents can see in and children can see out.

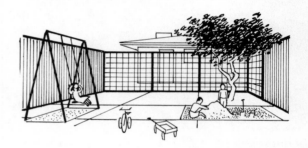

7. *Vines,* grown over a wire framework, can be functional as well as decorative. A warm breeze that passes through a moist vine fence into the garden usually aids in cooling the garden.

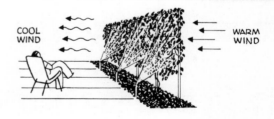

## The screen enclosure

If you enclose an area with screen—the old fly screen or one of its modern counterparts—you accomplish three things: wind control, insect control, and sun control. A square foot of most metal screening covers as much as 25 to 30 per cent of that area with metal. This metal barrier in turn cuts about 30 per cent of the sun's intensity and slows a breeze to a standstill.

When screen is used in both walls and roof, the enclosed area becomes a quiet, airy, protected place for people and plants. A screen roof will collect leaves and twigs and will need an occasional sweeping to keep it looking neat. Unless you are a stickler for neatness, however, the dappled shade pattern made by sunlight filtering through the leaves can be rather pleasant.

LAWRENCE HALPRIN
STRUCTURE BY WURSTER, BERNARDI, EMMONS

*In this screen porch on warm afternoons, you are protected from wind and insects as well as sun. Porch makes sheltered peninsula in outdoor patio area that*

*is easily accessible from both living room and dining room. Sense of enclosure is minimized by extending screen panels from roof to exposed aggregate paving*

*Same porch from outside. Enclosure built right over terrace so porch becomes shady transition between house interior, garden. Sliding glass door between*

*living room and porch can be left open during warm weather without fear of insect invasion. Deep roof overhang gives porch furniture year-round protection*

C. JACQUES HAHN, J. CHARLES HOFFMAN

*This completely covered terrace extends almost the full length of the south side of house, and all major rooms open on it. This section, off the living room, is fully* *screened. Planting in 4-foot planter inside wall shows interesting combination of umbrella plant (Cyperus alternifolius), Queensland umbrella tree (Brassaia)*

---

In designing the screened-in area, remember that the more lofty the overhead and the more generous the floor space, the more luxurious will be the enclosure. As you can see in the photographs above, there's a world of difference between this kind of enclosure and the old, cage-like screened porch.

Many homes lend themselves to screened rooms.

*Starting with an open patio*

*. . . or a patio and trellis*

*. . . you could build this protected room*

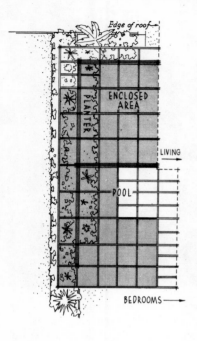

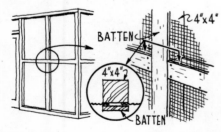

*This section of the completely covered terrace shown above opens off bedrooms. It is only partially roofed over with screen, leaving the walls completely open. Used primarily as the children's area for sunning and playing*

There are several ways to screen in a patio or terrace. The easiest, most economical method is to use roll screening. By applying the screening directly to the structure, you avoid the additional expense of separate frames for each opening. Tack or staple the screens on to stay if they must be left on in winter weather.

TENSION TYPE SCREENS | ROLLER TYPE SCREENS

Or you can build your own frames out of 1 by 2-inch stock, a suitable molding, and cut roll screening. Sketch indicates one method of attaching frames to structure. Screens can be taken down and stored in winter.

Instead of bulk roll screening, you can use tension or roller-type screens. Both types are more expensive than roll screening, but can be protected from winter weather. (Roller screens roll up out of sight, tension screens can be removed quickly.) Roller screens usually require professional installation.

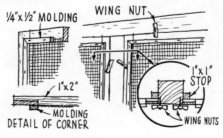

STRUCTURE BY RICHARD NEUTRA

*Screened area on house gets winter sun. In summer, house shades terrace from afternoon sun. Framework for screen cloth fits under overhang. Sliding door rides on overhead track. Roof is also screened*

*Sliding doors open living room into an outdoor all-purpose room. Screen panels are same size as glass panels*

STRUCTURE BY ALVIN B. MILLER

*Screened terrace allows for transition between upper house and lower studio addition. Screening acts as a mild windbreak, protects owners from hot western sun. Rockery planted with shade-loving plants*

*Same terrace from outside. Studio room on right, original structure at left. Pine is added wind-sun protection*

**128 Enclosing the garden**

HENRY VAN SIEGMAN

*Circular tree well of brick sets stage for colorful spring flower display in patio surrounded by pear orchard. Potted rose-pink azaleas around well, in fence sections*

# Ways to use raised beds, low walls

There are several good reasons why the landscape designer often makes use of raised beds and the low walls:

They give strength and permanency to design lines.

They give a "finished" look to the garden immediately.

They maintain order and neatness in every season.

They save hours of labor in the garden. See chapter on *Maintenance*.

Any flower or shrub planting bed that is raised above the ground level is a raised bed. It may be anywhere from 4 inches to 3 feet high. Sometimes it is free-standing; sometimes it is carried the full length of a fence or a wall of the house.

The low wall may be used to form a raised bed, or used alone to divide garden space, or used as a seat wall.

The low masonry wall is generally made of brick, concrete blocks, concrete, stone, or adobe.

Concrete blocks are the least expensive and the easiest for the amateur to use.

Poured concrete is the most plastic of the wall materials, and is favored where curves are called for. However, because of the forms and finishing it requires, it is neither an easy nor an inexpensive wall to build. See chapter on *Costs*.

Stone walls set up without mortar (dry walls) are natural to a garden, and you can plant in the soil between stones. For the best effects, the builder should have a love for stone, and he needs a good collection of stones from which to pick and choose.

The following photographs show typical installations.

The raised pool serves much the same function in the garden plan as does the raised planting bed. The adobe-walled pool shown in this photograph is the central feature of Sunset's patio. Pool is tile-lined

Adobe blocks are wide enough to be laid up dry. Here they serve as wall of raised bed on slope. Long-blooming ivy geraniums spill their color over it most of year

Adobe blocks set in mortar form low wall with pillars at intervals. For privacy, add panels of split redwood stakes. Cement blocks can be used in same manner

LOCKWOOD DE FOREST

*Wide brick terrace adjoining outdoor room will get more intensive use because plant materials are put un-* *der control in brick-walled raised beds. Ivy geranium in foreground; newly planted carissa in background*

FRED LANG

*Combined raised bed and low wall holds grade where elevations have been lowered. Pots set in soil can be changed seasonally. Grapestake fence in the back*

*In a retaining wall, raised bed, or foundation planter, brick is a pleasant material to live with. Here Convolvulus mauritanicus displays gray foliage, blue flowers*

Raised beds, low walls 131

*Concrete in serpentine form contrasts with natural rock and conifer planting. Its function here is to give dec-* *orative edge to parking area. Planted with Irish moss ground cover, junipers, dwarf spruce, grevillea tree*

*Concrete block wall 30 inches high retains raised bed. Feathery Lotus berthelotii cascades over edge. Violas, moraea behind. Espaliered calliandra on fence*

*Due to their uniformity, cast concrete blocks take well to geometric pattern in wall of raised bed. Spilling over wall is Lockwood rosemary; sea lavender above*

**132  Raised beds, low walls**

*Broken concrete, laid dry, retains soil; divides terrace and planted area. Hen and chickens in crevices. Cerastium and thyme ground cover above. Paving is asphalt*

*Another example of broken concrete laid dry. Drifts of helichrysum, santolina, good contrast with rough-hewn concrete. Ajuga ground cover. Hewn pole fence*

*Native rock in mortar solves serious grading problem. Curving red brick steps and white gravel mulch above wall provide color interest, suggest simple plantings*

*Dry wall of Columbia big stone rubble—making easy change of level—is at home on this Oregon hillside. Daphne cneorum is planted in foreground of raised bed*

*Classic example of raised bed shows importance of cap. Wall is 2 by 12-inch redwood capped by 2 by 6. Raised bed makes the high brick retaining wall less dominant*

*Redwood seat wall doubles as a retainer for raised bed. Wall, capped with 2 by 8, is 24 inches high, maximum for comfort. Daisies, zinnias provide summer color*

*Concrete block retaining wall steps down to raised bed, Xylosmas senticosa arches gracefully against wall, over wall. Giant ajuga between concrete stepping stones*

*Used brick wall, railroad ties hold slope. Cedar plant box in front is planted with tamarix juniper. Informal ground cover treatment complements railroad ties*

# Ways of roofing the garden

Overhead structures increase the amount of comfortable living space for people, and they also provide protected growing space for plants.

Let's take a brief look at the various types of structures before discussing each in detail.

To many gardeners, the most beautiful and useful overhead is a tree. Depending upon the kind of tree you select, you have your choice of deep or filtered shade, high or low shade, all-year shade or summer shade and winter sun. One wide-spreading tree can eventually shade a 60-foot garden. Six small trees will give you shade more quickly, and do it without dominating the garden.

For home owners with a sun problem that needs a solution right now, trees are too slow. An overhead for immediate sun control is the lath structure. You can control with exactness the amount of sun you or your plants will receive by the size and placement of the lath.

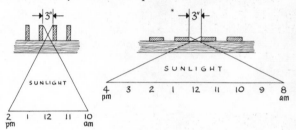

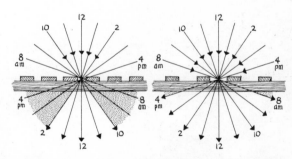

Another type of overhead structure is the vine support. This generally is a light structure that gives some protection while the vine is taking over. The lightly framed overhead offers the designer many opportunities for quick effects.

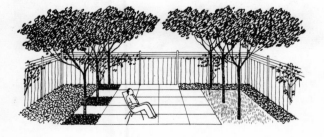

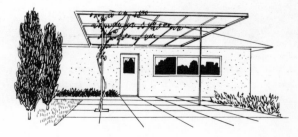

WALTER AND FLORENCE GERKE

*White-flowered wisteria vine transforms and lightens heavy structural extension of roof of house, provides cool summer shade. When leafless, vine detracts little* *from winter sun; gives grand show of spring flowers. In summer, a canopy of light green foliage gives filtered shade, casts lacy shadow pattern on brick paving*

Still another type of structure aimed at sun control is the overhead holding more or less perishable materials, such as reed, bamboo, netting, or canvas. Most of these are low in cost and, even when replaced every five years, are not too expensive.

Overheads that directly extend indoor space and are attached to the house are in another class. The open-air, all-weather rooms that they create usually should be designed and constructed with an eye to their future incorporation into the house itself. As a potential room of the house, this type of overhead should have an architectural similarity and continuity with the house.

You may decide to combine several types of roof enclosure in one structure. You may want a combination that will give you livable space in the rainy season, in the heat of summer, and in the cool, breezy season. Or you may vary your materials simply to achieve a pleasant effect.

Here's how the various types of materials have been used, how they are built, and how they fit into the garden plan.

## Lath

The term lath is used to cover a variety of materials. Common ⅜ by 1-inch lath will sag and twist if not supported every 24 inches. Small dimension lumber—1 by 1's or, preferably, 1 by 2's and 1 by 3's—is more satisfactory.

The use of lath has changed dramatically in the last few years. Ten years ago a lathhouse was a small structure built to protect plants. Today we make a distinction between the lathhouse (a plant shelter) and a lath overhead. The word "arbor" might be used to describe the lath overhead in some cases, but the trend is toward a "sky screen."

Here is a 4-step picture of the changes in the use of lath:

ORIGINAL LATHHOUSE

LATH SHELTER (OPEN ONE SIDE)

LATH SHADE (OPEN 3 SIDES)

LATH SKY SHADE & PLANT DISPLAY

The lofty overhead does not take up garden space as does the small lathhouse.

DOUGLAS BAYLIS

*Looking through lathhouse, with its nursery of plants, gives you the impression of following down a long, cool, garden corridor. This feeling is sustained in the roofed red brick walk that continues around the house*

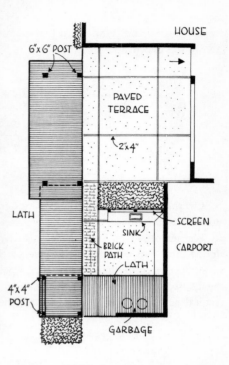

*Into a 21 by 23-foot open terrace, a small lathhouse and generous 13 by 23-foot work center were neatly incorporated. All 3 units designed and built as one, and joined directly to the house*

Illustrated in these photographs is a patio roof, lathhouse, and garden work center built as one unit. Although designed for a special situation, this idea and plan adapts itself to many situations.

Take the case of the older house with the garden at the rear of the house. Lathhouse and work center are built opposite the garage; the patio roof joins the two,

creating an open garden room that is part in the sun, part shaded by the patio roof.

On a narrow lot, the garden work center goes beside the house, completely out of sight from the patio. The lathhouse forms one wall of the patio. Opposite side is open to the garden.

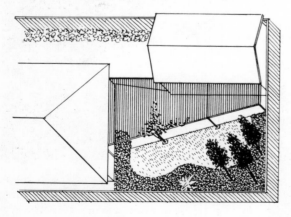

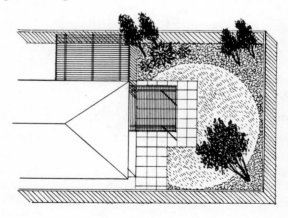

LATH HOUSE

PATIO ROOF

GARDEN
WORK CENTER

GARAGE

HOUSE

HOUSE

DOUGLAS BAYLIS

*Overhead view of 3-unit garden terrace showing how neatly separate units fit together. House at left and lower right form two walls of garden room; work cen-ter and lathhouse at upper left make third side; fourth side is open. Ceiling of garden room is partly sky, partly roof. Shadow pattern changes by hour, season*

*Looking from the work center to patio with an angled view of lath shelter. To make sure that the overhead remains crisp and clean, does not sag, 1 by 3's, spaced 1 inch apart, are used rather than lath*

*This patio is extension of family room. Facing south, it is protected on three sides from wind, usable even in winter*

Roofing the garden   139

*Structural pattern of roof allows complete freedom from posts. Beams anchored to posts in window wall. Steel rods through rafters provide cantilever structure*

*Overhead brought out from house at eave level. Gives lofty scale to this patio four steps below floor level. Space between roof and overhead left open for light*

On a wider lot, or where the house forms an ell, you can build the lathhouse in two sections, one on either side of the patio roof. In the sketch below, the "working" lathhouse at left is next to the garden work center, the "display" lathhouse at right is against the house.

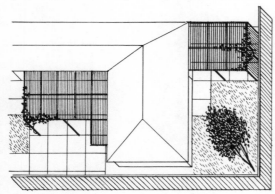

If yours is a one-story, simple, gable-roofed house, your patio roof can continue either or both of the two roof lines:

If your roof line is complicated, a flat roof is usually the best choice.

If your indoor floor level is well above ground level, so much the better. With roof level remaining the same and the floor level dropping, your garden room will be loftier and more open than any indoor room, as it should be.

**Woven reed and bamboo blinds**

These materials provide more densely filtered shade than the lath roof; they are preferred over wood lath by many home owners because the shade pattern is more natural and has less contrast. Both are effective wind screens. Neither is considered a permanent material. Wire woven reed is new to the West. We have seen 5-year-old installations in California that were still presentable.

Reed and bamboo are good materials for partially enclosing a high lath-covered frame. By various combinations of lath overhead and reed or bamboo, you can direct shade where you want it. The western sun can be par-

*Woven reed panels stapled to wood frames are suspended from spaced 2 by 6 beams. By varying the height of the panels, a more open feeling is maintained*

*Roof extends out from south wall of house. Bamboo on simple framework removable in winter. Shade pattern of bamboo is less busy than striped effect of lath*

---

tially or completely blocked depending upon how low you drop the reed on the west side:

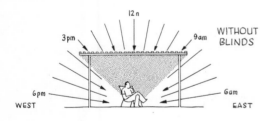

In some cases, adjustable protection is welcome on all sides of the overhead.

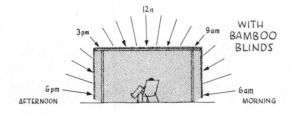

## Canvas

The virtue of canvas is its versatility. It can be held in place overhead with wires, pipe frame, or wood. If held on wires, it can be extended or folded back as the weather requires. When used as an overhead in hot summer areas, take care that a warm-air trap is not created beneath it.

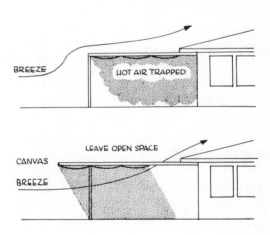

Many new fixtures for the construction of canvas shelters have been manufactured in recent years.

In the West where summer rains are no problem, there are other advantages in keeping overhead shelters two or three feet out from the house. Open space prevents the house from being darkened and allows full growth of plants along the house.

One of the smartest canvas installations consists of panels of canvas, fitted with grommets and laced to a pipe frame. An example of such an installation can be seen on pages 62-63.

**Roofing the garden 141**

OSMUNDSON-STALEY

DOUGLAS BAY

*Cabana-like canvas shelter is designed for shade until trees are large, and to divide adult's area from children's space. At back, two fixed canvas panels and flap on roller rebuff western sun, prevailing wind*

*Here horizontal and vertical sections of canvas, laced through grommets to pipe framing, give sun, wind shelter*

In most cities you'll find awning companies that specialize in the use of canvas in the garden. From them you can get anything from complete installation down to prefabricated units of pipe frame or panels with grommets.

### Reinforced plastic

Panels of glass-fiber-reinforced plastic solve several types of overhead problems. Because they form a rainproof roof without cutting out light, they are valuable in overheads in cool-summer areas where sunlight is never intense. In hot-summer areas, this material is used on the east side of the house. Don't use it, especially in light colors, as a sun filter where summers are hot.

Plastic panels are often used in combination with opaque corrugated material, such as asbestos board, and with aluminum panels. Because they admit light, they are useful in situations where a solid roof would darken the inside rooms of a house. Like this:

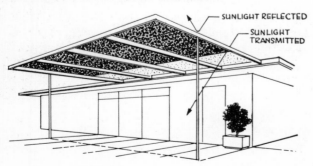

SUNLIGHT REFLECTED

SUNLIGHT TRANSMITTED

### Corrugated aluminum, steel, and asbestos

All of these materials give complete overhead protection. Both aluminum and steel are noisy in the wind if not carefully installed, and both materials expand and contract with heat and cold, loosening ordinary fastenings. Unless properly nailed on, they will leak around the nail holes. Check with your building materials supplier on the latest type of fasteners.

Corrugated asbestos and aluminum make cool roofs, while steel absorbs and re-radiates the sun's heat.

### Louvered window screen

The use of this material demands a careful study of sun angles before installation; the degree of shade depends upon the direction of the louvers and the time of day. It solves the problem of screening the wind without blocking ventilation; however, it gives no rain protection and, because leaves and small particles lodge in the tiny louvers, it can become untidy under trees.

Miniature louvers are built right into this screening material. It is made in a variety of finishes, the most commonly available and economical being aluminum. It is long-lasting and requires little maintenance.

### Ordinary fly screen

This is valuable where insects bother or where you need wind controls. A screened enclosure 10 to 12 feet high gets away from any feeling of being caged in, and creates a quiet, protected environment for people and for plants.

*Entrance drive overhead sheathed with plastic screen, is rain cover for parked cars, shades kitchen, bedroom from western sun. Plants are tree ferns, banana*

*Where frequent rains and cool summers are to be expected, panels of Fiberglas and plastic can be used for patio roofing. Posts are 4 by 4's, beams are 4 by 8's*

*Cool terrace roof on north side of house combines filtering action of lath with colorful all-weather protection of green Fiberglas plastic roofing. The plastic*

*covers roof of ½ by 3-inch lath nailed to 1 by 8 rafters on 12-inch centers. Additional cooling effect and wind protection are provided by vines trained over screen*

Roofing the garden 143

*In pipe-supported overhead, louvers can be set at different angles to shade house wall and filter sun when high over head. Louvers of lightweight wood, beams taper*

*In pool-side lath shelter cantilever structure of 2 by 8 posts, 6-foot centers, with tapered 2 by 10-inch rafters, roofed with 1 by 2-inch strips, creates shade for fuchsias*

LAWRENCE HALPRIN

*Combination of solid roof, partially open, and lath cover is designed to give a choice of weather as you move out from the living room to the spacious deck*

*Shadow pattern on paving shows how corrugated plastic covers only portion of the overhead frame, but cuts off the wind which formerly swooped over house*

# Color in the garden

Color is such an important and integral part of the garden that it's almost impossible to separate the two. In fact, the words "garden" and "color" are practically synonymous.

The word "garden" may recall something as general as green trees or a sweep of lawn, or something as specific as the first wave of yellow daffodils in the spring, or something as personal as a lilac bush in the neighborhood you grew up in. Chances are that you cannot look at a black and white photograph of a garden without "seeing" reds and yellows and greens and blues.

There's color in a garden before any flower, shrub, tree, or vine is planted. The existing house walls, paving, and fences—red brick, gray concrete, brown cedar, warm redwood, white-painted wood, stippled stucco—are and always will be a part of your color scheme.

So will the colors of distant backgrounds, and of important existing trees—red-barked madrone, gray-trunked oak, gray-green leafed eucalyptus or olive, dark green pine, blue-green cedar.

Happily, garden color schemes are not static. Some shrubs will change from light green to dark green to yellow through the seasons. The yellow-green of nandina will switch to crimson in the winter months.

The important thing in gardening is not to be frightened by colors. There are no "bad" colors. Choose to delight *your* eye.

You can follow with confidence a simple logical sequence in establishing a garden color scheme if you start with the colors of your backgrounds. They give you a strong reference point to turn to each time you must make a decision involving color in your garden.

In selecting your permanent plant material—shrubs, trees, and vines—to build the basic framework of your garden, you are also creating a basic color framework.

Your choice of basic framework plants will be determined by background colors. Every color that you move into your garden influences, and is influenced by, the background.

Let's take a look at the sketch of the entry to a small house of wood, stained dark brown. The dark brown, being the dominant color, is your reference point. You make your color decisions with that in mind. There are no rules; the choice should be based on your feeling about color. Here's one logical sequence:

1. Gray-green variegated *Pittosporum tobira* to lighten shadow.

2. Tubbed citrus—yellow-green foliage with accents in yellow or orange fruits; or tubbed yellow-green bamboo.

3. Clump of birches—silvery gray trunks against dark brown of house.

4. Gray ground cover under birch to pick up color of the bark and provide a contrasting panel of gray against red brick paving.

If you take the same entry arrangement with a white house, your choices in color might go in this sequence:

1. Medium green boxwood to absorb some of the reflected light.

2. Tubbed Kurume azaleas with accents of pink or red flowers—or *Pieris forrestii* with accents of new red foliage and white flowers.

3. Flowering crabapple with medium green foliage, accents of pinkish-white flowers, red or yellow fruits; or a mass planting of scarlet floribundas.

4. Ground cover of *Vinca minor* with accent of blue flowers.

Or when brick walls are dominant:

1. Blue-green junipers for contrast and accent.

2. Tubbed *Mahonia bealei* for bold gray-green foliage with accents of yellow flowers and bluish berries.

3. Deciduous magnolia, flowering cherry, or dogwood with white flowers for accent.

4. Ground cover of *Ajuga reptans* interplanted with drifts of gentian blue, spring-flowering grape hyacinth.

## Features for building color schemes

Other important existing features on which you can base your color scheme are:

- Rooms in the house, particularly those from which you look out on the garden.
- Fences, patio floors, other surfaces.
- A view of the ocean, a lake, mountains, desert, woods, or rock outcroppings.
- An important plant—perhaps a flowering fruit tree, dogwood, magnolia, Japanese maple, a clump of birches.

Choosing a particular lead or reference point isn't so important as following it consistently with a scheme in which colors and textures of plants are related to each other as well as to the important feature. For example:

*The interior color scheme.* You may use plants to carry interior colors into the garden, or interior colors may pick up the colors of plants outside.

Gray-green walls or rugs repeat the gray-green of eucalyptus, olive, white fir, or deodar cedar. Furnishings in silvery grays repeat the color of Russian olive (*Elaeagnus angustifolia*), pearl acacia, or the silver tree (*Leucadendron*).

Instead of dealing with large amounts of color, you may prefer to pick up accents by carrying the color of cushions, draperies, or pottery into the garden. For example, you may repeat the coral color of indoor cushions in coral geraniums; or the soft yellow of draperies in forsythia, daffodils, iris, or hunnemannia.

*Fences, patio floors, other surfaces.* Use plants to tie together the colors of the house and terrace or patio floors. If your house is dark-colored and the terrace is light, use foliage in medium color values as a transition. For example, with a dark gray house and a light gray concrete terrace, use medium value foliage plants like *Elaeagnus pungens*, Pfitzer juniper, Ledifolia azaleas, or certain rhododendrons.

*The view.* If your garden is on the coast, the silver grays of sedum, sempervivum, ice plant, saltbush, aloe, and buckwheat will pick up the colors of rocks and sand. The blues of ceanothus will mirror the color of the ocean in some of its moods.

## Building color around dominant plants

You can build the whole color scheme around dominant plants. You create pictures with plants, using these simple elements:

1. A background—a tree or group of trees.

2. Middle distance—usually medium height shrubs, dwarf trees, or evergreen perennials.

3. Carpet—ground covers, lawn, paving—alone or with low plants between.

4. Accents—seasonal color from bulbs, annuals, or perennials.

Here are three examples of color schemes built around dominant plants.

*Color scheme No. 1: Purple and gray with accents of soft yellow, blue, and red.*

Background: Purpleleaf plum *(Prunus cerasifera pissardii)*—dark purple-red leaves, pinkish-white flowers in spring.

Middle distance: *Teucrium fruticans*—silvery gray, lavender-blue flowers in summer.

Carpet: *Ajuga metallica crispa*—dark bronze leaves with metallic sheen and blue flowers in spring and early summer.

Accents: Pale lavender-blue bearded iris and soft yellow or white daffodils in spring. Red *Lobelia cardinalis* and lavender-blue *Aster frikartii* in summer and early fall.

*Color scheme No. 2: Gray-green and dark green with accents of blue, yellow, and salmon.*

Background: Gray-green European olive, or silvery gray Russian olive planted against a gray-green house.

Middle distance: Strawberry tree *(Arbutus unedo)*—dark green; pineapple guava *(Feijoa sellowiana)*—gray-green; variegated *Pittosporum tobira*—gray-green and white; *Senecio greyii*—gray-green leaves outlined and backed with felty white; *Correa pulchella*—deep green foliage, gray-green beneath, pink bell-shaped flowers.

Carpet: Sun rose *(Helianthemum)*—interplant groups of green and gray-green foliaged varieties with soft yellow or salmon-pink flowers; spaces for seasonal accents.

Accents: Yellow daffodils and tulips in spring. Clumps of blue delphinium in early summer. Salmon annual phlox or petunias in summer. Salmon dwarf chrysanthemums in fall.

*Color scheme No. 3: Light, medium, dark green and red, with accents of yellow and gold.*

Background: Staghorn sumac—foliage rich green in summer and brilliant scarlet in fall, velvety brown branches.

Middle distance: Oregon grape *(Mahonia aquifolium)*—glossy dark green leaves, with ruddy and bronze new growth; clumps of Siberian dogwood *(Cornus alba sibirica)*—coral-red branches and twigs, yellow-green leaves turning to red and crimson in winter, white flowers in spring; *Viburnum opulus nanum*—red maple-like leaves in fall.

Carpet: Wild ginger *(Asarum caudatum)*—large dark green heart-shaped leaves. Interspaces for accents.

Accents: Bright yellow winter aconite *(Eranthis hyemalis)* or yellow Dutch crocus and blue scillas or grape hyacinths *(Muscari)* in early spring. Blue-flowered *Ceratostigma plumbaginoides* and yellow dwarf chrysanthemums in summer and fall.

## What colors can do for you

In working out garden schemes it will be helpful to know what various colors can do for you. Here we discuss their qualities and list some of the best plants for bringing these colors into the garden.

Although annuals, perennials, and bulbs receive credit for most of the garden color, many shrubs and trees also contribute their share. For example, roses, camellias, azaleas, rhododendrons, and fuchsias are always reliable sources of color.

For complete information on all plants, refer to the *Sunset Western Garden Book,* the *Sunset Seasonal Garden Guide,* and *Sunset's How to Grow Roses.*

### Gray

Gray makes most colors sing, tones down those that shout. The gaudy red of the annual salvia, the red of geraniums or fibrous begonias, takes on a smart sophistication when supported by gray-foliaged plants. The strong yellow and orange of marigolds is softened and cooled by the introduction of gray plants.

Gray brings out hidden luminosity and sparkle in quiet colors. There is a soft glowing quality in the combination of gray with shades of soft yellow, pink, or blue.

Here are some of the most useful gray plants:

| | |
|---|---|
| *Achillea argentea* | *Helleborus lividus* |
| *Arabis albida* | *Lavandula officinalis* |
| *Artemesia* Silver King | *Lotus berthelotii* |
| *Centaurea cineraria* | *Nepeta mussinii* |
| *Convolvulus cneorum* | *Santolina chamaecyparissus* |
| *Gonospermum canariense* | *Senecio cineraria* |
| *Helichrysum petiolatum* | *Senecio greyii* |

Gray-foliaged annuals are not considered here, as the flowers are the important consideration and foliage lasts only one season.

### Blue

Blue has a cool, refreshing quality, especially welcome in warmer climates. While you can combine various shades of blue to make a satisfying border, the contrast of clear white will intensify and enliven most blues. Blue is particularly enhanced by its complementary color—yellow.

Here are plants in different shades of blue:

### MEDIUM BLUE TO DEEP BLUE

| Perennials | Annuals | Bulbs and bulb-like plants |
|---|---|---|
| *Aconitum napellus* | *Anagallis* | *Agapanthus* |
| *Anchusa* | *Anchusa* | *Anemone* |
| *Aquilegia caerulea* | Browallia | *Camassia* |
| Brunnera | Bachelor's-buttons | *Muscari* |
| Campanula | Cineraria | *Scilla sibirica* |
| Delphinium | *Cynoglossum* | Iris |
| Gentiana | Larkspur | |
| Lithospermum | *Lobelia erinus* | |
| Penstemon | Violas | |
| *Salvia azurea grandiflora* | | |

### SKY BLUE

| Perennials | Annuals | Bulbs and bulb-like plants |
|---|---|---|
| Delphinium | Forget-me-nots | *Leucocoryne* |
| Felicia | Nemesia | *Muscari* |
| *Linum perenne* | Nemophila | Heavenly Blue |
| Meconopsis | Nigella | *Scilla sibirica* |

### LAVENDER-BLUE

| Perennials | Annuals | Bulbs and bulb-like plants |
|---|---|---|
| *Aster frikartii* | Ageratum | *Colchicum* |
| Catananche | Aster | Crocus |
| Delphinium | Cineraria | *Gladiolus* |
| Eupatorium | Didiscus | Hyacinths |
| Michaelmas daisies | Larkspur | *Scilla* |
| *Nepeta mussinii* | Pansies | Iris |
| *Phlox paniculata* | Petunias | Tulips |
| Polemonium | Primroses | |
| Scabiosa | *Scabiosa* | |
| Trachelium | Stock | |
| Violets | Sweet peas | |
| | *Verbena* | |
| | Violas | |

### PURPLE TO BLUE-VIOLET

| Perennials | Annuals | Bulbs and bulb-like plants |
|---|---|---|
| *Anemone pulsatilla* | *Alyssum* | *Brodiaea* |
| Aubrieta | Aster | Crocus |
| Boltonia | Cineraria | *Gladiolus* |
| Delphinium | Larkspur | Hyacinths |
| Eupatorium | Pansies | Iris |
| Heliotrope | Petunias | *Scilla* |
| *Lavandula* | *Scabiosa* | Tulips |
| *Limonium* | Stock | |
| Liriope | Sweet peas | |
| Michaelmas daisies | *Verbena* | |
| *Platycodon* | | |
| Salvia | | |
| Stokesia | | |
| Violets | | |

## Pink

Pink—depending on the shade—can be soft and delicate or loud and garish. Pale pink is good with other pastel colors, especially blue, and with white. Salmon-pink is one of the easiest shades of pink to use. It contains enough

yellow to harmonize with yellow flowers; and it is very effective with clear light to medium blues. Coral-pink contains more red, is emphatic in itself and combines well with soft yellow and white. Rose-pink, which leans slightly toward the blue side, is pleasing with lavender and violet.

Floribunda and hybrid tea roses provide one of the most varied and reliable sources of pink.

Here are plants in different shades of pink:

### SOFT PINK

| Perennials | Annuals | Bulbs and bulb-like plants |
|---|---|---|
| *Anemone japonica* | Aster | *Canna* |
| *Astilbe* | Cineraria | *Cyclamen* |
| Chrysanthemums | Clarkia | Dahlias |
| *Dianthus* | Cleome | *Gladiolus* |
| Geraniums | Cosmos | Hyacinths |
| *Gypsophila* | *Dianthus* | Lilies |
| Fibrous begonias | Godetia | *Nerine* |
| *Heuchera* | Hollyhocks | Pink callas |
| *Impatiens* | Impatiens | *Scilla hispanica* |
| Peonies | Larkspur | Tuberous begonias |
| Pelargoniums | Petunias | Tulips |
| Penstemon | *Phlox* | |
| *Phlox paniculata* | *Primula malacoides* | |
| Primroses | Snapdragons | |
| *Sedum spectabile* | Stock | |
| Transvaal daisies | Sweet peas | |
| | *Verbena* | |
| | *Vinca rosea* | |
| | *Zinnia* | |

### DEEP PINK

| Perennials | Annuals | Bulbs and bulb-like plants |
|---|---|---|
| Chrysanthemums | *Aster* | *Amaryllis* |
| *Dianthus* | Cineraria | *Canna* |
| *Digitalis* | Clarkia | *Cyclamen* |
| Geraniums | Cosmos | Dahlias |
| *Heuchera* | *Dianthus* | *Gladiolus* |
| *Impatiens* | Godetia | Hyacinths |
| Michaelmas daisies | Hollyhocks | *Nerine* |
| Peonies | Larkspur | Tuberous begonias |
| Pelargoniums | Petunias | Tulips |
| *Phlox paniculata* | *Phlox* | |
| *Physostegia* | Snapdragons | |
| Primroses | Stock | |
| Transvaal daisies | Sweet peas | |
| | *Verbena* | |
| | *Zinnia* | |

### CORAL OR SALMON-PINK

| Perennials | Annuals | Bulbs and bulb-like plants |
|---|---|---|
| Chrysanthemums | *Clarkia* | *Alstroemeria* |
| *Dianthus* | *Dianthus* | *Canna* |
| Geraniums | *Godetia* | Dahlias |
| *Heuchera* | Hollyhocks | *Gladiolus* |
| *Impatiens* | Impatiens | Lilies |
| *Papaver orientale* | Petunias | *Nerine* |
| *Papaver nudicaule* | *Phlox* | Tuberous begonias |
| Pelargoniums | *Scabiosa* | Tulips |
| *Phlox* | Snapdragons | |
| Primroses | Sweet William | |
| Transvaal daisies | *Zinnia* | |

## ROSE-PINK

| Perennials | Annuals | Bulbs and bulb-like plants |
|---|---|---|
| *Armeria* | *Aster* | *Cyclamen* |
| *Astilbe* | Cineraria | Dahlias |
| *Aubrieta* | *Clarkia* | *Freesia* |
| *Bergenia* | *Cleome* | *Gladiolus* |
| Chrysanthemums | *Cosmos* | Hyacinths |
| *Dianthus* | *Dianthus* | Lilies |
| *Dicentra* | *Godetia* | *Nerine* |
| Fibrous begonias | Hollyhocks | *Scilla hispanica* |
| Geraniums | Larkspur | Tuberous |
| Michaelmas | *Limonium* | begonias |
| daisies | Nicotiana | Tulips |
| *Nicotiana* | Petunias | *Watsonia* |
| Peonies | *Phlox* | |
| Pelargoniums | *Primula malacoides* | |
| *Penstemon* | *Scabiosa* | |
| *Phlox* | Snapdragons | |
| Primroses | Stock | |
| | Sweet peas | |
| | *Verbena* | |
| | *Vinca rosea* | |
| | *Zinnia* | |

## White

White has a cool, refreshing, quieting influence in gardens. It is particularly valuable in hot climates. Touches of white give a light airy feeling. White pacifies and tones down bright colors. Combinations of white and green or gray have classic beauty and dignity. Following are some of the best white-flowered plants:

| Perennials | Annuals | Bulbs and bulb-like plants |
|---|---|---|
| *Achillea argentea* | *Alyssum* | *Acidanthera* |
| *Anemone japonica* | *Aster* | *Agapanthus* |
| *Arabis albida* | Cineraria | *Alstroemeria* |
| *Arctotis* | *Gypsophila* | *Anemone* |
| *Astilbe* | *elegans* | Calla lilies |
| *Bergenia* | *Helichrysum* | *Canna* |
| *Campanula* | Hollyhocks | *Chionodoxa* |
| Chrysanthemums | *Iberis* | *Convallaria* |
| *Delphinium* | *Malcomia* | *Cyclamen* |
| *Dianthus* | Pansies | Daffodils and |
| *Dicentra* | Petunias | narcissus |
| *Digitalis* | *Phlox* | Dahlias |
| Fibrous begonias | *Primula* | *Freesia* |
| *Francoa* | *malacoides* | *Galanthus* |
| Geraniums | *Scabiosa* | *Galtonia* |
| *Gypsophila* | *Schizanthus* | *Gladiolus* |
| *Helleborus* | Shirley poppies | Hyacinths |
| *Heuchera* | Snapdragons | *Iris* |
| *Iberis* | Stock | *Leucojum* |
| Iceland poppies | Sweet peas | Lilies |
| *Impatiens* | *Verbena* | *Ornithogalum* |
| *Kniphofia* | Violas | *Ranunculus* |
| Marguerites | *Zinnia* | *Scilla* |
| Michaelmas daisies | | Tuberous begonias |
| *Nierembergia* | | Tulips |
| Pelargoniums | | *Watsonia* |
| Peonies | | |
| *Phlox* | | |
| *Physostegia* | | |
| Primroses | | |
| Shasta daisies | | |
| Transvaal daisies | | |
| Violets | | |

## Yellow

Yellow is a happy cheerful color. On a dull overcast day, yellow flowers or foliage (of certain shrubs and trees) supply the sunshine. Soft yellows combine easily with many colors and are almost as useful as gray for making transitions between uncongenial colors.

Yellow introduces spring. Daffodils are the first flowers to bloom in many gardens. Yellow alyssum warms the early spring border.

Yellow, of course, appears in all seasons. There is the warm yellow of summer sunflowers and zinnias; the rich golden yellow of harvest chrysanthemums, the brilliant yellows of some climbing roses, and the fall foliage of many trees.

Look to these plants for good yellows:

### SOFT LIGHT YELLOW

| Perennials | Annuals | Bulbs and bulb-like plants |
|---|---|---|
| *Achillea taggetea* | *Calendula* | *Canna* |
| *Alyssum saxatile* | Hollyhocks | Daffodils and |
| *citrinum* | *Linaria* | jonquils |
| *Anthemis* | Snapdragons | Dahlias |
| *tinctoria* | | *Gladiolus* |
| Moonlight | | *Hemerocallis* |
| *Aquilegia* | | Iris |
| *chrysantha* | | Lilies |
| Chrysanthemums | | *Ranunculus* |
| Marguerites | | Tulips |

### CLEAR DEEP YELLOW TO GOLDEN YELLOW

| Perennials | Annuals | Bulbs and bulb-like plants |
|---|---|---|
| *Alyssum saxatile* | *Calendula* | *Alstroemeria* |
| Chrysanthemums | *Celosia* | *Canna* |
| *Coreopsis* | *Coreopsis* | *Crocus* |
| *grandiflora* | *Dimorphotheca* | Daffodils and |
| *Doronicum* | *Gazania* | jonquils |
| *Geum* | Marigolds | Dahlias |
| *Hunnemannia* | Nasturtiums | *Eranthis* |
| *Kniphofia* | Pansies | *Freesia* |
| *Linum flavum* | Snapdragons | *Hemerocallis* |
| *Potentilla* | Sunflowers | Iris |
| Primroses | Violas | Lilies |
| *Sedum* | *Zinnia* | *Ranunculus* |
| Wallflowers | | Tulips |
| | | Tuberous |
| | | begonias |
| | | Yellow callas |

## Red

Red is a color with many hues. On one side of spectrum red—a primary color—are hues containing small to larger amounts of blue such as crimson, carmine, and rose—and the darker hues such as claret, burgundy, and maroon.

On the other side of spectrum red are hues with different amounts of yellow such as scarlet, vermilion, terra cotta, and tile red. To simplify classification of flowers in hues of red we use these four headings: spectrum red (or real red); orange-red; rose-red; and darker reds.

Reds of high intensity—spectrum red, scarlet, vermilion—are warm and exciting. If used alone in large masses they dominate the garden. They are most useful and effective when combined with white, gray, and blue-gray. As with the pink, roses provide the widest and most dramatic range of reds that you can find.

Following are plants with red flowers:

### SPECTRUM RED

| Perennials | Annuals | Bulbs and bulb-like plants |
|---|---|---|
| Carnations | *Celosia* | *Anemone* |
| Geraniums | Corn poppies | *Canna* |
| *Geum* | *Gaillardia* | Dahlias |
| *Helianthemum* | Hollyhocks | *Gladiolus* |
| St. Mary's | Nasturtiums | *Haemanthus* |
| *Penstemon* | *Salvia splendens* | *Hippeastrum* |
| Poinsettias | *Verbena* | Lilies |
| | *Zinnia* | *Nerine* |
| | | *Ranunculus* |
| | | Tuberous |
| | | begonias |
| | | Tulips |

### ORANGE-RED OR SCARLET

| Perennials | Annuals | Bulbs and bulb-like plants |
|---|---|---|
| Columbine | *Alonsoa* | Dahlias |
| *Delphinium* | Nasturtiums | *Fritillaria* |
| *nudicaule* | *Physalis* | Kafir lilies |
| *Helenium* | *Zinnia* | *Gladiolus* |
| *Kniphofia* | | Lilies |
| *Lychnis chalcedonica* | | *Tritonia* |
| Oriental poppy | | Tulips |
| *Penstemon* | | |

### ROSE-RED

| Perennials | Annuals | Bulbs and bulb-like plants |
|---|---|---|
| Chrysanthemums | *Aster* | Dahlias |
| *Dianthus* | *Cosmos* | *Nerine* |
| Fibrous begonias | Hollyhocks | *Ranunculus* |
| *Heuchera* | Larkspur | Tuberous |
| Pelargoniums | *Linum rubrum* | begonias |
| *Penstemon* | *Nicotiana* | Tulips |
| Primroses | Petunias | |
| Sweet William | *Primula malacoides* | |
| Valerian | Snapdragons | |
| | Stock | |
| | Sweet peas | |
| | *Zinnia* | |

### DARK RED

| Perennials | Annuals | Bulbs and bulb-like plants |
|---|---|---|
| *Astilbe* | *Aster* | *Canna* |
| Chrysanthemums | *Cosmos* | Dahlias |
| *Dianthus* | Hollyhocks | *Gladiolus* |
| Michaelmas | *Nicotiana* | *Hippeastrum* |
| daisies | Petunias | Lilies |
| Pelargoniums | *Phlox* | Tuberous |
| *Penstemon* | *Salpiglossis* | begonias |
| Peonies | *Scabiosa* | Tulips |
| *Phlox* | Snapdragons | |
| Primroses | Sweet peas | |
| Sweet William | *Verbena* | |
| Wallflowers | *Zinnia* | |

## Orange

Orange, copper, and bronze occupy the range between red and yellow. Rich, warm, and glowing, but not garish, these are typical fall hues found at their best in autumn foliage of deciduous plants, but occurring also in rose blossoms and in the perennials, annuals, and bulbs listed below:

### ORANGE

| Perennials | Annuals | Bulbs and bulb-like plants |
|---|---|---|
| *Arctotis* | *Anagallis* | *Alstroemeria* |
| Chrysanthemums | *Calendula* | *Canna* |
| *Gazania* | California poppies | *Clivia* |
| *Glaucium* | *Coreopsis* | *Gladiolus* |
| Iceland poppies | *Cosmos* | *Hemerocallis* |
| *Kniphofia* | *Gaillardia* | Lilies |
| Oriental poppies | *Helianthus* | *Nerine* |
| Wallflowers | *Helichrysum* | *Ranunculus* |
| | Nasturtiums | *Tigridia* |
| | *Nemesia* | *Tritonia* |
| | Shirley poppies | Tuberous |
| | *Tagetes* | begonias |
| | *Tithonia* | Tulips |
| | *Zinnia* | |

### COPPER AND BRONZE

| Perennials | Annuals | Bulbs and bulb-like plants |
|---|---|---|
| *Calceolaria* | *Helianthus* | *Alstroemeria* |
| Chrysanthemums | *Helichrysum* | *Canna* |
| *Gazania* | Nasturtiums | *Gladiolus* |
| Primroses | Snapdragons | *Hemerocallis* |
| Wallflowers | *Tagetes* | *Iris* |
| | *Zinnia* | Tulips |

# Lighting the garden

Garden lighting should be considered from three points of view:

1. To illuminate paths, walks, steps, and living areas for use at night.

2. To illuminate and dramatize plant material.

3. To use light as a substitute for plants—in other words, to garden with light.

DOUGLAS BAYLIS

*Light sources are: frosted globes in roof of cabana; light box at table level, covered with aluminum honeycomb; spotlight under eaves directed against house*

To the home owner with undeveloped plant material, night lighting is sheer magic. With a few well placed lights, he can create a picture as romantic as Rio or Hawaii. A light panel in a fence, a shaded light on a post shining down on a pot of white petunias, the reflected light from canvas—these can transform an everyday little garden into another world.

Whether your garden is new and sparse or old and rich with plant material, the light you design with will be of these kinds:

*Direct light.* Light goes from source directly to the tree, vine, flower, pool, or whatever object is to be lighted. The direct source—the globe—in all cases should be hidden.

*Indirect light.* The light goes from the source to a reflecting surface which directs it to the area or object to be lighted. Direct the light to the ceiling of an outdoor room and let it reflect down, rather than directing the light from the ceiling.

*Glow light.* The light itself becomes the object to be seen and adds very little illumination. Light is covered with translucent material such as frosted glass, plastic, paper, or parchment.

Permanent outdoor lights must be weatherproof. There are a number of standard units available. For example:

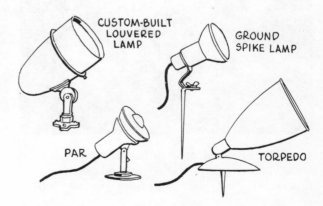

CUSTOM-BUILT LOUVERED LAMP

GROUND SPIKE LAMP

PAR

TORPEDO

ECKBO, ROYSTON, AND WILLIAMS

*When patio is extension of indoor areas, outdoor light plays important role of selecting picture you want to see. Here it's a raised pool and spreading oak tree*

ECKBO, ROYSTON, AND WILLIAMS

*Lights hidden back of raised bed play against textured fence screen. In background are Zabel laurel, camellias; foreground—Mugho pine, ivy geraniums, junipers*

*At corner of raised pool in Sunset's patio daffodils and cyclamen grouped around floodlight to screen light source, cut glare; cast nice shadow patterns*

Using the basic waterproof socket and connection, you can assemble many very effective types of light.

A piece of tin 10 inches square can be bent and fixed to the side of a post or a fence to give a soft light.

Wood pieces, 1 by 6 or 1 by 8, are used in the same manner as tin.

Large panels of light—using color—work well on a fence or wall.

Arranging for night lighting is best done by trial. The important thing is to avoid harsh light, to baffle the source of light.

You can see what night lighting will do for you very inexpensively with temporary lighting. At the far right are a few ideas:

Here are points to check in making a permanent outdoor lighting installation.

Underground wiring, limited for years to lead-sheathed wire or cable in watertight rigid conduit, is now available in a chemically coated variety that can be buried directly in the ground. No conduit is necessary. The nonmetallic trench cable is obtainable as single-wire, two-wire, and three-wire conductors.

If outlets are to be provided for outdoor appliances—such as electric hedge clippers, lawn mowers and trimmers, barbecue accessories—the outlet should be grounded

to minimize shock hazard. Outlet boxes attached to a conduit system are self-grounded, but those used with trench cable usually need to be grounded with bare copper wire. Three-hole outlets are recommended with grounded, outdoor installations. Many electric tools marketed for garden use are now sold with 3-wire cords and 3-pronged plugs.

Grounding of outdoor lighting circuits is a good practice, but not essential.

Trench for cables should be dug before walks and lawns are in. It's a good idea to carry out an extra cable for future extension. Bury cable at least 18 inches underground to avoid injuring it when spading the ground. Or, if shallower, protect the cable with a 1 by 3 or 1 by 4 board. Like this:

*Darting flames of torches on bamboo poles give the garden a festive air. In Hawaii they call it luau torch. Burns kerosene*

*Japanese lantern can be used with candle or light bulb. Paper sacks, with sand to hold them, often used as candle containers*

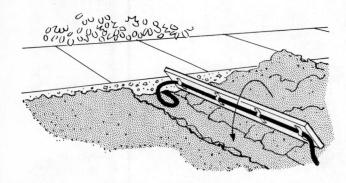

The cable must be given mechanical protection where it enters and leaves the ground. This can be done with conduit, pipe, or redwood frame. Like this:

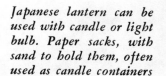

*Fiberglas plastic tacked and glued to circular piece of plywood. Veneer strip finish glued top and bottom. Use candle or lamp*

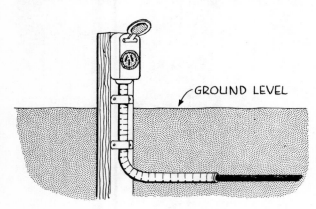

GROUND LEVEL

*Floodlight mounted in waterproof fixture set in tile floor of Sunset's terrace. Thick frosted glass diffuses light, lessens glare*

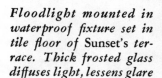

Terminate cable in weatherproof outlet boxes with spring shut gasket covers or screw cap covers. Generally, the weatherproof convenience outlets should be placed near the ground in several locations so that inexpensive portable lights can be used.

Switches may be mounted inside the house or garage. Weatherproof switches and combination outlets and switches are available. If outdoor type is used, inset in fence posts or wall as illustrated on the next page.

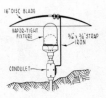

*Disc blade shields lamp in vapor-tight fixture, is placed low to bring safety to garden steps. Note the pebbled concrete surface*

Unshielded lamp mounted out of sight in eave of workshop to left

Two torpedo type fixtures in tree:

Lamp on ground behind fence structure backlights plants, plastic screen

Torpedo fixture on ground, shielded by planter

Unshielded PAR lamp screened by plants in planting bed,

STRUCTURE BY MORGAN STEDMAN

*Five lamps bring about this night picture. Source of light hidden in the planting beds and planters. Creating panels of light as in plastic at right is as important as the illumination of plants or structures*

*Don't underestimate the ability of candlelight to decorate your garden at night. Here hurricane lamps on white painted fence serve as markers for driveway*

Don't overload any household circuit. An average 15-amp circuit can safely handle only about 1,500 watts. This would mean a maximum of 10 of the 150 watt PAR lamps if no load is drawn off in the house. For normal lighting, No. 14 wire is large enough. When appliances are added, use No. 12.

Check local building codes. Get a permit from the electrical inspector.

# Heating the garden

Because the chill of the evening comes too soon in many outdoor living rooms, the inventive Westerner has worked out many heating schemes.

MORGAN STEDMAN

*An expanded metal basket contains charcoal. Simple steel frame holds basket upright where it can serve as a patio warmer just as effectively as a fireplace*

All successful devices are based on radiating heat to the people on the patio, rather than on heating the air.

The firepit is the most used device. In making one, don't get it too deep. As soon as the heat source is below the level of the patio floor, it's of no value to those sitting around it. Better have a shallow pit if you are planning a small fire.

A raised pit is more effective than a sunken one.

You are warmed by heat radiated from the walls of the raised pit as well as the fire itself.

The firepit is not so efficient as the old brick or stone outdoor fireplace. The advantage of the pit is that it provides a source for fire that more or less disappears when not in use. But if your outdoor room can take a fireplace unobtrusively, it is a better bet than a firepit.

A back wall for an open fire gives the same effect as a fireplace.

In the sketches and photographs on the next page are several schemes that have been used.

ARNOLD DUTTON

*Firepit is 5 feet in diameter. Circle contains 39 Roman bricks set in mortar. Hole was dug 20 inches deep, filled with crushed rock and top layer of pea gravel*

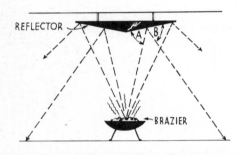

*Overhead heat reflector made of two pieces of stainless steel, with joint lapped, is angled to bounce back heat from brazier to the people who sit around it*

*Half circle of bricks*

*Raised pit, one side open*

*Raised pit and table*

The reflection and radiation of heat is all-important in garden heating. The half circle of bricks, for example, will radiate heat long after the fire dies down. If the concrete raised pit were faced with stainless steel, the radiation would be intensified. Evening sitting arrangement would be in front of the fire, of course. The objections raised with firepits of this type are the same as with fireplaces. If they are built to face away from the house, there is no daytime appearance problem. In all cases the sight of the open fire has a warming effect that is greater than the actual heat release. The open fire is important in night lighting, too.

*Folding aluminum screen, when placed around portable barbecue, reflects heat, stops cooling breeze. Aluminum will bounce back about 90 per cent of heat*

*In test of warming patio with reflective heat of aluminum roof, a sense of comfort was maintained with infra-red 250-watt lamps tilted at angle of about 70°*

The portable barbecue can be used as a heat source after the cooking is over. Of course, the greater the size of the brazier, the more heat will be radiated. The metal kettle type will keep shins and knees warm for an hour or more.

The warm floor panel, obtained by installing pipe in the concrete slab, or beneath tile or brick in sand, is being used to some extent. A heated floor will make a 55° air temperature feel comfortable if there is no wind and if the patio has an overhead cover.

The warm floor is not cheap. A hot-water heater, small pump, and a good hundred feet of pipe are needed. Complete installation of a 20 by 30-foot terrace heating system costs in the neighborhood of $600.

It's easier to warm a covered patio than one that is open to the sky. Sitting on an open terrace at night, you lose heat to the sky—more to a clear sky, less to a cloudy one. You lose heat to moving air in proportion to rate of movement. You lose heat to all nearby surfaces that are colder than you are.

With an air temperature of 55° to 60°, the open sky may be equivalent to a ceiling whose temperature is 32° to 39°. Underneath an overhead, the ceiling will be about the same as the air temperature.

Other ingenious home owners have worked out ways to use reflected heat. Note the overhead reflector cone above the fire in the photograph on opposite page.

Others have experimented with aluminum-faced panels, trying to "bounce" the heat so that when you sit before an open fire your back will be warm.

Research in the field of stored solar heat is going forward. It is expected that in a few years we will be able to use building blocks in the garden that will store heat during the day and release it for several hours after sundown.

*To heat patio, copper tubing is laid over concrete and gravel base and then covered with brick laid in sand*

*Finish of job pictured above. Radiant heat most effective where ceiling overhead stops heat loss to sky*

# Water in the garden

Water in motion gives a garden such a fresh breath that it is worth considering in almost any plan, and there are ways to get it at very little cost. In hot, dry climates where soaring temperatures outside tend to keep you inside, water cooling can make a big difference in how you use the garden.

You may think that the sight of a small garden pool or the sound of a sprinkler running makes you feel cooler only because it suggests a mountain pool or waterfall.

But it has more than a psychological effect on your physical comfort. A knowledge of the principles of evaporation and radiation will help you to control your garden climate.

## Evaporation

When hot dry air passes over water—on your skin, on the lawn, on the shrubs, on a terrace pavement—the water evaporates. To evaporate the water, the hot air uses up some of its heat, becomes cooler.

The drier the air, the lower the humidity and the greater the heat loss through evaporation.

This means that when a hot dry breeze moves through water, it becomes a cool breeze. Of course, if the humidity is high, evaporation is slight and the breeze is not cooled perceptibly.

But wherever humidity is low, you can reduce the temperature in your garden room by getting water into the air.

Even a garden sprinkler will do this, but at the cost of soggy ground and drenched surfaces.

For installations in a garden cooling system, look for spray heads that make a fine mist. There are many on the market, but they are not generally available at nurseries and garden stores. If your nurseryman won't order them for you, check with commercial growers. They use mist sprays in propagating beds, in greenhouses, and in shade houses.

Illustrated here are several types of spray heads. They are available in various nozzle sizes. Some throw such a fine fog that they use only 3 gallons of water an hour.

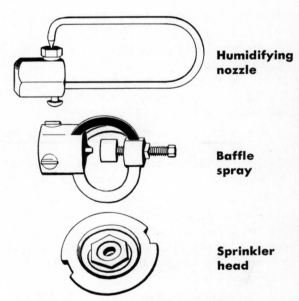

**Humidifying nozzle**

**Baffle spray**

**Sprinkler head**

Look around your garden for places to use the mist sprays and foggers. They use so little water that they can be operated constantly without creating drainage problems.

Vine-covered pergolas offer opportunities. For most efficient cooling, keep the vine damp on the windward side.

For double-duty, install a mist spray over moisture-loving plants in a lath shelter. Both you and your plants will love it!

*Note:* One of the main objections to mist sprays has been the likelihood of overwatering when operation is continuous. This objection can be overcome by adding automatic timers to the installation.

STRUCTURE BY JOHN MATTHIAS

*Where summer winds are hot, lath structure on windward side of garden rooms is equipped with mist spray nozzles. Lath slows wind to breeze; mist cools breeze*

*Two pipe lines with mist sprays change dry climate to moist one. Davallia, adiantum, polypodium ferns in baskets lined with tree fern trunk, osmunda, sphagnum*

HENRY VAN SIEGMAN

*In garden in Kyoto, Japan, center of interest is large pond. Stones make path across it, look as if placed by nature. Azaleas pruned to repeat shape of stones*

*To get sheet of falling water you must have perfectly level spillway surface. Sheet metal used here. Other flow surfaces are: aluminum, plastic, glass, and tile*

---

### Radiation

A hot object, surrounded by cold objects, loses heat to the cold objects.

If the pavement under your feet is cooler than you are, you lose some of your heat to it. If the garden wall, or the leaves of a vine, are cooler than you are, you feel cooler when you are near them.

Thus, to cool yourself, you should cool the objects around you.

This can be as simple as wetting down your patio floor with water, or spraying the fence or vines or trees around you. The longer the surfaces can be kept cool, the longer you will be cool.

FLOYD COWAN

*Pool recessed in wall of slate fragments. Water falls from ceramic fish head half hidden by fuchsias, flows to lower pool through small hole in rim of upper pool*

JOHN CARMACK

*Large pool is steel boiler head. Small circulating pump drops spray into a smaller bowl above that holds several glass floats which spin in the whirling water*

*Flowing water of a creek is a cooling sight and sound whether creek is natural or pump-controlled. Native spruce and Oregon grape are planted at head of stream*

OSMUNDSON-STALEY

*Three-level pool against masonry fence. Pump circulates water from lower basin through multiple jets into upper basin. Bamboo, dwarf Deodar cedar at left*

One product that is designed for spraying a small quantity of water just where you want it is a small-diameter plastic tube available in lengths of 100 feet. All necessary reducers and couplings are packaged with it.

Since the tubing costs but 10 cents a foot, you can carry a fine spray here and there throughout the garden for very little cost. Wind it over canvas roofs, along the fence, under lath, in the shade garden. (You punch the holes, so you get water only where you need it.)

Any masonry wall that absorbs water makes an efficient cooling panel when water is being evaporated from its surface.

In every scheme for garden cooling, remember that air temperature is only the measurement of how the thermometer feels. If the air is 90°, you can, with a sprinkling of water, cool the lawn and shrubs and surfaces around you down 10° to 20°, depending on the dryness of the air. With the cool surfaces around you, a 90° air temperature will feel more like 80° to you.

Obviously, no outdoor cooling method will change a 100° day to a 70° day. But come sundown and you move within the sight and sound of water that is cooling garden surfaces and the passing breeze, and you'll feel much cooler than the thermometer says you should.

# Low-maintenance gardens

Non-gardeners come in many grades. There's the non-gardener who has never gardened, is afraid of gardening, and doesn't want to study gardening or plants. "All I want," he says, "is to get a pleasant outdoor room. I suppose there will have to be some plants, but they should be the kind that can take care of themselves."

A more complex type is represented by the young family that is trying to keep in balance a growing interest in gardening. They find themselves delighted with gardening, but giving more and more time to it and less to reading, trips to the country, visiting with friends. They want a garden "that demands no more than its rightful portion of our free time." How to figure a "rightful portion"?

Another type is the overly ambitious gardener who started from scratch three years ago and has done such a wonderful job that neighbors and friends shower him with praise. He has given his project every spare moment of every day in the last three years. Suddenly he feels that the garden has trapped him. He's sick and tired of it. He's sure that to keep it in its present state of perfection will allow for no letdown—ever.

While all non-gardeners have in common a desire to cut down garden work, they don't mean it when they say they are willing to give up all garden interest. After demanding—and getting—a landscape plan without space for growing things, they may in a very short time develop a keen interest in every phase of gardening and may find themselves wondering why they ever insisted upon anything as dull as a minimum-maintenance garden plan.

Of course, there's no such thing as a work-free garden.

As long as there are plants of any kind, there will be work to do.

Over the years we've often been asked to prepare a check list on the relative amount of time required for certain typical garden tasks so that the home owner could look down the list and avoid, or select, features that will absorb his time.

There are real traps in such lists. "Relative amount of time" is deceiving. You may have to water a flower pot every day and weed a flower bed every month. If you're next to the flower pot every day and water is within reach, you'll spend less time on it than you do on the monthly weeding.

To place only a time value on weeding is not very realistic, either. If oxalis starts to overrun the garden, or quack grass or Bermuda grass has a foothold, weeding not only takes time but frays tempers.

As a class, vegetables take semi-weekly attention while they are young, and dusting when attacked by insects or disease. But swiss chard, zucchini, and corn are not at all demanding of time.

A gravel path must be weeded and raked frequently if you insist on spic-and-span neatness. But with some tolerance and an occasional spraying with diesel oil, the the gravel path drops out of the high maintenance class.

Time and effort in garden work depend more on the efficiency of layout and equipment than on anything else.

Roses, supposedly, are in the high-maintenance class because of spraying, pruning, watering, and weeding. But doesn't it depend on the rose? We've seen large border plantings of floribundas that require no more care than junipers.

Let's take a look into a small garden and see where the time is spent:

1. Hedge: Must be clipped often to be kept neat.

2. Annual border: Changed two or three times a year; weeded regularly; plants spill over lawn.

3. Espaliers: Need weekly attention during growing season.

4. Lawn: Walk divides into two narrow strips, multiplies edging and hand clipping tasks, design of walk encourages traffic to cut across corner.

5. Gravel from path gets into lawn, lawn mower.

6. Tree: Leaves falling on ground cover of sedum can't be raked, don't wash off easily.

7. Plant border and ground-cover area must be edged by spade.

Here's the same space redesigned for low maintenance:

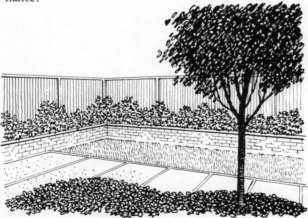

1. Raised bed, planted in informal, free-growing shrubs requires little attention.

2. Mowing strip of brick or wood eliminates hand-trimming of lawn.

3. New arrangement of lawn area cuts the edging job in half.

4. Tight-growing ground cover like ajuga or strawberry is easy to wash off with hose. Mounding juniper would allow the leaves to sift down out of sight.

5. Tree with small thin leaves is choice here. Leaves practically disappear.

6. Note that upkeep is reduced by changes in design more than in plant material.

Anyone interested in low maintenance should not overlook the raised bed and the mowing strip.

## Raised beds

The raised bed gives a permanent clean line between the grass panel and the flowers and shrubs. It gives the gardener a free choice as to what he wants to do with annual color. If he elects to plant a spring border, he can enjoy that without worrying about bare ground in late summer, fall, and winter—the raised bed masks the bare dirt.

Built-up beds are back savers. They are easier to weed, cultivate, and water. In gardens where there is a problem soil—too shallow or heavy, or poorly drained—the built-up bed filled with your special mix of top soil, sawdust, manure, or whatever, will change frustration and hard work into the pleasure of watching things grow.

GOOD DRAINAGE HERE...
ALTHOUGH NATURAL SOIL IS HEAVY

In areas where Bermuda grass is a problem, the built-up planting area almost does away with that terrible fight to keep Bermuda grass from taking over.

## Mowing strip

At the base of the built-up bed bordering the lawn, a 2 by 6 between the lawn and raised bed acts as a mowing strip. One wheel of the mower rides the strip. Grass is kept away from the bed; only an occasional edging is necessary.

Other uses of these devices are to be seen in photographs here and throughout the book.

## Children and maintenance

The same kind of planning as illustrated above to reduce upkeep will result in more livable gardens for children.

*The garden viewed from the living room. Here, children are the plants, and shadows of high spreading trees are the ground covers. The rock borrows from* *the memory of mountains. Water reflects the sky and its sound delights the ear. The warm colored floor is brick in sand laid tight in a basket-weave pattern*

The raised bed prevents damage from wheels, bikes, and dogs. No dirt washes into paths if the facing plank is properly installed. The unifying of lawn and paving areas gives more play space. There's no pick-up of gravel on shoes. However, if you believe that children have a right to play in the soil, don't pave all of the play yard.

### What's work and what's play?

Gardeners interested in low maintenance should remember this psychological quirk in garden work: A job that you can complete in half an hour seems easier than a half hour's work in a border that takes 4 hours to make shipshape. This happens where the garden is marked off in several small areas rather than long borders. Dressing up only one area gives the garden an immediate lift and gives the gardener a big reward for a little attention.

When looking for ways to cut down work in the garden, don't rush into planting changes, hoping that there are plants that will take care of themselves.

When a magazine, a book, or a friend talks about low maintenance material, they are talking about a relative thing. For example, ground covers as lawn substitutes will change your work from cutting to weeding. But hours per month may be the same or more. Weeds enjoy growing in strawberry, grass seeds itself in thyme and

Irish moss. About the only exception to the weedy rule are ivy and juniper, and they take time to reach the point where they completely cover the ground.

Enlarging paved areas and cutting down slightly on lawn areas saves practically no labor. Once the lawn mower is under way, the difference between cutting 3,000 square feet and 3,500 square feet is negligible.

It does make a lot of difference how the lawn areas are arranged. Small patches, half circles, or strips of lawn are annoying to cut and difficult to edge.

Don't pin your hopes for low upkeep on perennials. You may not have to plant them each year, but they do have to be cut back, or divided, or confined.

Not even shrubs can be counted on to behave as they should without attention. If they are to remain attractive over the years they must be pruned, or thinned, or shaped, fed, watered, raked up beneath, staked, and sometimes sprayed.

It has been suggested that the way to plan a low maintenance garden is to start on paper with a completely paved garden and remove sections here and there for the plantings you regard as minimum for beauty and comfort. Perhaps a better way would be to regard a few hours' upkeep each week as play.

ERIC ARMSTRONG, JANE TAYLOR

*No hand edging along the flower and shrub border or around tree. Brick is extended from covered porch to make easy-to-sweep corner with raised edge of border*

ECKBO, ROYSTON, AND WILLIAMS

*Vegetable beds, raised slightly for drainage. Paths wide enough for wheelbarrow, are always dry, weedless. Redwood 2 by 6's, sunk 3 inches, edge the beds*

DOUGLAS BAYLIS

*Maintenance is a matter of temperament. Some gardeners would rather care for a number of portable container-grown plants than keep a plant bed weeded*

THOMAS CHURCH

*Concrete mowing strip is continued around short section of fence that juts out boldly to create privacy in corner of garden. The grid squares are 9 by 9 inches*

SCOTT & IMLAY

*Brick meets concrete mowing strip to maintain clean lines that are easy to keep clean. The terrace is raised to the level of the living room floor. A cedar stake*

*fence separates the terrace from the service area in the background. The boundary fence is designed as a series of baffles to maintain an open feeling*

# How to select plant materials

Without a framework of permanent planting—one that is independent of the come and go of petunias, flowering trees, or any seasonal color—your garden can fall apart for weeks or months at a time.

In planning a new garden or remodeling an old one, you can avoid this common fault if you build in such a permanent planting framework. Up to a point, in working out your framework, you can look upon plant material and building material as interchangeable. For example:

You can pave with flat-growing plants or with asphalt. You can build walls with shrubs and trees, or wires plus vines, or wood and vines. If you wish to screen a portion of the patio from neighbors or wind, you can use panels of wood or canvas or plastic, or a frame supporting a vine or shrub.

If you wish to divide an area with an element that is from 12 to 16 inches high and about as wide, you can build a seat wall of wood, build a low brick wall, or plant a hedge.

However, there's a world of difference between selecting lumber for fences, walls, trellises, and roofs, and choosing plants for the same purpose. There is some organization in lumber sizes—from 1 by 1-inch to 12 by 12—and they don't change as they grow older. Plants not only increase in size and vary by the culture they receive, but they also vary in their proportions as they grow.

All the plants available to you, however, do divide themselves into definite functional groups. (See diagram below.) Out of these groups you select the forms needed for your garden frame. You look for the plants, in each

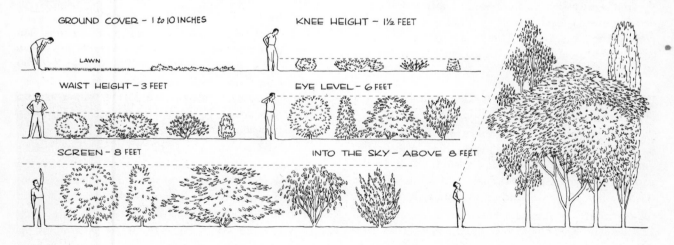

GROUND COVER - 1 to 10 INCHES     KNEE HEIGHT - 1½ FEET

LAWN

WAIST HEIGHT - 3 FEET     EYE LEVEL - 6 FEET

SCREEN - 8 FEET     INTO THE SKY - ABOVE 8 FEET

*When viewed close up there are thousands of different plants in the world, but when seen from a distance they classify themselves quickly into a very few forms. When you start to look for similarities in form rather than in leaf or in blossom, you are on your way to se-*

*lecting plants for landscape use. You look at the 8-foot screen group with the question of what width you can give the screen. You question the knee-height group for use as edgings or high ground cover. Or check for plants that divide space at waist height*

group, that meet these requirements for permanent garden material.

1. It must have good appearance throughout the year, regardless of how its appearance may change with the seasons.

2. It must be well adapted to your climate, exposure, and soil conditions. Temperamental and tender plants should have less important positions, where their loss will not destroy the garden scheme.

From the plants in each group that fulfill these requirements, you can choose those with texture and foliage that are in good relationship to each other and to your garden's background. Selection is not so difficult as it sounds if you have the courage to build the basic frame with great simplicity. If you fear that this simplicity will result in plainness, remember that everything you do with plants of character and structure, or with seasonal color in bulbs, annuals, perennials, roses, or your other favorites, will be more dramatic because of this simple background.

All but the most experienced gardener and designer will achieve more by the use of a few plants than by weaving an intricate tapestry of many.

Masses, solid and dense, or light and airy, can be built by interweaving many plants, modulating textures and foliage color, and synchronizing blooms in time and color. But the time to work out such borders is when you know plants so well and see them so clearly as texture and form that you don't need directions for grouping them.

In this discussion we are concerned only with the garden framework—against which you can do as you please, plant nothing or display favorite plants to your heart's content in the many ways suited to your framework.

Remember that the framework is built with blocks, masses, and lines. We are not looking at shrubs, for example, as individuals, but as multiples in a group.

To bring your possible choices of framework material into focus, we have grouped the shrubs, trees, vines, and ground covers by specific function in the garden. We have tried to narrow the field to a few of the very best choices in each classification.

In noting the climate adaptability in the following lists, we consider far more than the hardiness of the plant. A well adapted plant is one that will flourish and thrive with no more than average garden attention.

As in the *Sunset Western Garden Book,* we have divided the seven Western states into 13 climate zones.

1. *Intermountain.* Characteristic of this climate is a relatively short growing season, with below freezing

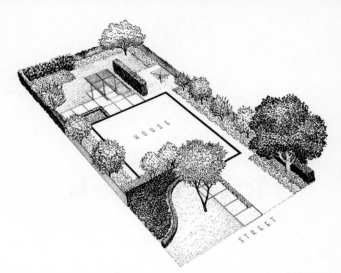

*Here is a small garden in which the plan is set firmly by plant and structure. Regardless of what season, it always holds its form. But there's nothing fixed in the plan except space relationships. Note in the section of the plan at right how plants and structure can be changed without changing the basic plan*

weather from November to March. The severity of the winter and the length of the growing season vary considerably. Where a plant is not adapted to the severe winter area of the zone, special mention is made of its adaptability.

2. *Columbia Basin.* The special climate typified by Walla Walla and Kennewick. Spokane area to the north and eastern Oregon area to the south have colder winters. In the following list, much the same material is suggested for Zones 1 and 2 because we are dealing with basic plants. Gardeners in Zone 2 can use with safety the plants recommended for the milder sections of Zone 1.

3. *Cool Puget; 4. Puget Sound; 5. Willamette.* The above three climates are regarded as one in the basic plant list. The variations in plant growth among the three west-of-the-Cascades climates is important when borderline plants are considered. We do not believe that the basic framework of the garden should be trusted to plants of questionable hardiness.

6. *Siskiyou-Sierra Foothill.* There is so much variation within this zone due to changes in elevation that gardeners should lean over backward and select the most hardy for the permanent framework, and lean forward to speculate with the incidental plant material.

7. *Central Valley.* The list is far short of all the plants that can be grown in this area. Here we rule out the many that will succeed if given special handling. Those recommended thrive in the Valley's summer heat and will take the most unusual winter.

8A. *Low Desert.* The Coachella and Imperial valleys of California and the Salt River Valley of Arizona.

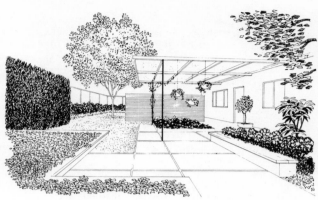

*In this view of back garden from plan on left, plant material rather than structure is emphasized. Hedge is used to set off patio rather than wood structure. Border plants allowed to grow natural rather than being confined by raised border. Many additional steps can be taken toward natural look if gardener desires*

*Here in the same area, the direction is toward more structure in order to eliminate maintenance. Raised seat wall takes place of the low hedge. At right, paving extended into corner of border to get away from hand edging of lawn. Paved area is increased. All planted areas are simplified, fewer varieties of plants*

---

8B. *High Desert.* The foothills neighboring the low deserts and the desert plateaus.

In most cases, plants adapted to these two above areas are given special mention in the list.

9. *Coastal Valleys.* The list does not include many of the shrubs and trees that are grown in the favored spots in this area. Again, we are not advising against planting them, but are merely saying that it's wise not to count on them for an essential permanent feature in your garden.

10. *Bay Area-North Coastal.* Here we emphasize plants that like fog and wind.

11. *Southern California Interior Valleys.* This is the climate of Riverside, San Bernardino, Redlands, and Pomona.

12. *Southern Inner Coastal.* Santa Ana, Pasadena, Sierra Madre, and portions of Los Angeles are typical of this climate. It is 10° to 12° warmer in midsummer than Zone 13, and 10° to 12° cooler than Zone 11.

13. *Southern California Coastal.* We recognize that in this mild, subtropical climate there is every reason to seek out the very tender plants that will grow in no other climate. We discuss them in the *Sunset Western Garden Book.* But in the following list of landscape plants we are most conservative and omit all but the very hardy permanent plants.

## List of basic plants

The following list omits dozens of favorite plants—those you regard as being essential in any garden. Remember that we are working out the background, the basic all-season framework, that should look as good in January as in June.

For that reason, in almost every case the ground cover or shrub recommended is evergreen. We accept that you will add the colorful deciduous material according to your preferences.

In climates where winter temperatures are severe and the list of evergreens is short, several deciduous shrubs must be included in the "framework" list. The following have many of the characteristics of the ideal framework.

Where the number of evergreen plants is limited, consider these shrubs: *To 3 feet: Cotoneaster horizontalis* with its wonderful display of shiny red berries long after the leaves have fallen. *To 6 feet:* Flowering quince (see it espaliered, page 117); Korean spice viburnum (upright, slightly irregular, and open); purpleleaf Japanese barberry (compact, upright). *To 8 feet or more:* Many of the dogwoods bring twig and branch color to the winter garden—bloodtwig dogwood, redtwig dogwood, Siberian dogwood, yellowtwig dogwood. The viburnums offer interesting structure in addition to flower display—common snowball, doublefile viburnum, European cranberry bush, and Japanese snowball. And of course, these all-time spring-flowering favorites—Cornelian cherry, forsythia, kerria, lilac, pearlbush, and philadelphus.

## Use Sunset Western Garden Book, too

The plant lists have been written to help in the *selection* of plants, not in their culture or identification. You can complete the plant information and add to the lists by consulting the *Sunset Western Garden Book.*

## Ground Covers

*Plants that have the ability to cover the ground with smooth flat mats, rough carpets, and foot-deep blankets*

### 1. *Ground covers that give a flat surface:*

**Ajuga.** CARPET BUGLE. Useful in large and small areas; in foliage colors ranging from dark green, variegated, to bronze, and in size from a creeping mat of small leaves to jungle ajuga with large upright leaves. Zones 3 to 13. Suffers from winter cold, but comes back strong by early spring. Sun or shade in mild climates, but best in filtered shade.

**Anthemis nobilis.** CHAMOMILE. Special use, low, flat, moss-like green cover that sends out a pleasing herb fragrance when stepped upon. Zones 1 to 13. As a lawn substitute in small areas, it will mound unless mowed and rolled a few times a year; as a fill-in between paving it needs occasional clipping. Full sun or light shade.

**Arenaria verna cæspitosa.** IRISH MOSS. For restricted use as a plush panel carpet of bright green. Zones 3 to 13. Needs more water than lawn, and becomes lumpy unless thinned occasionally. If petted constantly it's beautiful, but grass and weeds grow through it and must be hand pulled, one at a time.

**Cerastium tomentosum.** SNOW-IN-SUMMER. Very difficult to give a fair appraisal of this silvery-gray, 6-inch carpet. Zones 3 to 13. A very enthusiastic grower, it will spread far and wide unless confined. Must be clipped after bloom in early summer. Inclined to mat and die out in spots for short intervals. Do not overwater or locate in heavily sprinkled areas.

**Fragaria chiloensis.** WILD STRAWBERRY, SAND STRAWBERRY. Glossy, strong patterned, and informal. Zones 3 to 13, except in very hot, dry, exposures. Will grow to 6 to 8 inches high, but can be kept lower by regular mowing. May climb over less vigorous neighbors if fertilized. Sun or shade. Not easy to keep weed free.

**Hedera.** IVY. Number one ground cover in garden design. Zones 1 to 13. Gives thorough coverage relatively quickly in almost any soil or exposure; requires little maintenance—keeps out many weeds. Choose species or varieties according to effect desired. Use ENGLISH IVY *(H. helix)* for blanketing big banks or large areas under trees. Many horticultural forms, small to large leaves, dark green to variegated. Use HAHN'S IVY, a variety of English ivy, for small-scaled intimate garden areas. Has smaller leaves, finer in texture, softer in effect.

ALGERIAN IVY *(H. canariensis)* is the best ivy for hot areas—sun loving and fairly tender. Large, bold, widely spaced leaves. Excellent for raised beds or decorative close-up ground patterns.

ICE PLANT. For areas you want to neglect. Zones 7 to 13. Succulent, fleshy leaves, and profuse, intensely colored daisy-like flowers. Many kinds and colors.

**Pachysandra terminalis.** JAPANESE SPURGE. One of the best ground covers in heavy or dappled shade; fulfills same functions as ivy or vinca. Zones 1 to 13, but best adapted in Zones 1 to 5. Crisp, patterned, decorative foliage. Grows to a happy 10 inches in heavy shade, 6 inches in dappled shade. Burns in full sun.

**Sedum.** STONECROP. Most useful flat growing, succulent-leafed, clean-cut plants for close-ups, and even for lawn size areas. Zones 3 to 13; all-year appearance best in Zones 7 to 13. Happy in poor soils, dry soils, sun or shade, but does not like traffic. Combine well with other sedums and other succulents for decorative ground patterns. MEXICAN SEDUM *(S. amecamecanum)* has yellow-green foliage, yellow star-shaped blossoms in spring and summer. Grows to 6 inches. Uncluttered contrast with dark green ajuga, strawberry, vinca, or ivy. *S. spathulifolium* has soft silvery gray leaves with tiny, upright, bright yellow flowers in late summer. Fairly slow growing to a neat, disciplined 4 inches. In growth habit and foliage texture, natural for rock gardens and filling spaces in paving.

### 2. *Ground covers that give a mounding surface:*

**Achillea argentea.** SILVER YARROW. For special uses in Zones 1 to 13. Forms neat mounds 3 to 6 inches high, with silvery-gray foliage that has a silky luster; pure white flowers in spring and summer. Plant it in sun, shear back after bloom to keep compact.

**Arabis albida.** WALL ROCKCRESS. For special areas. Zones 1 to 13. Forms gray or variegated foliage mats to 6 inches; bears white flowers in airy clusters in spring that almost obscure plant. Sun or part shade; shade in hot, dry areas. To keep a compact, tight foliage mat, cut plants half back after blooming.

**Convolvulus mauritanicus.** GROUND MORNING GLORY. For special areas. Zones 3 to 13. A sun-loving, drought resistant, spreading plant that tolerates any soil condition. Small oval leaves, grayed with white hairs, on trailing stems that twine and spread, forming mounds 1 foot high, 3 feet wide. Use for simple, casual effects—on dry banks, trailing over a wall, or rock outcropping, along steps.

**Erica.** HEATH. For use in large informal areas or restricted space according to form. Zones 1 to 5, 9, and 10. Of the more than 50 species and varieties, over a dozen are less than 12 inches high. Low spreading, mounding growth habit, and succession of bloom, especially desirable in bank plantings. Several are useful along paths, steps, and driveways. Best in mass groupings with other heaths. To keep trim, prune lightly in spring. Need sun and acid soil.

**Euonymus fortunei.** WINTERCREEPER. Very important basic evergreen in cold winter areas. Adapted in all zones, but little used in Zones 12 and 13. Sun or shade. Responds to imaginative handling—as ground covers, vines, spillers, and leaners. Trails and roots like English ivy, but will form tight compact mats if trimmed. These varieties are most commonly seen: COMMON WINTERCREEPER *(E. f. radicans)* is used for its dependable pattern of 1-inch, oval, medium-green leaves throughout the year. May mound up. BIGLEAF WINTERCREEPER *(E. f. vegetus)* has glossy, medium-green, 1½ to 2-inch leaves. Chartreuse new growth in April and May. Tends to grow as a low, viny shrub, more irregular in growth habit than common wintercreeper. Other forms of *E. fortunei* have colorful leaves.

**Iberis sempervirens.** EVERGREEN CANDYTUFT. Not for a large area, but very useful and dependable in many situations. Zones 1 to 13. Low growing compact mounds 8 to 12 inches high, spreading to 2 feet. Excellent dark green foliage, long spring blooming season of snow white flowers, fresh looking throughout the year. Best in sun, but will grow in light shade. Shear back after flowering season to keep neat.

**Stachys lanata.** LAMBS EARS. For special use. Zones 3 to 13. Makes rough dense mat of soft, woolly, gray leaves, 12 to 18 inches high, and spreading wide if not checked. Needs sunny location. Bedraggled winter appearance.

**Thymus.** THYME. Spreading, creeping, mat-forming, aromatic relatives of the well-known culinary thyme which grows as a woody, 1-foot shrublet. Adapted in all zones. Full sun, light poor soil, sandy or clay soils if well drained. Best used in small areas—between paving, along paths, or for a change of texture and color with other ground covers. MOTHER-OF-THYME *(T. serpyllum)* which forms a tight flat mat of tiny dark green leaves overlaid in late spring and early summer with purplish flowers, has many varieties. These include white flowering *T. s. albus,* SILVER THYME *(T. s. argenteus),* carmine flowered *T. s. coccineus,* and gray leafed WOOLLY THYME *(T. s. lanuginosus).*

**Vinca minor.** DWARF PERIWINKLE. Will cover large areas, but should not be used where a neat, trim cover is wanted. Zones 1 to 13. Forms a 6-inch, slightly mounding mat of bright green foliage. In very fertile soils and with lots of water, will grow to 12 inches high. Can be held in check if clipped annually. Never as vigorous as the larger leafed *V. major.* Blue flowers in early spring and again in fall. Tight growth habit discourages weeds. Sun, or some shade in hot areas. Slow to get established.

*Semi-formal pattern of espaliered evergreen magnolia is in keeping with trim lines of gravel path and clipped English ivy ground cover. This tree is six years old*

*Soft charm is mood established in this planting of gray-green—olive trees and clipped English lavender hedge—highlighted by the silver-gray dusty miller*

*This young garden shows an unusual reciprocal arrangement between structure and plants. The strong structural design serves the useful purpose of provid-* *ing a handsome and exciting background for plants that have not reached maturity. Old almond tree in foreground matches structure in strength, character*

Plant materials 169

*3. Ground covers of shrubby character—giving an undulating or rippling surface:*

**Arctostaphylos uva-ursi.** KINNIKINNICK, BEARBERRY. Very attractive bank and even large area cover when well grown, but not reliable in careless hands. Zones 3 to 6, 9, 10, 12, and 13. Needs perfect drainage, sun, and mulch to speed up spreading. Bright glossy green leaves on reddish stems that spread wide and flat.

**Carissa grandiflora prostrata.** Seedlings of *C. grandiflora* showing low horizontal growth have been propagated and sold for ground cover use. Should not be depended upon to cover large areas except in frost-free coastal climates of Southern California. The highly polished leaves of good substance make an elegant cover as low growing as ivy. In some cases a few plants may break the horizontal growth habit and lift branches above cover's surface. Prune these back. Fragrant, waxy white flowers, edible red fruits. Sun or shade.

**Ceanothus.** WILD LILAC, CEANOTHUS. In this large group of native shrubs and tree-like shrubs, there are low growing species or varieties that are particularly well adapted to ground cover use. Effective flower display in spring. Zones 7 to 13. POINT REYES CEANOTHUS (*C. gloriosus*) is most useful. Forms dense mat 4 to 25 inches high, spreading to 5 feet. Dark green foliage, lavender-blue flowers in spring. Good green contrast with rocks, and repeats rock form. CARMEL CREEPER (*C. griseus horizontalis*) has deep green glossy foliage, blue flowers. Generally low and creeping, but varies from 18 to 30 inches high, with a 5 to 15-foot spread.

**Cotoneaster dammeri** (*C. humifusa*) BEARBERRY COTONEASTER. For an uneven woody ground cover. Zones 1 to 13. Forms a mat of long, trailing branches that root as they spread. Rarely over 6 inches high. Glossy bright green leaves, white flowers, scarlet berries. Hardy and vigorous. Sun or shade, moist or dry soil. Neat all year for close-up viewing. Effective as bank cover, trailer for walls, and in steep rockeries because it follows irregularities.

**Helianthemum nummularium.** SUN ROSE. Well suited for informal areas and on sunny slopes. Zones 3 to 13. Evergreen shrublets 6 to 10 inches high with dense, glossy green, or gray-green foliage. Flowers from April to June and again in fall. Forms available in many colors. Full sun. Disadvantage: In any planting a few will die out occasionally and need replacing.

**Juniperus.** JUNIPER. Low growing junipers create the most reliable of ground covers. Zones 1 to 13. Low maintenance. The two that you can be sure will not grow over 2 feet tall and can be kept to 1 foot are: TAMARIX JUNIPER (*J. sabina tamariscifolia*)—wide spreading, with sprays of rather fine, bright green foliage. Good contrast with Mugho pine in form, color, structure. WAUKEGAN JUNIPER (*J. horizontalis douglasii*)—moderately fast growing, best adapted in Zones 1 to 5. Rather than planting for immediate coverage, space junipers 3 feet or more apart and fill in with annuals until the shrubs blanket the area.

**Rosmarinus officinalis prostratus.** DWARF ROSEMARY. Reliable, perennially attractive dwarf evergreen shrub, covered with narrow, dark green aromatic leaves, sheeted with light blue flowers in winter and spring. Zones 4 to 13. Grows 4 to 8 feet across, 15 inches high. Full sun, light gravelly soil. LOCKWOOD ROSEMARY (*R. o. lockwoodii*) is similar to dwarf rosemary but has brighter green leaves and deeper blue flowers. Both are admirably adapted to bank planting, also good for large flat areas where an undulating surface is desired.

## Shrubs to 1½ feet

*Shrubs that form foliage mass or blocks for boundaries, strong vertical lines, low foundation plantings*

*1. Neat evergreens—all can be trimmed or shaped:*

**Berberis buxifolia nana.** DWARF BARBERRY. As the word *buxifolia* implies, this barberry has dark green foliage similar to box-

wood. However, it's hardier and more vigorous than boxwood, is sheeted with orange-yellow flowers in spring, purple fruits in fall, and will take full sun. Gets by in the mild sections of Zones 1 and 2; widely used in Zones 3 to 6. Grows moderately fast to 15 to 18 inches. Not as naturally neat as *B. verruculosa,* and must be pruned as it often becomes leggy.

**Berberis verruculosa.** WARTY BARBERRY. Clean, neat, substantial border and foundation plant, and most useful in this class in Zones 1 to 6. Dark green leaves, some turning red in winter. Same climate adaptation as dwarf barberry. Will grow to 3 feet but can be kept to half that height and no more than a foot wide. Should be used more in Zones 9 and 10.

**Buxus sempervirens suffruticosa.** TRUEDWARF BOXWOOD. Classic, traditional, low boxwood, valuable for its orderly habit, and ability to define precise design. Widely used in Northwest, but suffers from winter cold and burns in full sun. Difficult to keep attractive in California. Slow growing to 12 inches. Can be held to 6-inch width.

**Euonymus japonicus microphyllus.** BOXLEAF EUONYMUS. A good substitute for boxwood with wide climate adaptability. In extreme winters loses about half its leaves. Does well in the mildest areas of Zones 1 and 2, and thrives in California's interior valleys and in the high deserts. Gets into trouble in coastal areas because of susceptibility to mildew. Provides a dark green, medium texture block of foliage. Moderate growth to 2 feet; can be kept lower by trimming. Full sun.

**Myrtus communis compacta.** DWARF MYRTLE. Tidy, dainty looking, with clean, light green, glossy leaves. In California and Arizona, from seacoast to high desert, this is easier to grow than boxwood or euonymus, but subject to thrip and red spider. Slow to moderate growth to 1½ feet.

**Santolina chamæcyparissus.** LAVENDER COTTON. An aromatic gray shrub useful for blocks of fine textured foliage when you want a quick effect. Renew every four years. Hardy all zones. Full sun. Fast growth to 2 feet, clip to 1 foot to prevent ragged look and remove yellow flowers (if not desired). Best appearance with new growth in spring. There's a dark green species, *S. virens.*

*2. Neat when free growing—naturally low or can be kept low without changing nature of plant.*

Several of the shrubs and vines function in this low evergreen class for borders, boundaries, and low foundation plantings. See *Euonymus fortunei* and varieties, dwarf rosemary, heaths, junipers, star jasmine. Important also in this class are the low growing azaleas and rhododendrons which are discussed in the 3-foot and taller classes.

In mild winter areas, the following evergreen perennials are among the plants that serve well in this low growing class: evergreen candytuft, hellebores in shade, nepeta, dusty miller.

## Shrubs to 3 feet

*Shrubs that form mass or blocks of foliage for boundaries, space dividers, foundations*

*1. Neat, dense, evergreens—some need trimming, some naturally neat.*

**Berberis verruculosa.** WARTY BARBERRY. Described in the 1½ foot list. Slow growing to 3 feet, if not cut back.

**Buxus harlandii.** KOREAN BOXWOOD. Brighter green, more heat resistant than the English boxwood. Favored in Southern California and the interior valleys of Central California. Hardy to 5°. Rapid growth to 2 feet.

**Buxus microphylla japonica.** JAPANESE BOXWOOD. Most commonly planted boxwood in California. In Southern California, practically all boxwood sold in flats is Japanese boxwood. Turns bronze when winter temperature drops to 25°. Slow to moderate growth to eventual 4 to 6 feet. To 3 feet if trimmed. More dense than English boxwood, with lighter green leaves.

*This ingenious streetside planting sets this garden apart from all others in the area. A trim zig-zag clipped panel of silver-gray, blue-flowered teucrium* *has a strong contrasting foreground of dark green English ivy. With exception of clipping hedge twice a year, this is definitely a low-maintenance planting*

*Foliage alone—without flowers—can carry interest. Here fine-textured dwarf heather provides unusual contrast with patterned leaves of David viburnum*

*Restrained growth habit, and crisp, sharply defined quality of foliage make sarcococca ideal for close-up viewing in shady areas of terrace, or low foreground*

Plant materials 171

**Buxus sempervirens.** ENGLISH BOXWOOD. The taller counterpart of dwarf boxwood. Where it thrives, practically indestructible and ageless. Much used in Zones 4, 5, 9, and 10. Suffers some winter damage in 4 and 5. Slow growing to become a small tree 15 to 20 feet, but can be kept to 3 feet by regular shearing.

**Carissa grandiflora tuttlei.** See panel plants list. This horticultural variety, propagated from cuttings, is the most dependable of the Natal plums as to growth habit.

**Hebe buxifolia** (*Veronica buxifolia*). BOXLEAF HEBE. Medium fine textured foliage similar to boxwood, but leaves narrower and olive-green. Prefers cool coastal climates—Zones 4, 5, 9, 10, and 13—where it likes full sun. Moderate growth to 5 feet but can be kept at 3 feet. In warm areas, give plenty of water for best appearance.

**Myrsine africana.** AFRICAN BOX. One of the best groomed foliage plants in Zones 7 and 9 to 13. Full sun or part shade. Slow growing to 3 to 5 feet; can be held to 3 feet. Dark green, medium fine textured foliage. Leaves crisp and alert looking on wine red stems.

**Myrtus communis.** TRUE MYRTLE. Larger leaves and looser growing than dwarf myrtle (See 1½ foot list), rapidly reaching 5 to 6 feet. Can be kept to 3 feet by pruning about 3 times a year.

**Myrtus ugni** (*Ugni molinae*). CHILEAN GUAVA. Crisp, dark green, with much the same character and appearance as evergreen huckleberry. Adapted to Zones 9, 10, 12, and 13. Full sun on coast, light shade inland. Grows to 6 feet, can be kept to 3 feet. Good choice alongside patio or walk because of its elegance and its reddish edible fruits that smell like pineapple when ripe.

**Pachistima myrsinites.** MYRTLE BOXLEAF, OREGON BOXWOOD. This distinguished looking Western native is especially valuable where boxwood and other dark green, medium fine textured evergreens are damaged by winter cold. Grows moderately to 2 to 4 feet. Low and compact in sun, taller, more open in shade. Limited availability.

**Pinus mugo mughus.** MUGHO PINE. Reliable and invaluable for a solid, rounded, crisp-looking block of dark green. Adapted to all zones except deserts. Slow to moderate growth to 4 to 8 feet, but can be kept lower by pinching back new light green shoots each spring. More often used singly than in mass. An excellent plant for patios or terraces.

**Skimmia japonica.** JAPANESE SKIMMIA. A shade plant of distinction and character, reaching its greatest beauty in mild cool climates. Foliage yellows in sun. Hardy except in colder sections of Zone 1; an easy-to-grow material wherever azaleas thrive in Zones 3 to 6, 9, and 10. Dark green, glossy, medium coarse textured leaves held precisely on stiff stems. Brilliant red berries in early fall through December. Need male plant to get fruit on female plants.

**Taxus cuspidata nana.** DWARF JAPANESE YEW. One of the most valuable dark green plants for cold winter areas where few broadleafed evergreens are winter hardy. Will take more shade and moisture than other conifers. Grows very slowly—about 4 inches a year.

**Teucrium fruticans.** BUSH GERMANDER. A silver-gray, medium fine textured plant of many uses and great compatability with other plants—particularly effective with red foliage. Adapted in Zones 4 to 13. Generally considered to prefer full sun but in warmer climates does better in part shade. Moderate to fast growth. Attractive in its naturally loose stemmed form, but can be clipped severely to make dense and to keep at desired height. Lavender-blue flowers scattered throughout the year.

**Vaccinium ovatum.** EVERGREEN HUCKLEBERRY. A Western native with a trim polished look. Best adapted to Zones 3 to 6, but grows well wherever rhododendrons and azaleas thrive. Slow growing in sun; moderate in shade. Grows to 6 to 8 feet, but can be kept to 3 feet. It will give you a neat hedge or a clean looking, glossy, dark green foliage mass when untrimmed. New growth is bronzy. Blue-black edible berries.

*2. Free growing evergreens—shrubs that grow no higher than 3 feet, or can be kept that low without changing the nature of the plant.*

Unlike the shrubs in the above list of neat, dense evergreens, the following are not act-alikes. Some are open, some are dense; some give a regular outline, some irregular. Each has a special reason for being in the basic list.

**Abelia gaucheri.** EDWARD GOUCHER ABELIA. This is a newer and lower growing abelia, with foliage similar to that of *A. grandiflora* (See 6-foot shrub list). Lilac-pink flowers.

AZALEAS. There are so many forms of azaleas, both evergreen and deciduous, that they must be considered in every height group. The introduction of new hybrids developed for both cold winter and warm summer climates has so widened the selection that no area is without some candidates. New methods of growing azaleas—in pure peat or peat and sand—has largely removed the soil limitations. For which azalea to grow in your climate, see *Sunset's Western Garden Book*.

**Cistus hybridus** (*C. corbariensis*). WHITE ROCKROSE. This thrifty plant, lowest growing of the rockroses, is one of the best in the 3-foot class for marginal areas where water is scarce. Well adapted in Zones 7 to 13, either under desert heat or exposed to ocean spray and wind. Moderate to rapid growth to 2 to 3 feet to form a mound wider than tall. Rough, leathery, dark green, medium textured foliage; reddish-brown stems. Large white flowers with yellow centers.

**Cotoneaster conspicua decora.** NECKLACE COTONEASTER. Arching branches, strung in fall with bright red berries, form an irregularly outlined plant 3 feet high and wide. Adapted in Zones 3 to 13. Sun. Moderate to rapid growth. Dark green, fine textured foliage almost covered with white flowers in spring.

**Juniperus chinensis pfitzeriana.** PFITZER JUNIPER. Long established favorite useful for filling large areas with irregularly outlined masses of soft gray-green. Performs equally well in all zones, cold or hot. Sun or part shade. Must be pruned regularly to hold at 3 feet. Left alone will grow to 10 feet with 15-foot spread under favorable conditions. Don't try to hold width to less than 6 feet.

**Mahonia aquifolium compacta.** DWARF OREGON GRAPE. This semi-dwarf form supposedly stays naturally low, but it often needs same type of cutting back as its parent (See 6-foot shrub list).

**Nandina domestica.** HEAVENLY BAMBOO, SACRED BAMBOO. Not a bamboo, but has the same light and airy structure pattern. Pencil-straight stems with bamboo-like leaves held in horizontal position. Adapted in Zones 5 to 13; semi-deciduous at 10°; killed to the ground at 5°. Sun or shade; better color in sun. Slow growing to 6 to 8 feet, but can be held to 3 feet by pruning old canes to the ground. Mature foliage soft light green, pick up bronze and purple tints in fall, often turn fiery red in winter. Shiny red berries in fall. Give it planting width of 3 or 4 feet where light and open mass or accent is wanted.

**Raphiolepis indica rosea.** PINK INDIA HAWTHORN. Reliable, always attractive, and in constant demand for low foundation planting, foreground of taller shrubs, massed effect. Irregular form varies from open to dense. Best adapted in Zones 9, 10, 12, and 13, in sun or part shade. Grown in Zones 4 and 5, and in shade in 7 and 11. Slow growth to 3 to 5 feet (3 feet is more usual). Handsome dark green foliage; high crowned clusters of pink flowers, February through May, and again in fall.

RHODODENDRONS. Wherever they thrive, they are basic shrubs of elegant substantial character. Natural rhododendron climates are Zones 3, 4, 5, and 10. Use is spreading in Zones 7 and 9 by planting in pure peat. Give the plants filtered sunlight. You can find all shapes and sizes of rhododendrons for basic planting in the small garden. You can look to these for attractive habit of growth and all-year appearance: Red—Elizabeth and May Day; pink—Bow Bells, Racil, and Humming Bird; white—Bric-A-

*These three highly individual plants make an elegant coordinated group. Each is strong in pattern, texture, and color. Beautifully ribbed leaves of Viburnum da-* *vidii provide medium scale transition between large foliaged hellebore, foreground, and lacy leaves of fernleaf Japanese maple. Woven fence adds to pattern*

Brac and Cilpinense; yellow, orange—Fabia, Moonstone, Unique; blue, lavender—Blue Diamond, Blue Peter, and Blue Tit.

**Rosmarinus officinalis.** COMMON ROSEMARY. A sturdy aromatic shrub with fine textured gray-green foliage. Light lavender-blue flowers in winter and spring. Adapted in Zones 3 to 13. Will grow to 6 feet and as wide, but gives better appearance when cut back to 3 feet after bloom. A rugged plant for sunny areas that are difficult to water.

**Sarcococca ruscifolia.** A choice shade plant of wide climate adaptability. Zones 3 to 13. Loose, open growth habit with waxy green, medium textured foliage. Slow growing, it will eventually reach 5 feet. Fragrant small white flowers, January to March. Another species, *S. hookeriana,* grows even more slowly and compactly.

**Senecio greyii.** Probably the most valuable gray-green shrub in this class. Adapted to Zones 4 to 13. Moderate growth to 4 to 5 feet and spreading wider, but benefits from yearly pruning to keep well filled out with new growth at lower height and width. Best appearance in full sun, lean soil, moderate watering. Clusters of yellow daisy flowers in summer.

**Taxus.** YEW. Extremely valuable where winter rules out other evergreens. The yews in the 2 to 4-foot class are: SPREADING ENGLISH YEW (*T. baccata repandens*)—to 2 feet; and *T. media* —more vigorous and taller. Both are wide spreading but will stand any amount of trimming and shearing. (Also see dwarf Japanese yew in 1 to 1½ foot list.)

**Viburnum davidii.** Aristocratic shrub with deeply ribbed, sharply pointed, dark green leaves. Valued in Zones 3 to 5 where it is best adapted. Grown in Zone 10 where rhododendrons thrive. Needs special handling in Zone 9. Sun or part shade where summers are cool. Shade or filtered shade elsewhere.

## Shrubs to 6 feet

*Foliage mass and blocks for visual division of space, hedges, high foundations, barriers, backgrounds*

*1. Neat, dense evergreens—trimmed and natural*

**Aucuba japonica.** JAPANESE AUCUBA, GREENLEAF AUCUBA. A basic evergreen shrub for deep shade. Unusual climate tolerance. Used throughout Zones 3 to 13. Have seen it on north wall in Salt Lake City and in full shade in Phoenix and Tucson. Will grow to 10 feet if not pruned. Glossy green, coarse textured foliage gives lush effect. There are variegated leaf forms—used for brightening dark shady corners.

**Berberis darwinii.** DARWIN BARBERRY. One of the showiest barberries with its perennially attractive dark green, holly-like foliage, and showy orange-yellow springtime flowers. Hardy in all zones. Sun or part shade. Moderate growth to 10 feet but usually kept at 6 feet by pruning. Fountain-like growth habit if not trimmed. Spiny branches make it a formidable barrier.

CAMELLIAS. Although usually treated as individuals, some varieties of camellias make highly satisfactory hedges, space dividers, and shrubbery masses in partial shade. Because flowers are so dominant, many prefer to use them as special features rather than in the basic framework of the garden.

**Citrus.** The dwarf citrus, slow growing to create an 8 by 8 block of dense yellow-green foliage, can be used in the basic framework as a thick hedge, but for fruit production they are better off in a small orchard type planting, or as tubbed specimens. The MEYER LEMON gives valuable service in hedge and foundation planting in Zones 7 to 13. Variable in growth habit, but stands pruning.

**Ilex.** HOLLY. While the traditional ENGLISH HOLLY (*I. aquifolium*) is not easy to grow in the small garden, it is sometimes used as a hedge in Zones 3 to 6. CHINESE HOLLY (*I. cornuta*), less rigid, less spiny leaves, and self-fertile, is adapted to Zones 7 to 13, and is used as a basic plant where 6-foot width is not troublesome. BURFORD HOLLY (*I. c. burfordii*), with spineless leaves, is the most versatile of the hollies, and thrives in Zones 7 to 13.

**Leucophyllum texanum.** TEXAS RANGER. An important basic shrub in the hot interior valleys and low and high deserts where winter temperatures are above 10°. Slow growing, compact, round headed shrub to 5 to 12 feet, spreading 4 to 6 feet, that can be kept to 6 feet by clipping. Medium textured, silver-gray foliage, light rose-purple flowers in spring and summer.

**Pittosporum tobira.** TOBIRA, JAPANESE PITTOSPORUM. Thoroughly reliable, easy-to-grow in almost any soil in Zones 7 to 13. Sun or light shade. Medium-coarse textured, glossy, dark green foliage. Moderate growth to 15 feet unless held back by selective pruning of stems. Don't shear. The variegated form is most useful in plantings where its gray-green, white-outlined leaves provide a contrast to dark sombre greens. Less vigorous, its growth can be held to 5 feet. More shade tolerant, you can use it to brighten dark areas.

*2. Free-growing, medium-dense evergreens—can be kept to 6 feet without changing nature of plant*

**Abelia grandiflora.** GLOSSY ABELIA. A clean, thrifty shrub with arching branches clothed in glossy, medium fine textured leaves— bronzy in spring and fall. Creates a definite pastel effect when covered with whitish-pink flowers from July to October. Grown in Zones 4 to 13, but at its best in sun in Zones 9, 10, 12, and 13. Needs part shade in hot interiors. Use as an untrimmed hedge or in massed planting.

**Choisya ternata.** MEXICAN ORANGE. Provides a fresh clean block of glossy yellow-green. Used in Zones 4 to 13, but damaged at 15°, and should have part shade in the interior valley. Grows rapidly to create a rounded dense mass to 6 to 8 feet, spreading as wide. Can be kept to 6 feet by frequent pinching back; heavy shearing ruins pattern value of foliage. Clusters of fragrant white flowers bloom from early spring and into fall.

**Elæagnus pungens.** SILVERBERRY. A rugged individual with lots of character. Widely adapted in Zones 3 to 13. Grows slowly to 6 to 15 feet. Medium coarse textured, gray-green foliage on angular branches that can be trained to fit almost any situation— against wall, fence. Several variegated varieties—the leaves with silver margins, or blotched with yellow

**Escallonia rubra.** RED ESCALLONIA. The most used escallonia in the 6-foot height. Finds its best climate in Zones 9, 10, 12, and 13; especially good along seacoast. Full sun along coast, half shade inland. Grows rapidly to 5 to 6 feet and as wide to create a dense, compact block of glossy, dark green, medium textured foliage. Clusters of small red flowers in the warmer months. Can be held back and shaped by pruning.

**Mahonia aquifolium.** OREGON GRAPE. We haven't found a single place where this handsome native fails to perform satisfactorily. Will grow in sun, half shade, or full shade. Moderate to rapid growth to 6 feet and taller, but can be held at lower heights by cutting the taller growing stems to the ground. Oregon grape presents a foliage mass of irregular outline. New holly-like foliage is light green and bronzy, then dark green with a scattering of red leaves throughout the year. Large clusters of bright yellow flowers March to May.

**Nandina domestica.** HEAVENLY BAMBOO, SACRED BAMBOO. This light and airy shrub will reach 6 feet and more at maturity. (Also see 3-foot list.)

**Pieris japonica.** LILY-OF-THE-VALLEY SHRUB. Deservedly a favorite in Zones 3 to 6 where it grows to perfection. In California it thrives wherever rhododendrons are grown. Grows slowly to 6 to 10 feet. Dense in youth, rather open in character as it matures. Presents a lustrous, dark green, medium textured foliage pattern. Drooping sprays of greenish-pink buds in fall, pearly white flowers in early spring. Best when planted in groups.

**Prunus laurocerasus zabeliana.** ZABEL LAUREL. Dark green, waxy foliaged, and clean—a distinct improvement over the

*Trained as a tree, Leptospermum laevigatum—usually seen as a hedge or screen—reveals picturesque branching habit and shaggy trunk. Ivy grows on trunk*

*Direct opposites in plants often complement each other. Here a succulent, large-leafed showy sedum, is combined with narrow-leafed creeping rosemary*

*On a west facing terrace, the slender stems and light green foliage of bamboo in containers cuts the hot afternoon sun and softens the light in the living room*

coarser English laurel (*P. laurocerasus*). Adaptable to Zones 3 to 13. Sun or shade. Moderate growth. Grows to only 6 feet with equal spread.

**Xylosma senticosa.** An unusually adaptable shrub throughout Zones 7 to 13—along the coast or in desert heat. Hardy to 10°. Will take full sun or part shade. Moderate growth to 4 to 6 feet. Forms a dense mass of arching stems clothed with medium textured, lustrous yellow-green foliage. Bronzy new growth.

## Shrubs to 8 feet or more

### Evergreen foliage mass used as screens for privacy and for sun and wind control

#### Usually shaped or clipped

**Chamæcyparis lawsoniana.** PORT ORFORD CEDAR, LAWSON CYPRESS. A Northwestern native forest tree that makes a beautiful blue-green lacy hedge, windbreak, or screen. Can be topped at desired height. Best adapted to Zones 3 to 6.

**Cupressus forbesii.** FORBES CYPRESS, TECATE CYPRESS. Where strong and steady winds are a problem, this rates as a basic landscape plant. Adapted to Zones 7 to 13; will take ocean wind and desert heat. Grows rapidly to 20 to 30 feet, but can be held to an 8-foot hedge by pruning.

**Eugenia paniculata australis** (*E. myrtifolia*). AUSTRALIAN BRUSH CHERRY. Although eugenia's basic leaf color is green, the dominant effect during a good part of the year is that of rich red or bronze, contributed by the young foliage. Well adapted in Zones 10, 12, and 13. Grown in Zone 9, but is cut back by frosts now and then. Untrimmed, will grow to 30 feet but can be held to a narrow 6 to 8-foot column. Plants are sheeted with white flowers in spring, heavily fruited with purplish-red "cherries" in fall.

**Euonymus japonicus.** EVERGREEN EUONYMUS. Dark green, shining, clean, medium textured foliage has high value in areas where mildew is not a problem. Adapted in Zones 3 to 13. Needs full sun, mildews in shade and along coast. Moderate growth to 10 to 15 feet, spreading to 6 feet; usually held lower by pruning and shearing. Several variegated leafed forms are available.

**Leptospermum lævigatum.** AUSTRALIAN TEA TREE. A highly individualistic and serviceable plant capable of assuming many different forms. Adapted to Zones 7 to 13. Close planting forces straight tall growth for hedges or screens up to 15 feet. Grown as a single plant, with judicious pruning, it becomes, in time, a small distinctive tree with an irregular crown of gray-green medium textured foliage, and a twisted, gnarled trunk covered with coarsely shredded bark. It takes pure sand and coastal winds in easy stride.

**Libocedrus decurrens.** INCENSE CEDAR. Native Western conifer, open and quite yellow-green in its youth, becoming a thick dark green pyramid 75 or more feet tall when mature. Can be topped and trimmed to an 8-foot hedge. Adapted to Zones 3 to 13.

**Ligustrum.** PRIVET. Of the many privets, these two evergreen ones have the greatest landscape value in Zones 3 to 13. Both have coarse textured lustrous green foliage. GLOSSY PRIVET (*L. lucidum*) will grow to 25 to 30 feet as a small tree, but can be held at 8 feet for hedge or screen. JAPANESE PRIVET, WAX-LEAF PRIVET (*L. japonicum*) grows to 10 to 12 feet. Japanese privet has the smaller, shorter pointed, more glossy leaves that are pale beneath.

**Myrica californica.** PACIFIC WAX MYRTLE. A refreshingly clean, dark green, Pacific Coast native well adapted to Zones 3 to 5, 9, 10, and 13. Will take coastal wind and moist soil. Moderate growth to 10 to 15 feet or to a small tree 35 feet high. Can be pruned as desired.

**Pittosporum.** The following tall growing pittosporums have established themselves as three of the most valuable hedge and screening plants. Will grow to 8 feet or more in height without taking much garden space. Can be held to 3 feet wide. All three are best adapted to Zones 9, 10, 12, and 13. All prefer sun. KARO (*P. crassifolium*) has medium textured, gray-green foliage, and is particularly well adapted along the seacoast. TARATA (*P. eugenioides*) has medium coarse texture, and yellow-green foliage. TAWHIWHI, or KOHUHU (*P. tenuifolium*) has medium textured, light green foliage. The two latter varieties are the fastest growing.

**Prunus.** NATIVE EVERGREEN CHERRIES. Two natives that reliably fulfill basic landscape needs and accept garden conditions. Adapted to Zones 7 to 13. Both are slow to start, then grow rapidly to 10 to 15 feet, or to 35 feet as a tree. Both can be held to an 8-foot screen, 3 feet wide. HOLLYLEAF CHERRY (*P. ilicifolia*) forms a rather casual screen as holly-like leaves vary in size by the individual plants. However, the overall texture is crisp and curly. CATALINA CHERRY (*P. lyonii*) has smooth margined leaves that in mass give a smooth, more formal appearance.

**Rhamnus alaternus.** ITALIAN BUCKTHORN. Solid dark green mass, less lively, but just as reliable as the native evergreen cherries for which this rhamnus is an excellent alternate. Adapted to Zones 7, 9, 11, and 12. Fast growth to 20 feet and can be trained as a hedge or small tree. Takes sun or shade.

**Taxus cuspidata.** JAPANESE YEW. (Also see other yews in 3-foot list.) Grows very slowly to 8 feet or more as a bushy wide shrub, but will stand any amount of shearing to keep to height. Dark green, fine textured foliage; scarlet cup-shaped fruits in late summer or early fall.

**Thuja.** ARBORVITAE. Probably the most used and most mis-used conifer in the garden. However, where the number of hardy evergreens is limited, the several forms of thuja that can be shaped to make a hedge or screen are valuable. Fine textured green to yellow-green foliage; golden forms also available. All are slow to moderate in growth; all have tendency to turn brown in winter.

**Thuja plicata.** WESTERN RED CEDAR. This native forest tree is probably one of the most popular coniferous hedges in the Pacific Northwest, but it is not hardy east of the Cascades. Shallow-rooted, not suitable for a windbreak. Moderate growth. Can be kept trimmed to 8 to 12 feet. Bright green foliage.

### Shrubs that do not take up too much garden space even when allowed to grow naturally

BAMBOO. Ideal plants for screens, unduplicated where you want a light, delicate branching and foliage pattern. Hardiness by species. Sun or part shade. Fast when established and well watered. Will take any amount of pruning. In general leaves are green to yellow-green; various forms have yellow, yellow-green striped, or black stems. HEDGE BAMBOO (*B. multiplex*) and its varieties make excellent screens. Hedge bamboo grows to 15 to 35 feet and is hardy to 16°. ALPHONSE KARR BAMBOO is about the same height but is hardy to 20°. STRIPE-STEM FERN-LEAF BAMBOO grows only to 6 to 9 feet, and is hardy to 20°. CHINESE GODDESS BAMBOO is the lowest growing—4 to 6 feet—and is hardy to 20°. GOLDEN BAMBOO (*Phyllostachys aurea*) grows to 15 feet, and is hardy to 20°. One of the most widely grown, and drought resistant when established. BLACK BAMBOO (*P. nigra*) grows to 10 to 20 feet, and is hardy to 28°. Best in partial shade on sheltered south or west side of house.

**Pittosporum** (*P. crassifolium, P. eugenioides, P. tenuifolium*). See preceding list. These are slender, tall growing plants that can be held to 3 to 4 feet in width with very little pruning while they grow naturally to 12 feet or more.

**Podocarpus.** Although these are evergreen conifers, they are much more reminiscent of, and as useful as, medium fine textured, dark green broadleafed evergreens. Adapted to Zones 9, 10, 12,

C. JACQUES HAHN, J. CHARLES HOFFMAN

*This base planting of Murraya exotica makes a neat bright green panel against a light background, and is easy to keep low enough to clear the windows. Other*

*plants that can perform the same function are:* Choisya ternata, Pittosporum tobira variegata, *or boxwood. Here evergreen pear is espaliered between windows*

THOMAS CHURCH

*Variegated* Pittosporum tobira *is more restrained than the species. Unclipped, it makes a soft, full, undulating mass of foliage in this base planting panel.*

*Its gray-green and white leaves provide interesting and easy transition from concrete aggregate walk to the house wall; contrast well with brick surface*

and 13. If closely planted and allowed to grow naturally, they create a casual screen to 15 feet high and about 6 feet wide. Make handsome clipped hedges, and especially choice espaliers. Sun or light shade. Slow to moderate growth.

### Shrubs for tall screens where width is not a factor

**Arbutus unedo.** STRAWBERRY TREE. Generally used as an individual, becoming a distinctive small open-crowned tree when older. If your garden is large enough, can be used to create a rather rangy thick shrub screen. Best in Zones 7 to 13, desert or seashore. Grown in Zones 3 to 6, but damaged in severe winters. Sun. Slow to moderate growth to 8 to 20 feet, with equal spread. Height can be controlled by pruning, but do not shear. Medium coarse textured, dark green foliage. Clusters of small white or greenish-white flowers, and orange-red strawberry-like fruits appear at same time in fall and winter.

**Escallonia montevidensis.** WHITE ESCALLONIA. Substantial dense shrub that grows rapidly to 25 feet, and spreads as wide. Can be kept lower by pruning. Hardy to 18°. Wind hardy, and tolerates seacoast conditions. Sun or light shade. Medium textured shiny green foliage. Ample clusters of white flowers in late summer and fall.

**Feijoa sellowiana.** PINEAPPLE GUAVA. Not only is this hardiest of subtropicals handsome in foliage, but it is exotic in flower, and bears edible fruits. Thrives in Zones 7 to 13. Full sun, tolerates some shade. Grows moderately to 15 to 18 feet, spreading almost as wide. Can be held to 3 feet wide and 6 feet high by annual pruning in late winter. Gray-green to silvery, medium coarse textured foliage.

**Griselinia littoralis.** KUPUKA TREE. Wavy dark yellow-green foliage, less glossy than coprosma, which it resembles somewhat. Best in Zones 9, 10, 12 and 13, especially good for seacoast planting. Likes plenty of water; foliage is best in some shade. Rapid growth to about 10 feet, and spreading as wide.

**Nerium oleander.** OLEANDER. Sturdy, tough, attractive under hot, dry interior conditions, and colorful in flower from May to October. Naturals in Zones 7 and 8, but perform beautifully in the warm sections of Zones 9 to 13. Moderate growth to 20 feet high and 25 feet wide. Can be held to 8 to 10 feet by pinching out growing tips and cutting some branches to the ground each spring.

**Pyracantha.** FIRETHORN. In small gardens, pyracanthas are usually best espaliered. Most of them are rather rough thorny shrubs if allowed to grow naturally, and are best used as hedgerows or wide barriers. They are adapted to Zones 4 to 13. Full sun. Rapid growing up to 10 to 15 feet and as wide. Clusters of white flowers in spring. Red, orange, or yellow berries according to the form you choose.

## Panel plants for fences, walls, trellises

### Shrubs and trees that can be kept flat to give a 3 to 12-inch thick evergreen surface

**Carissa grandiflora.** NATAL PLUM. A cheerful, serviceable plant favored in milder climates for its shiny bright green foliage and red plum-like fruits. Adapted best to Zone 13 as young plants are damaged at 26°, but once well established will get by in all areas from low desert to the seashore. Where frosts come seldom, it is as serviceable as privet, and more interesting. While often grown naturally, it is most effective trained flat against a fence or wall.

**Coprosma baueri.** MIRROR PLANT. An invaluable shrub for gardens receiving coastal fogs and winds in Zones 10 and 13. Naturally grows to 10 feet with a 6-foot spread, and becomes straggly unless pruned. Looks its best when pruned to grow as a 12-inch thick panel. Medium coarse textured, light to dark green, very glossy foliage.

**Elæagnus pungens.** SILVERBERRY. (See 6-foot list.) Can be pruned and clipped to form a flat panel. Variegated forms have lively color interest.

**Euonymus fortunei.** WINTERCREEPER. (See ground cover list.) When allowed to climb, this species and its varieties form a spreading mass of foliage. A special advantage is the fact that it doesn't become so thick and heavy that it tears loose of its own weight.

**Podocarpus.** (See 8-foot list.) Close clipping transforms espaliered podocarpus into a flat soft textured panel.

### Shrubs and trees that can be trained as pattern plants

**Azara microphylla.** BOXLEAF AZARA. Fine-textured dark green foliage and fan-like growth habit makes azara a natural for refined pattern against walls, or for shadows against translucent screen. Best adapted to Zones 9, 10, 12, and 13. Grown in Zones 4 and 5 but damaged at 20°; also in hot interiors in shade. Slow growing at start, then rapid to 12 to 18 feet if not controlled. Requires regular pinching back and light pruning to direct growth.

**Chænomeles.** FLOWERING QUINCE. Although deciduous, it serves as an all-year pattern plant because of its interesting branch structure when properly pruned. Hardy everywhere, most valuable in cold-winter areas where evergreen pattern plants are few, and early flowers appearing on bare branches are reassuring. Choose a tall growing form for training.

**Elæagnus pungens.** SILVERBERRY. (See 6-foot list.) Can be trained in an informal pattern.

**Eriobotrya japonica.** LOQUAT. With patience, can be trained to form a dramatic, bold-foliaged pattern plant. Adapted in Zones 8, 9, 10, 12, and 13. Likes sun.

**Euonymus fortunei** and varieties. WINTERCREEPER. (See ground cover list.) Valuable for evergreen wall patterns in cold winter climates. Sun or part shade.

**Ficus carica.** FIG. Large dark green leaves are the strong feature from spring to fall. Smooth light gray branches make a winter pattern. Probably the easiest fig to train against fence or wall is the Mission fig. It's widely adapted throughout California. Requires less pruning to keep to shape and produce fruit than other varieties. Sun.

**Fuchsias.** Choose variety that produces long branches for espaliering. Best adapted to Zones 10 and 13. Part shade.

**Magnolia grandiflora.** SOUTHERN MAGNOLIA. This normally large tree can be trained to grow flat against a wall creating a rich glossy coarse textured pattern. Adapted to Zones 3 to 13, but best in Zones 7 to 13. Sun or part shade.

**Pyracantha.** FIRETHORN. (See 8-foot list.) Easy to manage, but needs frequent pruning to maintain structure pattern.

**Pyrus kawakami.** EVERGREEN PEAR. Willowy branches spread like a vine when trained against wall or fence. Prune often to keep pattern. Zones 7 to 13, but best adapted where fruiting pear is grown.

**Roses.** What the climbing rose lacks in winter interest, it makes up in color from late spring to fall. Try for as many horizontal branches as possible to get foliage and bloom spread from the base of the vine to the top.

### Evergreen vines for panels, wall and fence covers or tracery

**Bougainvillea.** Basic plant in Zones 12 and 13 where a long warm growing season encourages lush growth climaxing in a brilliant summer color spectacle. Will grow and bloom well in sections of Zones 9 to 11, but may be killed in cold winters. Blooms best in full sun. Strong growing to 20 feet, can be controlled by pruning. Medium textured dark green foliage. Many varieties from purple-red to magenta, and scarlet. Colors intense, require careful placement near other plants.

**Cissus.** A group of tender vines distinguished for handsome foliage, and best adapted to the mild areas of Southern California. Elsewhere several are popular house plants. EVERGREEN GRAPE

*A beautiful blending of foliage textures is seen here. There's enough contrast to be interesting and lively but it offers such a subtle gradation that no one plant* *is too dominant. Native salal is planted in foreground; Pieris japonica above; with a background of camellias, rhododendrons, Pacific wax myrtle* (Myrica), *pines*

(*C. capensis*), light green grape-like leaves burnished with copper, grows rapidly, needs constant pruning and pinching to keep under control. VENEZUELA TREEBINE (*C. rhombifolia*), less coarse in texture than evergreen grape; bright olive-green foliage with bronzy tones. Needs all-year warmth for fast growth. *C. hypoglauca*, hardiest of the group—to 23°; will grow to 15 feet in a season, in sun or shade. *C. striata*, finer in texture, looks like a miniature Virginia creeper; makes delicate tracery against plain surfaces.

**Clematis armandii.** EVERGREEEN CLEMATIS. Long garlands are draped with glossy dark green foliage, heavy with clusters of white flowers in spring. Zones 4 to 13. Slow to start but fast when roots are established. Sun or light shade. To create a pattern, select the branches to follow design and cut off everything else. Prune regularly during growing season to control vigorous new growth.

**Clytostoma callistegioides** (*Bignonia speciosa, B. violacea*). VIOLET TRUMPET VINE. A pastel counterpart of bougainvillea, with similar growth habit and use, forming a blanket of dark green foliage smothered with violet-lavender to pale purple trumpet-like flowers in April and July. Zones 7 to 13; treat as a perennial in colder climates. Sun or part shade. Needs support on a wall.

**Euonymus fortunei** and varieties. WINTERCREEPER. (See ground cover list.) Probably the most hardy evergreen vine. If given support, will climb and cover a flat surface with an even orderly mat of bright green waxy foliage. Grows in full sun or part shade.

**Gelsemium sempervirens.** CAROLINA JESSAMINE. Yellow-green, glossy, medium-textured foliage forms a full shrubby mass useful for covering flat surfaces. Fragrant yellow flowers in spring.

Zones 7 to 13. Sun. Moderate growth. With pruning, can be trained as a garland.

**Hedera.** IVY. (See ground cover list.) Among its virtues is its ability to convert a wire or wood fence into an evergreen foliage block. Hardy in all but coldest areas. Slow to start, once established, grows rapidly and needs control to keep it where you want it.

**Lonicera hildebrandtiana.** GIANT BURMESE HONEYSUCKLE. Handsome, robust, tall climbing vine that will rapidly cover a fence with dark green coarse textured foliage. Long tubular fragrant flowers are creamy white changing to yellow and orange before falling. Zones 9 to 10, 12 to 13. Sun.

**Lonicera japonica halliana.** HALL'S JAPANESE HONEYSUCKLE. Useful for a dark green foliage cover, growing rapidly and rampantly unless controlled. Fragrant summer blooming flowers change from white to yellow. Hardy except coldest sections of Zone 1. Evergreen in mild areas, semi-deciduous in colder locations. Sun or light shade.

**Polygonum aubertii.** SILVER LACE VINE. Excellent quick overhead shade provided by medium textured dark green foliage, crowned in summer and fall with a thick foamy mass of small white flowers. Hardy evergreen in Zones 7 to 13. In Zones 1 to 6, where it is usually cut back by frost, it is deciduous and treated as a perennial. Likes sun.

**Trachelospermum jasminoides.** STAR JASMINE. A versatile plant capable of serving equally well as a vine, foundation shrub, or ground cover. Polished green leaves on stems that are upright at the base, twining and vine-like as they elongate. Small white fragrant flowers bloom all summer. Zones 7 to 13. Sun for heaviest bloom; will grow in shade. Slow to moderate growth. With support it will climb to 20 feet.

### Deciduous vines for seasonal effects on walls, fences, overheads—especially where summer shade and winter sun is wanted

In climates where the choice of evergreen vines is limited, you must turn to deciduous vines as basic plants for covering vertical or horizontal surfaces. Actually most of the following vines, with the exception of *Hydrangea petiolaris,* are grown quite widely in milder climates also.

**Actinidia chinensis.** YANGTAO. A twining vine, clean and uncomplicated in structure, and easy to train in simple patterns. Uncrowded, medium textured leaves are velvety green and carried on dark red stems. Creamy flowers in August, followed by small edible fruits that taste like gooseberries.

**Campsis radicans.** COMMON TRUMPET CREEPER. Useful where you want to cover a large space with a blanket of green foliage with a summer overlay of orange-red trumpet-shaped flowers. All zones. Needs rigid control. Requires support only in the first year.

**Clematis.** Large flowered forms are dramatic when they bloom on the light delicate branching structure. Blooms appearing in summer and fall vary from white, through sky blue and violet-blue to rich crimson. Flower best in sun. Hardy in all zones, best adapted in cold winter climates.

**Hydrangea petiolaris.** CLIMBING HYDRANGEA. A vigorous climber, shrubby at the base, clinging to wood and stone by aerial rootlets. Heart-shaped green leaves, hydrangea-like white flowers in showy clusters in June.

**Parthenocissus.** Two familiar vines, as familiar and useful in their way as ivy, provide a thick foliage cover in spring and summer, and warm red fall coloring. Cling tenaciously to flat surfaces, in sun or part shade. All zones. BOSTON IVY (*P. tricuspidata*) has glossy green coarse-textured leaves similar to those of grape. VIRGINIA CREEPER (*P. quinquefolia*) with deeply divided leaves, is more graceful in feeling, forming interesting patterns and traceries when not allowed to become overgrown.

**Wisteria.** Vigorous, rapid growing, increasing in beauty with age, the wisteria is a peer among vines. With intelligent pruning, can be trained horizontally to form a garland or cordon, vertically as a curtain or screen. Dramatic display of fragrant white, lavender, or purple flowers in spring before the leaves appear.

**Others:** There's a variety of GRAPE for every climate—American type for cold winters, European type for mild winters and hot summers. In mild winter areas, don't overlook the CHILEAN JASMINE (*Mandevilla suaveolens*) if a deciduous vine is wanted. Provides white, fragrant, trumpet-like flowers from May to October.

## Large trees

### Large trees that will give a high foliage canopy—may eventually shade greater portion of smaller garden

#### Deciduous:

**Acer platanoides.** NORWAY MAPLE. Large, dark green, dense foliaged tree, forming a dome-shaped head. Favored tree for shading streets in hot summer areas. All zones. Moderate growth. SCHWEDLER MAPLE (*A. p. schwedleri*) offers rich red in young leaves, gold autumn foliage. Horticultural variety Crimson King maintains purplish-red leaf coloring throughout growing season. Major drawback of these maples is aphis causing honeydew drip.

**Acer saccharinum.** SILVER MAPLE. Open crown of light green, silvery backed foliage creating pleasant filtered shade. All zones, but particularly valuable in interior valleys and deserts. Rapid growth if given plenty of water.

**Alnus rhombifolia.** WHITE ALDER. Widespreading and ascending branches form a large head providing medium dense shade. Zones 3 to 13. Rapid growth—as much as 9 feet a year. Likes moisture.

**Ginkgo biloba.** GINKGO, MAIDENHAIR TREE. Attains distinction and character in maturity when it assumes an irregular, high crowned, dome-shaped head. Performance varies by zone. In Zones 1 to 6 quite slow. Moderate to fast elsewhere. Light shade. Leaves light green in spring and summer, buttery yellow in fall. Tolerates city smoke and smog. Best to plant only male trees grown from cuttings or grafts, as female trees have unpleasant smelling fruit.

**Gleditsia triacanthos inermis** Moraine. MORAINE LOCUST. Sturdy, long-lived tree, round-headed in youth, assuming a graceful elm-like vase shape when older. All zones. Rapid growing, drought resistant. Light to medium shade.

**Liriodendron tulipifera.** TULIP TREE. Very large, high-branched tree with wide spreading, well spaced branches and conical crown. All zones, but intolerant of drought and alkali. Moderate to rapid growth. Medium dense shade. Large light green leaves turn yellow in fall. Needs ample water. Susceptible to scale and aphis.

**Quercus borealis.** NORTHERN RED OAK. Spreading branches carrying large, deeply lobed leaves form a massive crown that provides medium heavy shade. Fall color dark red, ruddy brown, or orange. All zones. Rapid growth in fertile soil with lots of water.

**Quercus cerris.** TURKEY OAK. Broad conical crown giving good shade. Valuable for its comparatively short deciduous period. Zones 7 to 13. Rapid growth. Needs water when young; otherwise heat and drought resistant.

**Quercus coccinea.** SCARLET OAK. Spreading irregular crown, open branching habit providing light to medium shade. All zones. Brilliant scarlet foliage in fall. Colors best in Northwest. Fast growing in deep soil. Deep rooted and withstands drought.

**Quercus garryana.** GARRY OAK, OREGON WHITE OAK. A native with broad rounded crown, gives medium shade. Zones 3 to 6, 9 and 10. Moderate growth.

**Quercus lobata.** VALLEY OAK, CALIFORNIA WHITE OAK. Native becoming a large and imposing tree with broad rounded crown, formed by spreading, drooping, often tortuous branches. Zones 6 to 13. Slow to moderate growth. Gives medium shade.

**Salix babylonica aurea.** GOLDEN WEEPING WILLOW. Graceful tree forming round head with drooping branches. All zones. Rapid growth. Light green foliage turns yellow in fall. Golden yellow branches make attractive winter pattern.

**Ulmus parvifolia.** CHINESE ELM, (includes form: EVERGREEN CHINESE ELM). A tree with some of the character of the weeping willow, but darker green, less pendulous. All zones. Very rapid. Evergreen in mild climates. Variable in form—erect to weeping. Medium dense shade. Stake and prune for shape first 2 or 3 years.

#### Evergreen:

**Quercus agrifolia.** COAST LIVE OAK. Best known evergreen oak in California, becoming a large tree of noble proportions—round headed and wide spreading. Zones 9, 10, 12 and 13. Moderate growth. Gives dense shade.

**Quercus ilex.** HOLLY OAK. A clean looking tree—smaller than the coast live oak, but with a similar rounded head. Crisp dark green holly-like foliage. Zones 9 to 13. Moderate growth. Salt air and wind tolerant; little maintenance.

C. JACQUES HAHN, J. CHARLES HOFFMAN

*Three ground covers, contained by header boards, make a pattern that breaks the monotony in a long streetside area. A panel of dark green Ajuga reptans* *grows along path. Medium dark green Hahn's ivy is carpet against house. Bright green dichondra in foreground. Note how textures are repeated to unify area*

**Quercus virginiana.** LOUISIANA LIVE OAK. Large leaves, dark green and shining above, whitish beneath, make a rounded spreading canopy giving moderate shade. Zones 7 to 13. Especially valuable tree for Southern California including high desert. Rapid growth.

## Medium sized shade trees

*Trees that will not dominate the garden*

*Deciduous:*

**Albizzia julibrissin.** SILK TREE. A hardy tree with an exotic character suggestive of the tropics—not unlike the jacaranda in foliage texture although leaflets are lighter yellowish-green. Zones 2 to 13; especially 8, 9, 10, and 11. Rapid growth. Very wide spreading tree of low branching habit; can be trained to form umbrella-like canopy giving pleasant filtered shade. Pink fluffy flowers, June, July, and August. Takes alkaline soil and lawn water.

**Betula pendula** *(B. alba).* EUROPEAN WHITE BIRCH. Graceful tree forming a slender pyramid of pendulous white-barked branches. Clear yellow fall color, winter interest in leafless branch structure. All zones except 8. Moderately rapid.

**Fagus sylvatica atropunicea.** PURPLE BEECH. Distinctive, unmistakable with its rich reddish-purple leaves and handsomely spaced branches—the lower ones sweeping the ground. All zones except hot interiors. Frequently planted in zones 1 to 5. Slow to moderate growth.

**Fraxinus americana.** WHITE ASH. Straight-trunked symmetrical tree with a dense wide crown of dark green, light-backed foliage giving dense shade. Zones 1 to 6. Moderate growth. Leaves burn in hot windy areas.

**Fraxinus pennsylvanica lanceolata.** GREEN ASH. Smaller than the white ash, with compact oval crown casting dense shade. Zones 1 to 6. Moderate growth. Also subject to leaf burn.

**Fraxinus velutina glabra.** MODESTO ASH, SMOOTH ASH. Useful for shade in warmer areas after it reaches maturity as a round open-headed tree. Zones 3 to 13. Subject to wind damage, and in California's interior valleys to ash blight (a form of anthracnose) usually associated with moisture. Moderate growth. Tolerates alkaline soil.

FRUIT TREES. Climate determines your choice of variety. Many, like apple, give wonderful shade in addition to fruit. Most fruit trees are fairly rapid growing.

**Jacaranda acutifolia.** JACARANDA. Lacy, soft-textured bright green foliage in an open irregular oval head, decorated in summer with large upright clusters of lavender-blue flowers. Zones 11 to 13, favorable spots Zone 9, fair in Zone 8. Moderate to rapid. Deciduous period short. Despite some litter from flowers a pleasant tree for the patio where it receives protection from wind. Stake first few years for erect growth.

**Morus alba.** WHITE MULBERRY. Forming a broad round head of thick dark green foliage, the mulberry is uniquely fitted to give dense shade. All zones. Rapid. Fruitless forms—free of litter from white or violet fruits—are especially adapted to hotter, drier sections of Zones 7 to 13. High winds cause breakage of brittle branches.

**Nyssa sylvatica.** SOUR GUM. Brilliant red fall color—even in mild areas—is the high point of interest in this tree which forms a spreading irregular crown after starting out as a rather gawky youth. All zones. Slow growth. Gives medium shade.

**Pistacia chinensis.** CHINESE PISTACHE. Exciting in autumn when the rounded open foliage crown turns to brilliant orange and scarlet. Zones 6 to 13. Performs best where summers are long and hot. Moderate growth. Gives light shade. Needs staking for 3 to 4 years as it's an erratic grower when young. Sometimes late in leafing out.

**Sophora japonica.** JAPANESE PAGODA TREE. Green branches clothed in dark green foliage form a wide spreading crown that provides light shade. Yellowish-white flowers from July to September. All zones. Slow growth.

**Tilia americana.** AMERICAN LINDEN. Compact narrow crown of dark green heart-shaped leaves give dense shade. All zones except 8—intolerant of drought. In mild winter sections, leafless period lasts 4 months. Slow to moderate growth.

**Tilia cordata.** LITTLE LEAF LINDEN. Smaller in all respects than the American linden. Same climate adaptability as the American linden. Slow growing.

*Evergreen:*

**Ceratonia siliqua.** CAROB, ST. JOHNS BREAD. Sturdy, compact, round headed tree providing a small area of medium dense shade. Zones 7 to 13. Excellent in Southwest and desert areas. Slow growth. Remains shrub-like for many years; remove lower branches for a tree you can walk under. Tolerant of drought, wind, and alkaline soils.

**Maytenus boaria.** MAYTEN TREE. Branchlets covered with small, shining, pointed leaves similar to smilax (the common name of smilax tree is sometimes applied to mayten tree) hang gracefully from upright branches, forming a narrow, irregular, dome-shaped crown reminiscent of weeping willow. Zones 7, 9 to 13. Fond of moisture, intolerant of hot, dry conditions.

## Small shade trees

### Trees suitable for patio or terrace

*Deciduous:*

**Acer circinatum.** VINE MAPLE. Western native, similar to, and in many ways as beautiful and interesting as the Japanese maple, but without some of the latter's faults, such as susceptibility to windburn and dieback. Light green leaves, orange-scarlet in fall. Zones 3 to 6. Slow growing, many stemmed, or single trunked. Inclined to be more vine-like in shade. Likes moist rich soil.

**Acer ginnala.** AMUR MAPLE. Graceful, small neat tree that is often used as a substitute for Japanese maple. Hardy all zones, but can't take extreme heat. Best adapted in Zones 1 and 2. Slow to moderate growth. Gives light shade.

**Acer negundo variegata.** SILVER VARIEGATED BOXELDER. Silver-margined, light green leaves crowded into a small rounded head lighten shadows and contribute a glow to gardens that are predominantly green. Provides light shade. Hardy all zones. Stands heat but appreciates water. Grows moderately fast.

**Aesculus carnea.** RED HORSECHESTNUT. A well behaved tree for summer shade. Use in protected areas of Zone 1 and throughout coast and coastal valleys. Foliage burns in dry winds. Moderate growth. Round head of large dark green leaves casts dense shade. Soft pink to red flowers April-May. *A. c. briotii* has scarlet flowers.

**Cercis canadensis.** EASTERN REDBUD. Round headed with strong horizontal branch pattern; light green foliage gives light shade. Rose-magenta flowers on bare branches in early spring. All zones, although flowers may be damaged by late frosts. Moderate growth.

**Cornus florida.** FLOWERING DOGWOOD. Horizontal branches form a wide umbrella-like head with leaves arranged in tiers.

Creamy white flower bracts in May; red leaves and fruits in fall. *C. f. rubra* has pink bracts. Best adapted to Zones 3 to 6. Not for desert areas. Moderate growth. Bright green foliage gives light shade.

**Cornus nuttallii.** PACIFIC DOGWOOD. Western native, strikingly handsome in cool moist climates of Zones 3 to 6 where it forms a narrow irregular pyramid up to 50 feet. Slow to moderate growth. Gives light shade. Greenish-white to cream flower bracts in spring. Yellow and red fall foliage is accompanied by red-orange seed buttons.

**Cratægus lavallei (C. carrierei).** CARRIERE HAWTHORN. Erect rather narrow tree having dark green foliage highlighted with white flowers in spring; large orange-red berries in fall. Light shade. Hardy in all zones but not adapted in hot dry areas; fall color poor in mild sections. Moderate growth.

**Cratægus oxyacantha paulii.** PAUL'S DOUBLE SCARLET HAWTHORN. Round dense head gives light to medium shade. Clusters of red double flowers in spring. Climate and growth rate as above.

**Cratægus phænopyrum (C. cordata).** WASHINGTON THORN. Open structure gives light shade. White flowers in May. Shiny red fruits in fall, remain on until Christmas. Climate and growth rate as above. The horticultural variety Autumn Glory has larger fruits.

**Diospyrus kaki.** ORIENTAL PERSIMMON. Beautifully formed round headed tree, glorified in fall first by yellow and red foliage and later (in November) by bright orange fruit on bare branches. Zones 7 to 13. Slow growth.

**Elæagnus angustifolia.** RUSSIAN OLIVE. Irregular crown of silver-gray narrow leaves gives light shade. Effective in winter when the dark brown bark and angular trunk stand out sharply without competition from foliage. Will grow in all zones, but best adapted and most effective in cold areas. Rapid growth.

FLOWERING CHERRIES. Many forms, flower colors, and rates of growth, depending on variety. At their best, flowering cherries give a superb display of flowers in spring, rich leaf coloring in fall. Admirably adapted in Zones 1 to 6, quite good in Zones 7, 9, and 10.

FLOWERING CRABAPPLES. Trees of variable habit, coloring, structure and shade pattern. Varieties with single and double white, pink, or red flowers, and yellow, red, or purplish fruits. Adapted in all zones but best performance usually in Zones 1 to 6.

FLOWERING PLUMS. Useful for contrast and accent provided by purple or bronze foliage. Upright vase-shaped structure gives light and narrow area of shade. White or pink flowers on bare branches in spring. Good in all zones. Rapid growth. *Prunus blireiana* is highly favored because it is fruitless and does not cause litter.

**Kœlreuteria paniculata.** GOLDENRAIN TREE. High, open, umbrella-like head throws light shade; carries clusters of bright yellow flowers in June and July. All zones except coldest areas of Zone 1. Slow growth. Especially valuable because of its ability to overcome arid and alkali soil conditions.

**Kœlreuteria formosana.** CHINESE FLAME TREE. Similar in growth habit to the goldenrain tree, differing mainly in moderate rate of growth, finer textured foliage, and ornamental orange or red capsules in late summer and fall. Also less hardy—adapted in Zones 6 to 13. Head high and shape carefully to train as shade tree.

**Lagerstrœmia indica.** CRAPE MYRTLE. A large shrub that can be trained into a vase-shaped tree that gives light shade. Slender trunk and light colored bark reminiscent of eucalyptus. Wonderful display of pink, rose, red, or lavender flowers in July, August, September. Zones 7, 8, 11, 12, and warm dry spots in Zones 9. Slow growth rate. Needs full sun; mildews on coast.

*An orderly, precise pattern planting is confined within grids. Squares of light green Mexican sedum alternate with dark green ajuga. Clipped yearly after bloom*

*Circular gray stone path is an effective foil for trim clipped planting of pachysandra ground cover at base of oak. Ivy-covered stone wall half encircles area*

**Liquidambar styraciflua.** SWEET GUM. Highly adaptable, deservedly favored for its neat pyramidal habit and exciting fall coloring. All zones. Moderate growth rate, slow in cold winter areas. Burns in hot dry wind.

**Magnolia soulangeana.** SAUCER MAGNOLIA. Open, irregular growth habit, often with several stems. Many varieties usually differing from the species only in flower color. Zones 3 to 13. Slow growth.

**Oxydendrum arboreum.** SOURWOOD. Slender growth habit—often multiple-stemmed—with slightly spreading head richly clothed with long, narrow, glossy leaves. Graceful, pendant clusters of white flowers June to September. Fall foliage brilliant scarlet to orange. Best in Zones 3 to 6; difficult in Zones 7 to 13. Needs acid soil. Slow growth.

**Rhus typhina.** STAGHORN SUMAC. Shrub-tree—dramatic and picturesque at all seasons, especially in fall when ablaze with brilliant scarlet foliage topped with clusters of crimson red fruits. Best performance in Zones 1 to 6. Moderate to rapid growth. Can train and prune to a high crowned tree that can be walked under. Withstands extreme heat, cold, and poor soil.

**Sorbus aucuparia.** EUROPEAN MOUNTAIN ASH. Round crown of gray-green foliage gives light shade. White flowers in spring, followed by orange berries that remain on the tree from July or early August until winter. Best adapted to Zones 1 to 6. Moderate growth.

*Evergreen:*

**Cinnamomum camphora.** CAMPHOR TREE. Fairly formal looking tree with compact oval crown on a thick straight trunk. Yellowish-green leaves, new growth red. Best in Zones 9, 10, 12, and 13. Will grow in Zones 7 and 11. Slow growth. Gives dense shade. Strong wooded, wind resistant, needs only minimum pruning.

**Crinodendron patagua** (formerly *C. dependens*). WHITE LILY TREE. More like a large shrub than a tree in its youth, also when older unless pruned to get tree form. Clean wavy edged leaves look like miniature editions of live oak foliage. Zones 4 to 13. Moderate growth rate. Small white flowers carried in great profusion in June and July are followed by cream and flame colored fruits.

**Eriobotrya japonica.** LOQUAT. Bold dark green foliage forms dense round crown, heavy and solid in effect, giving a small area of deep shade. Zones 7 to 13, except in extreme hot dry sections. Moderate growth. Most effective as an espalier.

**Hymenosporum flavum.** SWEETSHADE. Refined, slender tree with open shiny-foliaged crown providing light shade. Fragrant yellow flowers in early summer. Zones 9, 10, 12, 13, borderline in Zones 7 and 11. Slow to moderate growth.

**Magnolia grandiflora.** SOUTHERN MAGNOLIA. Highly glossed leathery leaves crowded into a rounded crown—spreading only on older trees—gives medium shade. Large white fragrant flowers in summer. Zones 3 to 13. Slow growth. *M. g. lanceolata* is a dwarf form of southern magnolia, otherwise the same.

**Olea europæa.** OLIVE. A tree of great charm and interesting character, especially when very old, when it assumes an irregular spreading head with knobby, gnarled trunk and branches. Train and thin to create open framework for look-through quality and light shade. Zones 7 to 13. Moderate growth rate when young, becoming slower as it matures.

**Schinus terebinthifolius.** BRAZILIAN PEPPER TREE. Rounded crown of shining, bright green foliage, becoming wide-spreading and more open with age. Zones 8 to 13. Winter damaged in areas where temperatures drop below 20°. Moderate growth. Prune and train to encourage picturesque quality. Provides medium shade. Brittle, protect from wind.

# How to estimate costs

Across the bottom of these pages we show a breakdown of the cost of landscaping a large lot. The total cost is high. We have put more into this garden—more shrubs and paving—than is actually needed. You can take a far simpler approach and build a far less expensive garden. But we don't want to mislead you about costs. Whether you complete the whole job at once or finish it on the installment plan over a period of years, a *complete* garden will cost as much as an automobile. All the options, from hiring all work done to doing all possible work yourself, are within the range of automobile costs.

We give you this item-by-item breakdown of costs to help you figure out possible alternates.

The prices we quote are average through the West. Your building supply store's prices on some items may be higher or lower, and your contractor can point out instances where we are out of line in your community. But, in general, these prices are accurate enough to help you make choices between inexpensive and costly materials.

Many factors in the contractor's costs are so variable that we can give only general averages for typical situations. The accessibility of your home, your temperament, the nature of your soil, the sources of supply in your locality, the size of the job, are just a few of the factors that may raise the contractor's costs—and, of course, his price for doing your job.

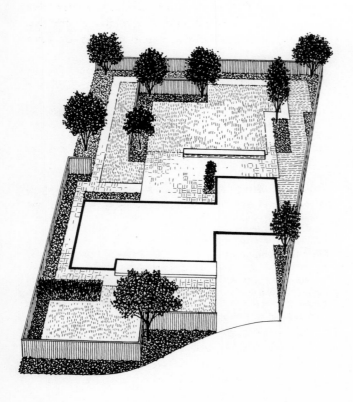

## Cost of complete garden done in three different ways

Column No. 1 shows the cost of the garden for the owner who demands the best and hires a landscape contractor to do the job. Column No. 2 is for the same garden, also installed, but with less expensive materials. Column No. 3 prices are for materials only—all labor is supplied by the owner.

### Preparing the site

| No. 1<br>By Contractor | No. 2<br>By Contractor | No. 3<br>By Owner |
|---|---|---|
| Soil handling, grading, drainage | Cost will depend on conditions—varies from nothing to thousands of dollars. | |

### Planting

**Trees**

| | | |
|---|---|---|
| 5 @ $20.00—$100.00 | 8 @ $10.00—$80.00 | 5 @ $4.00—$20.00 |
| 3 @ 15.00— 45.00 | | 3 @ 3.50— 10.50 |

**Shrubs and Perennials**

5 gallon cans

| | | |
|---|---|---|
| 104 @ $5.00—$520.00 | 5 @ $5.00—$25.00 | |

1 gallon cans

| | | |
|---|---|---|
| 110 @ $2.00—$220.00 | 209 @ $2.00—$418.00 | 214 @ $1.30—$278.20 |

There are eight trees and 214 plants in each development. In No. 1, the owner demands an immediate planted effect, so he buys good-sized plants and trees from the nursery. In No. 2, he still gets quick effect, but he must

With total costs what they are, most of us are forced into some compromises. We can spread the cost over three years or more; we can stretch the landscape dollar by temporarily substituting inexpensive materials for standard items. Before getting directly into costs, let's consider various ways of getting started and scheduling the work and expenditures.

## How to set up your own timetable

Moving from the original idea to the finished result, there are numerous possible stopovers. Where you will stop over and how many months or years you will spend on the whole installation will depend on your bank account, your available time, your regard for your back, and your plan. There are as many options as there are people. Here are the most likely ones:

*De luxe plan:* Start with a definite idea of what you want in relation to your particular site and house. Hire a landscape architect whose work pleases you. Be sure you understand the landscape architect's plans. Get bid from landscape contractor recommended by landscape architect. Stand back and let the landscape contractor finish the job under the landscape architect's supervision.

*Combination plan:* Proceed as above, but specify that the landscape contractor will do only the heavy work, such as grading, drainage, putting in fence posts, building frame for deck or overhead shelter. You take it from there, doing some of the paving, filling in the fence, putting in plant material and lawn.

*Spread the cost:* If you are going to do most of the work yourself, there are many advantages in spreading the project over 3 years or more. It's easier to carry out a plan to its full completion.

For example, if you plan for a large patio and set the boundaries within header boards immediately, you won't be too easily tempted to cut its size just because you can't buy all the permanent paving materials immediately. If your pattern for a patio calls for three times the amount of brick you can afford the first year, you can substitute sand, gravel, crushed rock, or ground cover in the squares you can't fill with brick, and complete the plan the second and third year.

If your plan calls for an overhead structure covered with plastic, solid roof, or any expensive material, consider building the frame and covering it later. The cost of posts and beams for the patio roof, or sky shade or arbor, is usually less than that of the covering materials.

---

give up some expensive plant material to reduce costs. In No. 3, he starts with small trees and plants at minimum cost and is willing to wait for natural growth.

## Lawns and sprinkler system

| No. 1 By Contractor | No. 2 By Contractor | No. 3 By Owner |
|---|---|---|
| Lawn, 3,000 square feet @ 13c—$390.00 | @ 13c—$390.00 | @ 2c—$60.00 |
| Sprinklers, 3,000 square feet @ 12c—$360.00 | | |

In No. 2, the owner saves by omitting the sprinkler system. To cut prices still further in development of No. 3, the owner plants the lawn himself. Prices for lawns will vary so much by the condition of the soil and its needs for mulching, fertilizing, etc., that the above can be only a general statement. The cost of a standard sprinkling system is for galvanized pipe installation.

## Paving

| No. 1 By Contractor | No. 2 By Contractor | No. 3 By Owner |
|---|---|---|
| Driveway, asphalt, 600 square feet @ 20c sq. ft.—$120.00 | $120.00 | $120.00 |
| Service yard, 650 square feet | | |
| Asphalt @ 20c sq. ft.—$130.00 | Gravel @ 15c—$97.50 | Gravel @ 3c—$19.50 |
| Patio and path, 1,400 square feet | | |
| Concrete (ex. aggregate) @ 40c sq. ft.—$560.00 | Concrete @ 30c—$420.00 | Concrete @ 15c—$210.00 |

Note that the price for the driveway is the same in each development. The asphalt paving of a driveway requires so much work, skill, and special equipment that few home owners would want to undertake it. For that reason, we quoted the contractor's price in all three gardens.

## Low seat wall, 30 feet long

| No. 1 By Contractor | No. 2 By Contractor | No. 3 By Owner |
|---|---|---|
| Brick @ $3.00 lin. ft.—$90.00 | Wood @ $2.50—$75.00 | Wood @ $1.00—$30.00 |
| Concrete @ $3.00—$90.00 | Concrete @ $3.00—$90.00 | Concrete @ $1.20—$36.00 |

Cost is reduced in development No. 2 by substituting wood for more expensive masonry. In garden No. 3, the wood wall is built by the owner.

## Fences

| No. 1 By Contractor | No. 2 By Contractor | No. 3 By Owner |
|---|---|---|
| Wire, 5 feet high, 100 feet @ $1.30 lin. ft.—$130.00 | @ $1.30—$130.00 | @ 80c—$80.00 |
| Board, 6 feet high, 187 feet @ $2.25 lin. ft.—$420.75 | @ $2.25—$420.75 | @ $1.30—$243.10 |

The same fences are used in each plan of development. Price reduction in garden No. 3 is achieved when the owner himself takes on the job of building the fences.

## What to do first?

The landscape contractor sets up a schedule of operations based on getting the job done in the least amount of time with the least amount of labor. Some of his planning also makes sense for the home owner doing all or part of his own work. Here is the contractor's usual pattern:

*Preliminaries:* Before doing any work on the site, he locates and orders plant material. If construction of a lathhouse, trellis, overhead, or workshop is in the plan, he gets a building permit. He checks to see if trucks and machinery can get in; checks soil, grade, and drainage; orders lumber.

*Earth moving:* He does all the work that involves soil handling by machine. This includes all earth moving in or out, all rough grading, all drainage ditches, holes for fence posts, and holes for large trees.

*Rough carpentry:* He has carpenters build forms for steps, foundations, walls; set up headers for concrete paving, asphalt, rock, gravel, brick.

*Masonry:* Concrete is poured or bricks laid in patio and in main walks.

*Large trees:* Any that must be moved by truck are planted at this stage.

*Fences:* These are installed, leaving one section open for delivery of smaller plant material, fertilizers, lumber, etc.

*Finish carpentry:* Carpenters build raised beds, seats, overheads, trellises.

*Final planting:* Shrubs, vines, and small trees are planted.

*Lawn:* Areas are given final grading and fertilized. Sprinkler systems (if any) and lawns are installed.

## Three-year timetable

The good logic of the contractor can't be followed to the letter in a three-year project.

There's a natural urge to fix up the streetside immediately—even if nothing more than putting in a lawn.

Generally, the next drive is to get the fence up, even if it means wheeling in concrete and other materials later.

Following the fence job, the beginner attends to jobs aimed to keep the family out of the mud. Often this means that the entire back yard is put into lawn with the idea that it will be changed later.

If this schedule is followed without a plan, you are likely to lock yourself into a garden that you will find hard to change. Once the entire back yard is in lawn, any change takes a lot of courage and tough digging.

Trees should be planted the first year. You probably will pay no attention to this sage piece of advice and will wait three years before you plant them. Somehow, it's almost impossible to decide on trees when you first begin to garden. You feel that trees will take too long to make a showing, and you need shade immediately. So you put off planting. In the third year you plant the tree that would be shading you and your house had you planted it when you first moved in.

After watching hundreds of families make their choices between patio or back yard lawn as their first project, we are sure that those who tackle the patio first are more satisfied. They get a resting spot sooner. Where there are children of the sandbox-wading pool age, a large paved area provides a more usable playground than a lawn.

## Estimating costs

Prices used in the three-plan estimate and those listed elsewhere in this chapter are for the year 1956. Cost information was gathered from 15 cities and towns, but no attempt was made to arrive at an "average." When you shop for materials, you will find that prices of many items will be lower or higher than quoted. Prices listed are for rough estimating. Prices are in most part comparative. When exceptions exist they are so noted. In general, sand, gravel, and all masonry material are cheaper inland than in the coastal states; lumber is cheaper in the coastal area.

## Overhead materials

*Insulating fiber board.* Use for sheathing on overhead structures. Costs 30c a square foot for a 2 by 8-ft. sheet, 2 in. thick.

*Aluminum, corrugated.* Available in smooth surface or in an embossed finish that cuts glare. Net coverage on rafters is 2 feet. Use special aluminum nails with neoprene sealing washers. Always nail on top of groove. Available in 6, 8, 10, and 12-ft. sheets, 26 to 48 in. wide, at 14c to 20c a square foot.

*Aluminum, 5V-crimp.* For roofs of lower pitch. Available in smooth surfaces or embossed finish. When two outside V's are lapped, water-tight air lock is developed. Same sizes and costs as corrugated aluminum.

*Canvas, awning* (heavy cotton). Complete overhead awning supported by pipes can be installed for $1 to $1.50 per square foot.

*Shingles.* #1 cedar cost $4.40 a bundle, 4 bundles cover 100 square feet. *Asbestos* are $7.00 a bundle, 3 bundles cover 100 square feet. *Asphalt* cost $2.80 a bundle, 3 bundles cover 100 square feet.

*Roofing paper.* Mineral surface asphalt, 90-lb. weight. One roll covers 100 square feet at a cost of 3½c to 4c per square foot.

*Bamboo blinds.* Will hold up better outdoors if varnished. Available in various widths and lengths, at 6c to 8c a square foot.

## Overhead and fence materials

*Cement asbestos board.* Sometimes used in fence panels. Best used in overhead structures. Available in 4 by 8 and 4 by 4-ft. sheets, both flat and corrugated, in the following thicknesses: ⅛ in., 13c a square foot; 3/16 in., 15c; ¼ in., 17c.

*Glass fiber plastic panels.* Come in wide range of colors, flat surfaced or corrugated: 4 to 12 ft. long, 26, 34, and 40-in. wide. Costs 60c to $1.25 sq. ft.

*Wire woven reed,* tight weave. Comes in rolls 6 ft. 4 in. wide, 25 ft. long, $12 to $15 a roll. When used in screen fences and overheads, will last about 5 years without becoming ragged.

*Lath.* Many items come under the general terms of lath, lattice, battens. Sometimes items sold for other purposes, such as "car strips," are offered as lath. Fir and redwood lath are available. Costs vary according to grade and locality. Better estimate cost of from 8c to 11c per square foot for lath covering.

*Light members* such as 1 by 2's and 1 by 3's are used instead of lath in fences, trellises, and overheads where warping, sagging, and splitting of regular lath would be annoying. Estimate 20c to 25c a square foot depending on grade and spacing.

*Boards.* Fir, redwood, and cedar are available in many grades and wide range of prices. Cheapest for overhead sheathing at about 10c a square foot. Better grades 15c and up.

*Plywood.* Available in 4 by 8-ft. sheets. Some suppliers offer multiple sizes. Use only *exterior* grades outdoor. Grade AA is good both sides; no knotholes or open defects. Use for outdoor furniture, fences where both sides are exposed to view, and where natural finish is desired. Grade AC ("Plyshield") is good one side; other side has small holes and patches. Greatest volume is in this grade. Use for garden structures, outdoor table tops, sheathing for overhead structures. Approximate prices:

| Grade AA | Grade AC |
|---|---|
| ¼″ 20c sq. ft. | 15c sq. ft. |
| ⅜″ 24c sq. ft. | 18c sq. ft. |
| ½″ 28c sq. ft. | 25c sq. ft. |
| ⅝″ 30c sq. ft. | 27c sq. ft. |
| ¾″ 36c sq. ft. | 32c sq. ft. |

*Tempered hardboard.* Most common sheet size is 4 by 8 feet, but it can be obtained in smaller sizes, or in larger sizes, by special order. Use for fence panels, overhead sheathing. *Perforated sheets* are convenient for walls of storage areas; perforations fit standard hardware clips and hooks for hanging up garden tools. Available in 4 by 8-foot panels. Prices:

| Solid sheets | Perforated sheets |
|---|---|
| 1/8″ 11c sq. ft. | 19c sq. ft. |
| 3/16″ 15c sq. ft. | 24c sq. ft. |
| 1/4″ 18c sq. ft. | 28c sq. ft. |
| 5/16″ 21c sq. ft. | |

## Fence and enclosure materials—Wire

*Insect screen.* See pages 126, 127, 128, for examples of installations. Insect screen material is receiving more attention from manufacturers and designers. The following prices of screening are for screen in rolls. Tension screen is slightly higher in cost. Aluminum, 15c to 20c a square foot; galvanized steel, 8c to 12c; plastic coated fiber glass, 15c to 20c; bronze, 20c.

*Louvered sun screen.* Aluminum, 29c to 36c; bronze, 85c to 90c.

*Wire.* A simple panel or fence frame filled with wire not only stops traffic but provides support for plants. Wire panels often used where privacy is not needed immediately and a solid fence would be annoying. Prices:

*Poultry netting:* 1-in. mesh, 20 gauge, 12, 18, 24, 30, 36, 48, 60, and 72-inch wide, runs from 4c to 23c a lineal foot, or from $4.20 to $22.60 for a 150-ft. roll. 2-in. mesh, 20 gauge, 24, 30, 36, 48, 60, and 72-inch wide, runs from 5c to 11c a lineal foot, or from $4 to $10.80 for a 150-ft. roll.

*Non-climb wire,* 12½ gauge. 4 ft. wide, 25c lin. ft., $19.50 for a 100-ft. roll; 5 ft. wide, 30c lin. ft., $25, 100-ft. roll; 6 ft. wide, 35c lin. ft., $29.50 a 100-ft roll.

*Wire mesh.* Hardware cloth (½ by ½-in. mesh), 19 gauge, 24, 30, 36, and 48 in. wide, 38c to 76c lin. ft.; 1 by 1-in. welded mesh, 16 gauge, 3-ft. width, 30c lin. ft.; 1 by 2-in. welded mesh, 16 gauge, 3-ft. width, 25c lin. ft.

*Chain link.* A 6-foot high fence complete with top rail and line posts, 11 gauge wire, $1.60 to $1.80 lin. ft.; $2.22 to $2.40 lin. ft., contractor installed. Without top rail, but line posts included, $1.30 to $1.50 lin. ft.; $1.90 to $2.10 contractor installed. Obtainable in galvanized steel or, at higher cost, in aluminum.

Chain link, 11 gauge wire, is now being sold separate from steel posts and can be stapled to wood posts. Costs about 70c lin. ft. of 6-foot fence.

## Flooring Materials—Hard Surfaced

*Brick:* There's a wide fluctuation in costs depending upon the area and distance from brick kilns. In Salt Lake City, for example, common brick costs $24 to $36 a thousand as compared to $50 to $60 a thousand in the San

Francisco Bay area. Outdoor paving costs, however, do not have that wide a spread. In cold winter areas where there is frost, brick should be laid in mortar on a 4-inch concrete slab. Furthermore, in cold areas, outside brick must be hard baked and costs $57 and higher per thousand. Cost installed in inland areas is much lower than prices quoted below. These costs are for the coastal areas.

| | You do | Contracted |
|---|---|---|
| Brick in sand | 25c-30c sq. ft. | 85c-$1.10 sq. ft. |
| Brick in sand on 2-inch concrete base | 30c-40c sq. ft. | $1.10-$1.35 sq. ft. |
| Brick in mortar on 2-inch concrete base | 32c-45c sq. ft. | $1.90-$2.25 sq. ft. |

*Adobe blocks:* Not obtainable in many localities. Costs within trucking distance of manufacturing plant: 17c sq. ft. self-installed; $1 sq. ft. contractor-installed.

*Asphalt:* Hot-mix asphalt can rarely be successfully applied by the amateur; but cold-mix—providing you can borrow or rent a heavy roller—can often be successfully applied by the homeowner.

| | You do | Contracted |
|---|---|---|
| Hot mix 1½ to 2 in. on 4-in. base rock | | |
| More than 1000 sq ft. | .... | 15c-22c sq ft. |
| Less than 1000 sq. ft. | .... | 25c sq. ft. |
| Cold mix. 1 to 2 in. on 4-in. base rock | 9c sq. ft. | 28c-35c sq. ft. |

*Tile.* The least expensive of the tiles is the foot square, ⅞ inch thick, patio tile distributed in northern California. It costs about 30 cents each. Can be laid inexpensively in sand-cement mixture but better method is on concrete. Other tiles vary in size and type and price by locality.

*Flagstone:* In warm-winter areas, preferably laid on 2-in. concrete slab but sometimes laid on sand or soil. In cold-winter areas, laid on 4-in. slab. Cost ranges from 35c to 60c sq. ft. if you do the labor to $1.65 to $2 if a contractor installs the flags.

*Concrete:* A 3-in. thickness is adequate for most areas, but a 4-in. slab is easier to pour if you are using 2 by 4 headers.

| | You do | Contracted |
|---|---|---|
| Plain finish with broomed surface | 12c sq. ft. | 30c to 35c sq. ft. |
| Plain, broomed surface with color-hardener | 17c sq. ft. | 40c to 45c sq. ft. |
| Exposed aggregate | 12c sq. ft. | 40c to 50c sq. ft. |
| Exposed aggregate with acid stain | 17c sq. ft. | 45c to 50c sq. ft. |

If concrete is to be poured inside permanent headers, add cost from chart that follows.

*Header boards or forms*

| | You do | Contracted |
|---|---|---|
| 2 by 4 redwood or cedar forms to remain in place. (Includes 1 by 2 by 12-in. redwood stakes spaced 4 ft. apart) | 10c-12c lin. ft. | 35c-40c lin. ft. |
| 1 by 4 redwood or cedar forms to remain in place. (Includes 1 by 2 by 12-in. redwood stakes spaced 4 ft. apart) Use ½ by 4 in. forms doubled for curves. | 6c-8c lin. ft. | 30c-35c lin. ft. |

*Materials for concrete*

| | You do | Contracted |
|---|---|---|
| Cement | $1.25 sack | $4.80 bbl. (4 sacks) |
| Sand and gravel mix | $3.40 ton covers 70 sq. ft. 3 in. | $4.60 yard covers 90 sq. ft. 3 in. |
| Transit mix. Prices vary by delivery distance, formula. Min. delivery usually 1 yd. | | $12 to $14 yard 1:3:4 mix; 100 sq. ft. 3 in. |
| Dry mix (sand, cement, gravel) in 60 and 90-lb. sacks. | | $1.25 up per 90-lb. sack, covers 8 sq. ft. 1 in. |

*Rentable equipment for handling concrete*

*Concrete mixers.* (Gas or electric-driven) 6 cubic feet (takes ½ sack of cement) with a 1-batch hopper: $7.50. Same size without hopper: $5. 3 cubic feet: $2.50.

*Wheelbarrow.* Rubber-tired, heavy duty, contractor's type: 75 cents.

*Cement buggy.* A 2-wheeled rubber-tired dump cart that holds 2 wheelbarrow loads: $1.50.

*Vibrator.* A vibrating rod to compact concrete in the forms: $5.

*Trowels, edgers, markers, floats,* and miscellaneous hand tools: 50 cents to $1.

## Flooring materials—soft surfaced

*Loose aggregates.* Customs in handling and prices vary by area. In some localities, these materials are sold by the ton, in others by the yard. Minimum deliverable quantity also varies by locality.

*Base rock, pea gravel, fill material.* Called by different names according to local supply—"redrock" in San Francisco Bay area, "fill material" in Seattle. A cubic yard covers 100 sq. ft. 3 in. thick. Costs average $2 to $3 a yard, or a sq. ft. cost of 2c. Contractor cost installed, from 10c to 20c a sq. ft. Cost less in inland areas. (Pea gravel generally laid ½ in. thick on 3 in. of water-bound base rock.)

*Tanbark.* Cost varies by distance from tannery. Starts at about $13.50 a ton, $9 a yard. About $14 a yard 100 miles from a tannery.

*Crushed rock.* About $2.70 to $4 a ton, or $4 to $7 a yard. One ton covers 70 sq. ft. 3 in. deep. A yard covers 90 sq. ft.

*Roofing rock.* Available in colors. $1.50 to $2 a sack. Six sacks will cover 100 sq. ft. 1 inch deep.

*Pumice.* Cost depends upon distance from source. $6 and up per yard.

## Decks

Decks have long been thought of as expensive ways to get an extension of indoor living space on hillside homes. Lately, landscape architects and home owners are using decks for extensions of indoor rooms even when these are but a foot or more off the ground. They are finding that such decks can be built for a very reasonable cost—only a little more expensive than a permanent paving.

A deck such as illustrated on page 54, constructed of 2 by 3-in. decking on 2 by 6-in. joists, supported by a 4 by 6-in. beam and 4 by 4 posts on concrete piers, costs less than $1 a square foot for materials.

## Plant Material

Cost of plants is difficult to tabulate for the reason that cost is a combination of size and the kind of plant. The slow-growing and rare plants are, of course, more expensive than easy-to-propagate fast growers. The following cost tables split between the extremes.

| | You do | Contracted |
|---|---|---|
| Shrub, 1 gal. container | $1.00- 1.30 | $1.70- 2.00 |
| Shrub, 5 gal. container | 3.50- 4.50 | 5.00- 5.25 |
| Tree, 5 gal. container (incl. 2"x2"x8' stake) | 3.50- 4.50 | 6.25- 7.50 |
| Tree, 15 gal. container | 10.50 and up | 17.50 and up |
| Ground cover (ivy, strawberry, ajuga, etc., planted 12 in. o. c.) | 5c to 7c sq. ft. | 10c to 12c sq. ft. |

In areas where plants are sold "balled and burlapped," rather than in containers, you can estimate plant costs in a rough way with these prices:

| Size | You do | Contracted |
|---|---|---|
| 12 in. to 15 in. | $1.50- 2.50 | Add 33 per cent |
| 15 in. to 18 in. | 2.50- 3.50 | to retail price |
| 18 in. to 24 in. | 3.50- 5.00 | for installation |
| 24 in. to 30 in. | 4.00- 6.00 | of average job |
| 30 in. to 36 in. | 4.50- 8.00 | |

## Low walls—retaining walls, seat walls

Because the construction of walls depends upon the foundation necessary, the soil, and wall height, it is difficult to give even a rule-of-thumb key to estimating.

Probably the most inexpensive retaining wall is the wood wall of 4 by 4-inch posts with a facing of 2-inch redwood or cedar. If you have such a wall built by a contractor, expect to pay about $1.20 per square face foot. If you do the work, the cost would be approximately half of that.

A *concrete block wall* is not very much more expensive. You can get it built for $1.50 or less per square face foot. Blocks are available in the following sizes and at the following prices:

4" x 8" x 16"—about 16c each.

8" x 8" x 16"—about 26c each.

8" x 16" x 16"—about 32c each.

A *brick wall,* 8 in. thick, can be built at about $2.25 to $2.50 per square face-foot; 12 in. thick, $3.25 square face-foot. Material cost is less than half.

A *fieldstone wall* costs about $3.60 per square face-foot. Material cost is less than half.

## If you need help

Don't hesitate to ask the help of your building inspector. In most cases he will be glad to help you with your problem in addition to checking to see if your structure meets city standards.

Landscape contractors can be engaged on a partial construction basis. You can contract for the basic frames of fence, overheads, panels, etc., and then do the finishing yourself.

### PHOTOGRAPHERS

Ben J. Allen: pages 122 (right), 134 (bottom right), 136. Jerry A. Anson: pages 64 (bottom), 159 (top left), 164 (top right). William Aplin: pages 12, 74 (top left, right), 79, 126, 127, 140 (top right), 143 (bottom), 177 (top), 181. Aplin-Dudley Studios: pages 73 (top left, right), 102, 104 (top), 107 (left), 120 (right), 131 (bottom left), 133 (top right, bottom left), 156 (bottom), 164 (top left). Morley Baer: pages 13 (bottom), 14 (bottom), 40, 41, 43, 54, 73 (middle left), 74 (bottom), 88, 89, 112 (left), 119 (right), 123, 130 (bottom, left and right), 132 (top), 142 (top right), 151, 164 (middle left), 175 (top right). Ernest Braun: pages 13 (top), 16 (top), 46, 47 (top, bottom right), 52 (top right, bottom), 53 (right), 56, 57, 58, 62, 64 (top), 73 (bottom, left and right), 78, 81 (top), 84 (top, left and right, bottom right), 90, 91, 94, 95, 96 (right), 104 (bottom right), 111 (right), 118, 125, 138, 139, 140 (top left), 143 (top left), 144, 153, 155, 163, 169 (top left, bottom), 171 (top), 173, 175 (left, bottom right), 183 (left). Tom Burns, Jr.: pages 16 (bottom), 82, 83, 128, 141 (top right), 143 (top right). Carroll C. Calkins: pages 44, 45, 48, 77 (right), 171 (bottom, left and right). Clyde Childress: pages 39, 49, 84 (bottom left), 122 (left). Columbia Studios: pages 87, 133 (bottom right). Robert Cox: pages 129, 141 (top left). Barry Evans: page 157. Philip Fein: pages 50, 52 (top left), 53 (top left), 111 (left), 154 (top right). Richard Fish: page 132 (bottom left). Frank L. Gaynor: page 107 (right). Jeannette Grossman: pages 109 (left), 179. Art Hupy: page 104 (bottom left), 117, 121, 154 (bottom). Russell Illig: page 106 (left). Theodore Osmundson: pages 86, 103 (bottom), 142 (top left), 160 (bottom right). Maynard Parker: page 131 (top). Rondal Partridge: page 15. Chas. R. Pearson: pages 80 (right), 103 (top), 160 (bottom left). George F. Peterson: page 106 (right). Lorry Ray: pages 92, 93. John Robinson: pages 80 (left), 97 (top, bottom right), 103 (middle), 109 (right), 119 (left), 120 (left), 131 (bottom right), 132 (bottom right), 134 (top left), 159 (bottom right), 160 (top left), 164 (middle right, bottom), 177 (bottom), 183 (right). Julius Shulman: pages 128 (top, left and right), 159 (top right). Douglas M. Simmonds: page 156 (top). Blair Stapp: pages 97 (bottom left), 98, 99, 100, 110, 116, 130 (top). Ralph Stevens: page 169 (top right). Shan Stewart: page 47 (bottom left). Roger Sturtevant: page 152 (top). R. Wenkam: page 14 (top). Mason Weymouth: pages 51, 59, 108, 112 (right), 153 (bottom). COVER: (top row, left to right) Clyde Childress, Ernest Braun, Maynard Parker; (bottom row, left to right) John Robinson, Ernest Braun, John Robinson.

# Index

Bold face page numbers refer to principal references.